THE
BATTLE
OF
ST.
BART'S

ALSO BY BRENT C. BROLIN

The Failure of Modern Architecture
Architecture in Context
Sourcebook of Architectural Ornament
Flight of Fancy: The Banishment and Return of Ornament

THE BATTLE OF ST. BART'S

Brent C. Brolin

William Morrow and Company, Inc.

NEW YORK

Library of Congress Cataloging-in-Publication Data

Brolin, Brent C.
　　The battle of St. Bart's / Brent C. Brolin.
　　　　p.　　cm.
　　Includes index.
　　ISBN 0-688-05938-4
　　1. St. Bartholomew's Episcopal Church (New York, N.Y.)—History.
2. Historic buildings—Law and legislation—New York (N.Y.)
I. Title.
BX5980.N56B76 1988
283'.7471—dc19　　　　　　　　　　　　　　　　　87-34789
　　　　　　　　　　　　　　　　　　　　　　　　　　CIP

Printed in the United States of America

First Edition

1　2　3　4　5　6　7　8　9　10

BOOK DESIGN BY KATHLEEN CAREY

Contents

THE BATTLE OF ST. BART'S

CHAPTER

I

LATE on a cool October afternoon in 1980 a mustached gentleman in a bowler hat walked across New York City's Park Avenue, at Fiftieth Street. The trim figure, precise gait, and emotionless face gave no hint of his mission. James Sinclair Armstrong—former undersecretary of the navy, former chairman of the Securities and Exchange Commission, and now attorney with the Fifth Avenue law firm of Whitman & Ransom—was going to see his rector.

The Reverend Thomas Dix Bowers is the titular leader of a flock of some 1,500 Episcopalians who worship in a remarkable setting in a remarkable metropolis. The immediate goal of Armstrong's purposeful afternoon stroll was St. Bartholomew's Episcopal Church. This salmon-hued neo-Byzantine structure, perpetual witness to the presence of the Christian God in the most secular of

American cities, is embedded in a forest of corporate towers. It seems an incongruous bit of architectural yesteryear.

The domed sanctuary occupies the north side of the half-block site. Shouldering up against its southern wall, just opposite the Waldorf-Astoria, is the Community House of St. Bartholomew's Church, a low building with appropriately modest architectural pretensions. It is set back from Park Avenue, behind a small garden (at the edge of the sidewalk) and a generous terrace. Almost everyone who knows the church's name at all calls it St. Bart's. No disrespect is intended to the early Christian martyr who was flayed alive somewhere in Turkey in the first century A.D.

Entering the Community House through the small, mid-block doorway of Fiftieth Street, J. Sinclair Armstrong walked down a nondescript corridor, past a switchboard operator, who was also the security check, and into an old-fashioned, manually operated elevator. It rose slowly, audibly objecting to its task. The doors opened, and Armstrong left the dingy decor of the interiors that are accessible to the general public and made his way past the rector's secretary to a large, comfortably appointed office with plush carpeting and inviting furnishings.

The rector greeted Armstrong warmly and openly, as he does all his parishioners. Father Bowers was born and raised in Norfolk, Virginia, schooled at the Virginia Military Academy, and, after a stint in Korea as an artillery observer, at Sewanee (University of the South), and Virginia Seminary. As of that afternoon, the rector had been a resident of New York City for two years, although he had been a frequent and admiring visitor to the city for several years before; in the parlance of his trade, he was "called" to St. Bart's. With a robust, fleshy physique, Bowers looks like a Fielding character: dark hair surrounding a full face and ruddy cheeks, eyes close set and sparkling. He is lively and broadly smiling, outgoing and backslapping. His easy familiarity—even with people he meets for the first time—might seem the facile glad hand to anyone who has not ventured west of the Hudson or south of Jersey, where folks view that manner with less suspicion than New Yorkers do.

After an exchange of greetings, the rector and his distinguished parishioner got down to the matter at hand. St. Bartholomew's Church sits on an extraordinarily valuable piece of land. Weeks before this meeting, an "unidentified major American corporation" had offered to buy the Park Avenue property, buildings and all, for $100 million. The rector and vestry were considering the proposition. This meeting was to see if Armstrong would support his rector in the undertaking.

It was not the first time someone had asked Armstrong to consider the development question. It had been on his mind for some weeks. His ninety-eight-year-old father, Howard S. Armstrong, had asked him to look into it soon after the offer became public.

Armstrong declined to join the rector's camp. He recalled the rector's saying, "Sinc, I'm gonna make war on you."

"I've known five rectors of this church," responded the gray-haired parishioner, "and the rectors of St. Bartholomew's don't make war on their parishioners."

This rector has.

*　　*　　*

Philip Alston, an Atlantan and longtime friend of Tom's, knows him as a fighter: "Tom Bowers has never approached his ministry as a popularity contest. He's never gone out to purposely offend anyone, but when he advances an idea he doesn't back away from it, and I think that's his greatest strength."

Secretary of Defense Caspar W. Weinberger, who has known Armstrong since their days on the *Harvard Crimson*, described his mettle in similar terms: ". . . he is very tenacious once he has made up his mind as to the right course to follow, and I know he is willing to support his views with major and continuing investments of his very considerable mental resources. It is entirely characteristic that he would continue with the battle of St. Bartholomew's for so many years, and indeed I do not believe he would ever give up having concluded that the proposed building program is wrong."

*　　*　　*

The Reverend Thomas Dix Bowers makes you feel like calling him "Tom" from the very first time you meet him. The jovial rector is an ecclesiastical lightning rod of sorts. To his followers he is a frontline fighter, a Christian soldier in the holy war against poverty and privation, prejudice and indifference. His battleground of choice is the city; his fortress, the besieged urban church. In the heart of hostile territory, Tom Bowers tries to carry on a ministry to the socially and economically disenfranchised while his church reels under economic burdens created by rising costs, a dwindling congregation, and deteriorating buildings.

To his detractors, Tom Bowers is "an ambitious, unprincipled hotshot, who couldn't wait to get started in New York." Lester Kinsolving, Episcopal priest and syndicated religious columnist, said Bowers "came from Atlanta and landed in La Guardia running, but he found the money for his programs just wasn't available at the church, and there was no quick way to get it." That was when development appeared on the church's agenda, according to Kinsolving.

Tom Bowers won his battles at two previous posts, in Washington, D.C., and Atlanta, Georgia. He rejuvenated faltering parishes and created loving communities actively involved in caring for others. More important for the future of his church, Tom brought the young back into the fold. He won that skirmish in the battle for the urban church for the same reasons he won the others: because people loved Tom Bowers and he could convince them to do things they never thought they could. Tom could inspire. His supporters in the landmarks controversy see him as a blessing to New York City, a man who is on God's side of every issue.

Tom Bowers displayed another gift, too, one that is at least as important in the "Kingdom Business," to use the rector's own phrase. He raised money as easily as Georgians raise peaches. "If he went and did the talking, he could persuade anybody to give everything they had," said Patty Weatherly, his secretary of many years in Atlanta.

With the victories came the spoils: love and praise from his parishioners and a well-deserved sense of accomplishment and self-esteem. For his rare combination of notable talents, Bowers also gained the affection and respect of many who watched from outside his parishes. When New York called the rector away, Atlanta held a "Tom Bowers Day" to acknowledge his contribution to the community at large.

The thrust of the most recent campaign in Tom Bowers's Christian war, the Battle of St. Bart's, is much like his earlier ones. "There are two great commandments in the Bible," the stocky rector will tell you. "The first is to love thy God. The second is to love thy neighbor as thyself." Jesus did not choose to be a king or a simple miracle worker or even an economic savior. Jesus chose to be the Messiah. He chose to save the people. The mission of the modern-day church is to stimulate that ministry, which means "being concerned with the needs of humanity."

The second charge, loving your neighbor, means ministering to the poor—feeding the hungry, clothing the naked, and housing the homeless. It also means providing counseling and other services to the community, nurturing the recovering alcoholic, the battered spouse, the teenager with a drug problem, and the family in need of a sympathetic ear if it is to remain a family—in short, tending to the countless social ills that commonly distress modern society.

According to the rector and vestry, two facts of urban life prevent St. Bartholomew's from carrying out its mission. First, it is no longer the wealthy church it was when the Astors and Vander-bilts sat in its pews. Second, office buildings have replaced apartment houses that surrounded it in the 1950's and 1960's, pushing out the church's potential constituency and replacing the twenty-four-hour population of the neighborhood with an eight-hour one. Parish rolls dwindled from 3,000, just after World War II, to around 1,500 by the time Reverend Bowers arrived. That exodus, claimed the rector and vestry, deprived St. Bart's of its economic base, just as the flight of downtown retailers to suburban shopping malls deflated urban tax bases in those same decades.

The unforeseeable demographic disaster was accompanied by the more predictable pains of architectural old age: deferred maintenance. Church fathers commissioned a survey in 1985 which told them it would take $12 million to complete the "essential repairs" to their deteriorating buildings. Difficulties in raising money from a depleted congregation, combined with the great sums needed to keep the buildings from falling into ruin, created a one-two punch that would KO the parish unless it found a fertile new source of income. Without one, the church treasurer predicted bankruptcy by 1990.

Since St. Bart's is a prestigious church in a city with many well-to-do Episcopalians, outsiders wondered why a more traditional approach, fund raising, might not be a feasible alternative. As the former church of the Vanderbilts and other American nobility, it already had an endowment of $11 million when the dire bankruptcy prediction was first made, as well as a tradition of raising substantial sums from parishioners when it was necessary. But the magnitude of the needed repairs gave pause to the most optimistic of fund raisers, said Bowers. He and his loyal troops had tried but found it impossible to raise that kind of money through traditional channels. Nor could the rector convince private foundations and corporate donors to support his church's cause. St. Bart's ability to continue as a "dynamic force in the community" was in jeopardy. If it did not develop its property, the whole landmarked complex would be lost.

That was the kernel of the problem that brought J. Sinclair Armstrong and Thomas Dix Bowers together on that October afternoon in 1980. The church said it faced imminent financial disaster. If it expected to carry on God's work, it had to find money. And a developer had just offered St. Bartholomew's $100 million.

The will of the church, personified in the rector and vestry, was to try to profit from its real estate holdings to better serve God.

There was one problem. The sanctuary and its adjoining Community House, terrace, and garden were a New York City landmark. Tom Bowers was not just a soldier; he was a soldier under fire. The Landmarks Law victimized his church. It deprived St. Bartholomew's of needed income from its property, and that prevented it from carrying out its Christian mission of ministering to the poor.

It was not permitted to change so much as a brick or tile on the exterior without first jumping through a set of carefully documented administrative hoops. At the heart of that procedure was the notion of "appropriateness." Would the alteration—the replacement of the Community House with an office tower—"affect or not be in harmony with" the rest of the landmark?

If the New York City Landmarks Preservation Commission found the replacement harmonious, there would be no difficulty. It would grant a certificate of appropriateness, and St. Bart's could demolish the Community House to make way for the new building and financial security. If the commission found it an inappropriate alteration, the church could revise the design, or it could apply for relief from the Landmarks Law on the basis of "insufficient return," claiming the designation caused it financial hardship. Proving hardship is a complicated and delicate procedure, and how the owner of a landmark goes about doing that will be a topic for later discussion.

From the church's first submission, the commission provided the rector with his own version of the trials of Job. The church presented two tower designs. The landmarks commission rejected both. The church then applied for relief from the law under the hardship provision, and that, too, was rejected. Ultimately St. Bartholomew's filed a suit against the City of New York for $110 million, claiming the Landmarks Law deprived it of its First Amendment right to exercise its religion freely.

The church faced fierce opposition to its development plans from the start. When the third rejection came down from the landmarks commission, five years after the development plan was announced, opponents were quick to point out that St. Bart's was nowhere near the bankruptcy it had predicted for itself. In spite of an allegedly desperate situation, the church was in better financial health when its hardship plea was rejected than it had been when the first dismal prognostication was made. (Its portfolio increased in value by nearly $1.5 million between 1985 and 1986, and its budget was balanced.)

Opposition to the development of St. Bartholomew's came from loud and diverse sources. Outside the church it consisted of preservationists, architecture buffs, professional organizations connected to design or planning, and a healthy slice of the general public. Virtually every New York City politician came out foursquare against development. Pro-preservation forces generally state their case simply: No one should touch the buildings, terrace, or garden.

Within the church it coalesced in a group called the Committee to Oppose the Sale of St. Bartholomew's Church, Inc., headed by the same J. Sinclair Armstrong who declined his rector's invitation to join the development team in October 1980. The committee has a membership of close to one thousand. It draws from inside and outside the church, claims that a third of the voting members of the parish contribute to its coffers, and routinely draws that portion of the vote in parish elections. (The internal opposition changed its name from the Committee to Preserve St. Bartholomew's Church, Inc. [October 1980], to the Committee in Opposition to the Sale of St. Bartholomew's Church, Inc. [1981], and finally to the Committee to Oppose the Sale of St. Bartholomew's Church, Inc., which will be used here.)

The committee has held to the view that the landmark is sacrosanct but has enlarged the platform beyond the architectural question. From the beginning, its members claimed church fathers were acting irresponsibly by squandering church money on a speculative scheme that had no chance of success. More than $2 million had been spent on various development-related expenses by the time the commission issued its third rejection. The church's lawyers estimated a court battle challenging the constitutionality of the Landmarks Law would cost an additional $300,000 to $600,000, if it went all the way to the U.S. Supreme Court.

Armstrong and his fellow committee members also alleged legal improprieties in the way the rector and vestry presented the development project to the parish. Thanks to an early move by Armstrong, the church adopted a bylaw requiring parish approval of the sale or lease of church property. Two votes were ultimately taken. In December 1981 the congregation approved a development deal by 21 votes out of more than 700. In September 1986 parishioners signaled their approval again, this time with 60 percent of the vote. In both instances the committee claimed voters were vaguely informed at best and perhaps intentionally misinformed by the church.

*   *   *

The Protestant Episcopal Church of America is hierarchical, like its parent, the Church of England. The diocese is the political unit. There are ninety-eight Episcopal dioceses in the United States, governed by as many bishops. The dioceses are divided into parishes, each headed by a priest, or rector, who is charged with caring for the spiritual life of his or her congregation. Vestries, elected by secret ballot and composed of laymen and laywomen, serve as agents and legal representatives of the parish in matters concerning the property of the religious corporation and in the relations of the parish to its clergy. Junior and senior church wardens are chief counselors to the rector and have powers similar to those of officers in a secular corporation.

Given the Episcopal command structure, parishioners would seem to have little opportunity to meddle in parish affairs. Yet the unique origins of this New World Protestant sect encouraged a certain testiness on the part of the internal opposition of St. Bart's.

The Protestant Episcopal Church of the United States is a new branch on the Protestant tree, an offspring of the American

Revolution. The Church of England had been on this continent for almost 200 years when those hostilities broke out. It held its first services near Hudson Bay, in 1578, and no scrap of paper signed at Yorktown could erase its presence.

The Constitution did away with established churches—those favored by the state and supported by taxes levied on the general population—for there was to be no "Church of the United States" as there was a Church of England. But most of the colonies continued to favor one or another sect, even after striking a blow for religious freedom, and the Anglican Church was high on the preferred list. (Connecticut, Maryland, Massachusetts, and New Hampshire continued to have established churches after ratifying the Constitution. Massachusetts gave up its established church, the Congregational, only in 1833.) The structure that remained in the former colonies could not be tied too closely to the Anglican Church, and it became, therefore, the Protestant Episcopal Church ("Episcopal," as in "episcopacy," or rule by bishop). It remained part of the Anglican Communion, however. That worldwide network is headed by the archbishop of Canterbury and consists of former mission churches which have chosen to maintain their ties to England.

Nevertheless, the American church evolved somewhat different views from the mother church about organization and where power should be lodged. Compared with the more rigidly hierarchical Anglican Church, the American wing of the Anglican Communion, according to the *Encyclopaedia Britannica,* turned into a "democratic institution in which the laity have practically as much power as the clergy." Part of that difference was no doubt due to geography. During its first 200 years in the American colonies, the Church of England never had a resident bishop but remained under the direct control of the bishop of London. It is not surprising that some degree of self-reliance evolved when guidance from the church hierarchy could be six months in coming. The first American bishop was not in place until almost a decade after the Declaration of Independence. A bishop can be consecrated only by another bishop, and after the Revolution, all those belonged to the

Church of England and consequently administered an oath of loyalty to the British king, hardly tolerable to the fledgling American church. Eventually it took advantage of an ancient enmity within the British Isles and, in 1784, convinced the bishop of Aberdeen to consecrate the Reverend Samuel Seabury (1729–1796) first bishop of the Episcopal Church of the United States. From that pioneer beginning the individual Protestant Episcopal churches in America have tended to operate with more autonomy than their sister parishes in England.

The decision to become an Episcopalian, a choice made by many famous Americans, involves some awareness of moving onto a higher social plateau. Episcopalians have always been in positions of political and economic power in our country; two-thirds of the signers of the Declaration of Independence, including Ben Franklin, were members of this church. At least three of America's finest nineteenth- and early-twentieth-century architects—Bertram Grosvenor Goodhue (architect of the present St. Bartholomew's), Richard Upjohn, and Stanford White—all chose to become Episcopalians. Few people who considered status when changing denominations thought of becoming Methodists, Presbyterians, or Lutherans, let alone Baptists.

Membership in other sects often reflects the ethnic composition of a city: Roman Catholic churches are in Polish, Italian, and Irish neighborhoods; Lutheran enclaves, in the Swedish and German quarters; and so on. The membership lists of Episcopal churches read like random samples from the telephone book. Although the sect is traditionally associated with white Anglo-Saxon Protestants, its prestige, combined with the ease of social migration in the new democracy, conferred an ecumenical character on the Episcopal Church, which kept it from being identified with a single ethnic group. The Roosevelts and Vanderbilts were Dutch Reformed before becoming Episcopalians in the 1820's and 1830's. A large Huguenot contingent included the famous Reveres, of Boston's equally famous (Episcopal) Old North Church. The Havemeyer family, of sugar-refining wealth, was originally German. Even Admiral David Farragut, a staunch supporter of the Episcopal Church, traced his ancestry to Catholic Portugal. The Episcopal Church is still the church of choice for many non-Episcopalians. The standard joke in this small sect is that its church marries and buries more people each year than it has members. (There are about 2 million Episcopalians in the United States.)

It was in an independent spirit befitting the new Episcopal Church that New York City's first St. Bartholomew's came into being. On January 10, 1835, a group placed a notice in a local religious periodical saying that services would begin in a rented room on the nineteenth of that month. Church historians say St. Bartholomew's was part of a movement to stem a rising tide of High Churchmen, who threatened to bring the Protestant church back into the fold of its old enemy the Roman Pope. (In Episcopal terminology, "Low Church" implies a preference for a less elaborate liturgy, with more emphasis on the sermon. "Just prayers and sermons," said one priest, "an intellectual trip.")

The first St. Bartholomew's Church, at the corner of Lafayette Place and Great Jones Street, was ready for occupancy in 1836. A critic of the day called it "very plain, and destitute of architectural beauty." However unpretentious the architecture (no doubt part of the Low Church bias against ostentation), the location of the church was well chosen. Its neighbors included Peter Cooper, a descendant of the Dutch family that had settled the island before New York was New York, John Jacob Astor, and the more recently arrived (socially and financially) Commodore Cornelius Vanderbilt. The social tone set by the first congregation of St. Bart's was to stay with it through two moves uptown.

Within a few decades—and in a scenario that was replayed nearly a century later—the lively commotion of commerce replaced the sedate residential character of Great Jones Street. In 1870 St. Bart's decided to look for a new home. Other Episcopal churches had already moved north to escape the bustle of downtown. St.

Bart's might have gotten as far uptown as St. Thomas did (Fifty-third Street and Fifth Avenue) had the Commodore's son, William H. Vanderbilt, not pegged the price of a lot on Madison Avenue and Forty-fourth Street too low to turn down. The second home of the young congregation was completed in 1872. Designed by James Renwick, in the Romanesque style, it was a more commanding structure than the first St. Bart's.

At that point in the history of the parish, the roster of St. Bartholomew's communicants included Henry Clay Frick, the railroad mogul; Charles W. Harkness, whose family gave tens of millions of dollars to Harvard and Yale universities; William D. Sloane (of the W. & J. Sloane department store family); and, of course, the next generation of Vanderbilts. It was not old money, but there was a lot of it.

Yet St. Bartholomew's was not just a church home for wealthy and socially aspiring New Yorkers. The social conscience of New York Episcopalians was well developed and generously exercised. The young St. Bart's followed the pattern set by Trinity, Wall Street. The mother church of the diocese had long provided spiritual and physical care for the downtrodden; in the early eighteenth century Trinity's catechists were already teaching young women and blacks to read and write. Like many churches in the late nineteenth century, St. Bartholomew's accounted for a fair portion of its annual operating expenses by renting pews, yet set aside free pews for the poor. Toward the end of the century, under the guidance of the extraordinary David Hummel Greer (rector from 1888 to 1904) and aided by the beneficence of its wealthier parishioners, St. Bartholomew's developed an extensive battery of mission, or outreach, programs. Cornelius Vanderbilt bought three lots to the south of the church in the late 1880's. With the help of a $250,000 gift from his mother, Mrs. William H. Vanderbilt, the church built the St. Bartholomew's Rescue Mission and Parish House among the tenements and saloons of East Forty-second Street. It opened in 1890, and the church added three additional lots a few years later to expand the facility. By the end of the century Cornelius Vanderbilt had given another $500,000 to provide long-term income for the Parish House and a like sum to support its missionary work.

Before Greer left St. Bart's to become bishop of New York, his church was offering Sunday programs in Swedish, Chinese, Armenian, and English to almost 2,000 young people and caring for the immigrant population of the city in a variety of other ways. The outreach ministry eventually embraced industrial schools, guild clubs, missionary societies, kindergartens, an employment bureau, a girls' boardinghouse, a clinic, and a loan association. In 1919 Mrs. T. J. Symington, of Baltimore, financed the renovation of the clinic into a hospital for gastrointestinal diseases.

When parishioners questioned the secular nature of their church's involvement, Greer answered: "It is spiritual, not always in its methods, but always in its aims." Long before the Reverend Tom Bowers arrived, St. Bartholomew's had a strong record of outreach ministries.

The Vanderbilt lot on Forty-fourth Street and Madison Avenue was a good deal financially but proved unsound geologically. By 1914 the church's second home was sinking into Manhattan at an alarming rate. Once again, however, the mixed blessings of commerce came to the church's rescue. Land values had increased substantially, enabling the church to sell well and purchase the brewery site on Park Avenue and Fifty-first Street which it still occupies.

An odd set of coincidences determined the look of the third St. Bartholomew's Church. Cornelius Vanderbilt, a major benefactor, died suddenly in 1899. Wanting to leave a lasting memorial to her husband, his widow donated an ornamental porch to the Madison Avenue church. The addition was magnificent. Designed by Stanford White, the porch is one of the few things that can be attributed to that flamboyant architect with any certainty. Daniel Chester French sculpted the seated Christ above its main portal, a figure that may have been the model for his later statue of the seated Lincoln, in the Washington, D.C., memorial.

The congregation learned about the inadequate foundations more than a decade after the porch was added. Mrs. Vanderbilt offered to pay to have her husband's monument moved to the new site on Park Avenue if it were used as the architectural frontispiece for the third St. Bartholomew's. By felicitous coincidence, the architect of the new building, Bertram Goodhue, was moving out of his Gothic phase into one that proved quite compatible with Stanford White's porch. The main body of the new St. Bartholomew's was to be neo-Byzantine.

In view of the present battle over its real estate, it is interesting that the rector and vestry of 1914 almost had a tower put on their site. One of three proposals Goodhue presented included an income-producing apartment building next to the church. Another scheme used only the front half of the site, so the two lots on the side streets could be sold off. A third plan, the one that carried the day, used the entire site for the church and its architectural accoutrements. A spokesman "denied that any attempt had been made to rival Saint Thomas's either in cost or architecture."

Bids for the original design came in higher than expected, and construction began on a modified design only in early 1917. The materials used in the new building included several varieties of European marble, whose delivery was delayed by the war. As a result, although the church opened for services in October 1918, the dedication took place in 1923. The Community House, terrace, and garden were finished in 1927, but only when the dome over the sanctuary was added, in 1930, was Goodhue's design complete.

So it remained, through the Depression, the war years, and the postwar boom. No one thought of changing the church, for it was the jewel of lower Park Avenue. There was certainly no reason to think something outside that church—home to so many powerful families—could threaten its life, least of all an upstart city agency like the Landmarks Preservation Commission.

*   *   *

Unlike most municipal agencies, the Landmarks Preservation Commission does not deal in quantities. Its province is not tons of garbage, miles of subway track, or per capita muggings. In the lackluster wording of the law that gave it life, the landmarks commission is to concern itself with preserving buildings and places of a "special character or a special historical or aesthetic interest or value." In short, the landmarks commission deals in that disturbingly unquantifiable commodity called "aesthetics."

"Unquantifiable" must not be confused with "intangible." It so happens that the aesthetic qualities of the finer old and new buildings of New York City are quite tangible assets in the minds of many and had been the focus of intense interest for at least three decades before Mr. Bowers and his vestry decided to improve their Park Avenue property.

When the Landmarks Law was adopted in 1965, it was only the official manifestation of an increasingly potent public interest in saving the physical remnants of the city's past. Historians say the acquisition of General Washington's Revolutionary War headquarters, at Newburgh, New York, launched the preservation movement in the United States. If so, the cause was slow in getting up to speed, for the headquarters building was purchased and restored in 1850.

According to the second chairman of the New York City Landmarks Preservation Commission, architect Harmon H. Goldstone, the origins of the commission can be traced almost as far back as those of the historic preservation movement. Goldstone says the seeds of the Landmarks Preservation Commission are found in the early decades of this century. In 1916 a private organization known as the Municipal Art Society suggested introducing walking tours to acquaint the general public with the city's architectural heritage. The suggestion was not taken up until the 1950's, however, around the same time other important preservation-related events were taking place. Three major exhibitions of New York City architecture appeared in as many years in the early fifties. It was an unusual coincidence, even in such an art-conscious city, and suggested that the public had reached a new plateau of awareness. By the late 1950's a private organization called the New York Community Trust was placing plaques on distinguished buildings. More important, in terms of the nuts and bolts of preservation on a grander scale, the Municipal Art Society was compiling a list of buildings of architectural merit in the five boroughs. The results came to the public eye in 1963, when the society published *New York Landmarks*, by Alan Burnham. Edward R. Finch, Jr., was on the board of directors of the Municipal Art Society at the time. Later a vestryman of St. Bart's and supporter of development, Finch noted with bitterness that Burnham's book included St. Bartholomew's, but as a third-rank landmark.

The intensified interest in the finer architecture of the city would have been frustrated without a statute to protect what remained of the legacy. The groundwork for that legislation was laid in June 1961, when several prominent citizens, including Jack Felt, then chairman of the City Planning Commission, Harmon H. Goldstone, and Geoffrey Platt, an architect who later became the first chairman of the landmarks commission, approached the mayor, Robert Wagner, with the idea of forming a commission to protect the city's landmarks. Shortly thereafter Wagner formed the Mayor's Committee for the Preservation of Historic and Aesthetic Structures. Within five months the committee had submitted a single page of recommendations—a substantial feat for a group with a title that long, said Goldstone.

Within three months the city's Board of Estimate had provided a modest budget appropriation of $50,000. Six months later the mayor appointed a twelve-member commission, headed by Platt. Between the summer of 1962 and May 1964 the legislation was hammered out, a process which involved countless conferences between the commission's subcommittee on legislation and the legal counsel of the city and the careful examination of landmarks statutes from forty-nine other municipalities. In April 1965, almost four years after the idea had been presented to the mayor, New

York City's Landmarks Law was on the books. The commission was given a three-part charge:

- Identify potential landmarks.
- Designate them.
- Make certain they are cared for after designation.

When the law was being written, the small staff of the newly formed commission was providing grist for later years, by searching the city for prime examples of the architectural styles that have highlighted its history. Identifying historically significant buildings in a city with more than 850,000 lots was (and still is) no simple task. St. Bartholomew's high visibility, afforded by its unique site, ensured it an early date with the commission. It received the call less than a year later. Dr. Terence J. Finlay was the rector at the time.

Old friends like Rob Morris, now treasurer of the Committee to Oppose, call him Terry and speak of him fondly as "one of the last of the great Edwardian rectors, a charming man, superb preacher, and good pastoral caretaker [with] as much business acumen as you would expect of a superb preacher and pastoral caretaker."

Business acumen or no, Finlay flatly opposed the landmark designation from the beginning. When advised of the commission's interest, the rector discussed it with the vestry and concluded that the church wanted no part of a designation. With a hint of disdain, Finlay told the commission how he and his vestry felt about the honor: "May I point out that several years ago this matter was brought before our vestry and it was decided that we did not wish to be included in any such designation nor to have any plaque attached to the building. I would, therefore, suggest that you omit St. Bartholomew's Church from such designation."

The young commission ignored the sweetly naïve suggestion. It held three hearings over a nine-month period and issued the designation report for St. Bartholomew's Episcopal Church on March 16, 1967.

For more than a decade St. Bartholomew's Church appeared able to live with its unwanted designation. Only after the arrival of Reverend Tom Bowers, and the series of events his coming set into motion, did the landmark status of St. Bart's become the focus of a battle that may be settled only by the Supreme Court of the United States.

*   *   *

Tommy Bowers had a close relationship with religion from his youth. While his family worshiped at First Lutheran, in Norfolk, Virginia, Tom was a solo-singing choirboy at St. Paul's Episcopal Church. Those who grew up with him were not surprised he chose the ministry. Tom's warmth and concern were traits that surfaced often in recollections of his childhood friends. "One of the most genuine, lovin' people I've ever known," said Bob Albergotti, who shared many experiences with the young Bowers. Albergotti described one scene, which had a Tom Sawyer–like quality about it: "As youngsters we were huntin' one day; we were in our teens, I guess. Tommy shot this bird, and afterwards he was heartbroken. He picked this little bird up, and I remember how tears just run down his eyes. He was just that tender, that sort of a lovin' person." Tommy was also smart, did well in school without noticeable effort, according to his longtime friend, and was well liked by his schoolmates.

Albergotti and other friends from Tom's early years did not hesitate to say that the tenderness in this "very kind, gentle person" was coupled with a strong will and a frank tongue. Tom was known for telling people what he believed. He never said anything for effect or to manipulate. "He'll tell you what he thinks about anythin' . . . straightforward, honest, ethical."

Tom's father, apparently concerned about a few boyish brushes with authority, arranged for his son to attend the Virginia Military Institute—the West Point of the South. Tom was graduated in 1949 with a degree in electrical engineering, one of the most disciplined and demanding majors offered. After he had worked a few months for General Electric, the Korean War brought Tom to the secular battlefield. Sixteen months overseas exposed him to suffering and agony that had a profound effect on his life. When he returned to Norfolk, habits that had once satisfied —the old friends and the country club—would no longer do. At the suggestion of a friend from his choirboy youth, Dr. Moultrie Guerry, rector of St. Paul's Episcopal Church, Tom considered the ministry. Guerry, a trustee of the University of the South, at Sewanee, convinced the admissions department to take Tom on twenty-four hours' notice, sight unseen. He earned a bachelor of Arts degree in 1953 and went on to the Virginia Episcopal Seminary.

Tom eventually married Margaret Harris Pendleton, the eldest child of a family prominent in local and state politics. Margaret is from the western mountain country of Virginia, stocky and solid, with a strong personality and good humor. "The perfect mate for Tom because of her love of partying," said one friend. Her style is broad, and like her husband, she can appear somewhat larger than life. She is an energetically engaging hostess and tremendous fun to be with, as a New York admirer put it. She is also a great cook and ran a gourmet cookware business while Tom was rector of St. Luke's in Atlanta. Margaret made no public statements about the controversy that eventually overtook their New York church, but friends said she was always ready to give counsel to Tom. The couple have four children, all of whom attended or are attending Sewanee. The eldest, also Margaret, married an Episcopal priest.

Tom Bowers's first church, or rather churches, were on the eastern shore of Virginia: St. George, in Pungoteague, and St. James, in Accomac. There he began a style of ministry that became his trademark. "Tom Bowers creates some sparks," said Philip H. Alston, a friend and former parishioner from Atlanta, and that is just what he did on the eastern shore.

It was in these years, said the rector in a 1980 interview, that he began to believe a responsible clergyman could not turn a blind eye if his church was in a segregated community. In a typically confrontational manner, and although some people swore they would leave the church, Tom baptized a black cleaning woman who worked for him and befriended an injured migrant worker, making certain the local hospital took him in.

St. Albans, a large church in Washington, D.C., called the still-young Tom Bowers from the hinterland of Virginia to serve as its assistant rector. His first position as head of a major parish was in an affluent church on Foxhall Road, in Washington. He came to St. Patrick's in 1961 and found a somewhat atypical Episcopal church. A fair percentage of its members were not even Episcopalians, but military families of various Protestant denominations whose jobs had brought them to Washington. In other ways, however, St. Patrick's was perfectly normal for Episcopal parishes of the time. It was not a very lively church, for example, and it was not a "young" church. Richard S. Beatty, a Washington lawyer who eventually became the senior warden under Tom, recalled that when he (Beatty) and his wife first visited the church, a helpful parishioner introduced them to the "other young couple."

Beatty had begun attending St. Patrick's only a week before Tom took over. He found the new rector attractive from the start. "Tom had a very direct and personal way of engaging a person, which made me feel as though he understood me, and saw things that I thought were valuable in me, right away, in ways that practically nobody ever had." For his part, Bowers found someone he could communicate with in Beatty and promptly asked him to run for the auxiliary vestry, although the new arrival had not yet even decided to become an Episcopalian. That was a pattern the rector took with him to later parishes. He liked having people around who agreed with him, regardless of how long they had been in his church. It was not a novel approach to the politics of life, religious or secular, but it would add to the pool of resentment that slowly accumulated when Tom came to St. Bartholomew's, perhaps partly because a few members of the opposition may have coveted the prestige of a vestry post.

The changes Tom brought to sedate St. Patrick's came rapidly and appear to have been possible because he could go head to head with people and convince them his road was the right one. That talent eventually endeared him to most of his Washington parishioners, but there were some rough spots.

In 1966 Tom brought in a black priest as an assistant, the first black priest in the history of St. Patrick's. Jesse Anderson had been rector of the Church of the Advocate, in a part of Philadelphia known as the "jungle." He elected to move on but wanted to go to a church interested in inner-city problems. Paul Moore, Jr., the present bishop of New York, was then a suffragan (assistant) bishop in Washington, and Anderson contacted him to see if there was a post in the Washington diocese that might suit him. Knowing Tom wanted to start an urban ministry at St. Patrick's, Bishop Moore suggested Reverend Anderson contact him.

Black clergy were rarely invited to join white Episcopal churches in the mid-1960's, yet when St. Patrick's was interviewing for the position of assistant rector, Tom picked Anderson over four other candidates. He was the only black and, by his own admission, had the least impressive urban credentials. There were some objections. One church member told Tom that when Jesse came in, he would go out. There were also telephone death threats to the rector, and sixty to seventy parishioners left the congregation. But the vestry stood behind Tom and his new assistant.

What happened once Anderson had arrived on fashionable Foxhall Road helps explain something of how Tom Bowers works. The black priest found "no concept at all of what [the urban scene] was" and no plan for getting involved—just a strong desire. People from all periods of Tom's past said he was not so much an initiator of programs as a catalyst. As Anderson put it, Tom's "greatness" was in his willingness to try anything. So, while Tom and the vestry extended the invitation, Anderson developed the outreach program.

The rector and vestry envisioned some kind of hookup between St. Patrick's and a black urban church. With that in mind, Anderson spent the better part of the summer of 1966 in the black neighborhoods of Washington, D.C., looking for a place to open a mission. He got to know the communities, figured out what to do and where to do it, and eventually established the Southeast Enrichment Center.

The center was an outreach ministry, a program that originated in the parish but extended beyond it. Outreach has played an important role in each of Tom Bowers's churches; one might even say that the outreach ministries of his churches have been responsible for most of the rector's fame or notoriety. The ones he later started at St. Bartholomew's became the focus of considerable attention from friend and foe alike.

St. Patrick's financed the enrichment center the way most churches finance their outreach programs: Some help comes from the parent organization; the rest from external sources. The seed money for the center, along with the assistant rector's salary, came out of St. Patrick's operating budget. Anderson recalled that being between $20,000 and $25,000. Once the center had been established, outside grants and gifts covered its operating expenses and staff salaries, except for Anderson's.

The chemistry between Tom Bowers and those of his flock who objected to his innovations was sometimes explosive. As assitant rector, Jesse Anderson also participated in day-to-day parish life. Tom had him celebrate the Eucharist one Sunday, and afterward a middle-aged lady kept Tom pushed up against the side wall of the nave for almost forty-five minutes, while she railed at him for letting a black priest give communion. Tom took all this calmly and eventually told the lady Jesse would also be celebrating at Thanksgiving. "I hope you'll be there," said the rector. In a testimony to the rector's powers, the irate lady came to the Thanksgiving service and brought her entire family to take the bread and wine offered by St. Patrick's black clergyman.

Anderson preached on occasion, and he described one Sunday when he "let 'em have it," expressing some cynical views about how far the government would go in supporting the black community. His chewing out did not sit well with a retired general and vestryman named Clovis Beyers, once an aide to General Douglas

A. MacArthur. Later that day Anderson received a call from the rector, who told him General Beyers would like to speak with him, in the rector's office, at eight o'clock sharp the next morning.

The way Tom orchestrated that meeting showed his preference for direct confrontation over subtle diplomacy. There was no attempt to smooth things over. The rector was 100 percent behind his clergyman but did not play the negotiator. He placed the combatants across from each other and left them to settle things themselves. The exchange was not decisive: The general advised Anderson that there was no way for him to win the fight if they (the blacks) went to war, to which the priest replied: "I know that, General, but you'll be in one hell of a battle."

Tom once got the church involved in a Head Start project, which was even less palatable to some members of the congregation than having a black assistant. Vestryman Richard Beatty said it involved busing black children from the inner city to the church each day during one summer, and created fears of rape and pillage among some members of the congregation, although the children were only four and five years old. Hundreds of parishioners turned out at a vestry meeting, demanding to know who was responsible for bringing the blacks into their neighborhood. "He made a lot of people fighting mad. Tom didn't mind that. I think a part of him really enjoys it. He's got a bit of 'I don't mind tweaking anybody's nose' in him."

If Tom introduced serious controversy into the quiet parish of St. Patrick's and caused some defections, he also recruited new members. A few people from Washington's international community came to see a refreshing curiosity: an integrated church in America's capital. Others, particularly among the young, were attracted by the rector's open, friendly style.

One aspect of his first rectorate is particularly interesting considering the events at St. Bartholomew's. Tom showed that he possessed in abundance a skill most clerics only dream of: a warmth and intensity that enabled him to convince parishioners to give to their church generously and often. "He was a very good fund raiser," said Beatty, "extremely good." He was so convincing he had outsiders giving to the church. One man, to whom Tom had once ministered, gave between $5,000 and $10,000 every Christmas, at a time when the top pledges among parishioners were around $2,000. Raising money was so easy for him that when Reverend Anderson heard his former chief was going to St. Bartholomew's, he immediately assumed its parishioners were looking for someone with a proved ability to attract money.

Tom's remarkable gift was fortunate, for it balanced a tendency to spend on a somewhat immodest scale. Anderson remembered that St. Patrick's budget was well above that of other Washington churches of comparable size during Bowers's tenure.

Tom's reputation as a mover and shaker soon spread through the Episcopal community, and on the weekend of July 4, 1971, he was expecting visitors. A few weeks earlier Brad Currey and another vestryman from St. Luke's, in Atlanta, had phoned to say they would like to pay a call. The visitors were participating in a rite that goes on hundreds of times each year, as one parish tries to lure a clergyman away from another.

"Dressed the best we could," they rang the rectory bell. Tom opened the door himself and found two men who looked like IBM executives. "Then this ruddy-faced, wide-eyed, bright-eyed sort of stocky fellow turned around and shouted up the stairs: 'Margaret, did you call the undertakers?' "

At dinner that evening they talked about the church in Atlanta. If it was not moribund, Currey told the potential rector, it was close to it. The vestryman recalled using a phrase that turned up with machinelike regularity whenever parishioners on either side of the St. Bart's controversy tried to explain why that church had invited Tom Bowers to New York. St. Luke's needed "shaking up," said the vestryman from Atlanta.

The polite playacting that accompanies the search for a new rector—the "Hi, we're just visiting from an out-of-town parish" approach—fooled no one. Tom knew what Currey was up to from the first telephone call. Currey himself said he had not been too coy. There seemed to be little sense in dancing around the subject

33

since Tom didn't seem to be that type of fellow. But the directness of the gentlemen from Atlanta did not help. Tom said he wasn't interested in leaving St. Patrick's. It took them months before he finally agreed to come.

Hayes Clement, a senior warden under Bowers at St. Luke's, later spoke of a few of the attractions that might have made Tom's break with St. Patrick's less painful. Among them were the opportunity to run serious social programs in a real urban setting (the church was near downtown Atlanta), the "potential in terms of financial resources," and the congregation's open-mindedness and willingness to take risks. Salary and other financial incentives also play a part in attracting a a rector, of course. "When you're looking for a top rector in the Episcopal Church," Clement continued, "you go and steal him from another church, that is the simplest way of saying it."

The Reverend David Gordon, stewardship officer for the diocese of New York, compared the process of looking for a rector with "headhunting" in the corporate world. Gordon is a good-looking, fatherly figure, who spent most of his ministry in the far West before coming to New York. When he entered the ministry in 1951, a vestry that was looking for a new rector would meet with the bishop, pick two or three names by the end of the evening, and have one of them on the job within a month. Financial incentives were rarely an issue in those days, said Gordon. "I guess people assumed parishes were doing what they could do and accepted what [money] there was if they wanted the call."

The process of "calling" a rector is more refined today. The vestry starts off with word-of-mouth recommendations, moves on to examine written and informal résumés, and then interviews candidates. If the right person is reluctant to come, direct and indirect financial incentives—"perks" in the business community— are laid on the bargaining table. That was what happened in Tom's case. As one longtime friend put it, they sweetened the salary until it was too good to pass up. An ex-parishioner from Atlanta couched it more delicately: Tom came to St. Luke's because it was "a step up" in terms of both the size of the parish and "compensation and that sort of thing."

St. Luke's Episcopal church was on Peachtree Street, in downtown Atlanta. If one believes the stories that are now part of the legend of Tom Bowers, when he arrived at St. Luke's it was suffering the fate of many other urban churches, a slow economic death brought on by white flight.

The facts are not as clear as legend. According to Patty Weatherly, the church was dying on the vine, and Tom turned things around. But Weatherly arrived a year or so after Tom. Those who were there before the new rector did not hesitate to describe St. Luke's as a strong parish. There was some maintenance to attend to and perhaps a few "underfunded programs," said Hayes Clement, but the church operated at a profit and never ate into its endowment. If membership and pledging were down a bit before the new rector came, Clement suggested the church had probably brought it on itself. St. Luke's had been sponsoring a number of suburban churches for several years by the time Tom came, and that might have given some parishioners the idea of leaving. Even Brad Currey (who emphasized the down side when trying to lure Tom from Washington) gave roughly the same estimate of St. Luke's financial affairs. It might have been "runnin' a bit on the rims" but was by no means broke. The church always took care to fit its programs to its budget.

Whatever the case, the population flow shifted toward St. Luke's after the new rector was installed. Tom's down-home style drew people from all over metropolitan Atlanta and its outlying suburbs. Patty Weatherly moved to Atlanta in 1973, when her husband transferred from the Midwest to a new job with Monroe Auto Equipment Company. Tom had made such an impression on the folks in Atlanta by that time that a friend of Weatherly's suggested she and her husband drive the twenty or so miles into the city one Sunday just to listen to the rector. "We went down to hear him and were hooked," said Weatherly. Although they lived well outside what could reasonably be called a parish boundary, Mr. and Mrs. Weatherly became active members of St. Luke's, as did many other citizens of metropolitan Atlanta.

Shortly after that first visit Patty Weatherly received a telephone call from the rector. Would she like to become his secretary? She had decided not to take a job in Atlanta, but her resolve evaporated when she talked with the charming rector. "He was just so homey over the phone he sounded like he would be a fun person to work with." And Patty Weatherly did, for the next five years, until St. Bartholomew's called Tom Bowers to New York.

It was demanding work in some respects. "If someone needed him, he was up and gone at the drop of a hat," and he would stay as long as the need lasted. On the other hand, his staff was not under the pressure of regular day-to-day demands from the boss— not because his standards were lax, as Weatherly put it, but because he delegated authority. "That's what I want done," he would say. "Do it any way you like."

That is not to say that anyone ever doubted who was in charge at St. Patrick's. The Episcopal installation ceremony leaves no room for that. The keys to the church are presented to the new rector while the officiating priest reads this passage from the Bible: "I place the key of the house of David on his shoulder; should he open, no one shall close, should he close, no one shall open." (Isaiah 22:22.) The rigor with which a rector exercises that near-absolute power varies with the personality, of course, yet even a strong rector can have difficulties. Once in charge, the new rector is engaged in a continuing dialogue with the vestry about the secular operation of the parish, including which of his programs it will fund and how the money will be raised. Parish politics is like politics outside parishes, and it is not uncommon for rectors to clash with someone on the vestry and to have a pet project nixed. But Tom seemed to have a special knack. His projects were not always welcomed when first presented, but in St. Luke's Tom managed either to convince the opposition or to get them out, just as he had in St. Patrick's. But that was something he could not accomplish in New York.

His success in Atlanta may have been partly due to coincidence: Tom Bowers was the right man in the right place at the right time. He took over from a "headmaster" type. "Ed Tate was a shy, brilliant theologian," Clement volunteered, "but couldn't remember people's names, and read his sermons." (Reading sermons in an Episcopal church is unprofessional, like an actor with script in hand on opening night.)

If Tate lacked magnetism in his sermonizing, he had done his best in the early sixties to get St. Luke's to reach out to the community, but with little success. "Here was a mild, meek man who was just catchin' all kinds of abuse. Although he paid with a part of his own hide, he did get the church to begin to look a little bit outward." But that was the early sixties, and serious social outreach was not yet fashionable. Tom Bowers arrived in the early seventies, several years after the official policy of the national Episcopal Church had shifted toward social activism, and managed to take St. Luke's much further out into the community than most souls in the congregation ever thought possible.

For the ordinary parishioners, Tom's approach to religion was quite different from what they were accustomed to. He enjoyed his religion and made it fun to be in church. The youthful, sometimes naïve ethos of the sixties pervaded his ministry; the ferocity of the Old Testament's vengeful Jehovah gave way to a delight in God. Tom did not ignore the laws, but the spirit in the church shifted from repentance to joy. (His critics at St. Bart's called it the "feel good" approach to religion.) By the time he had been in Atlanta a year, the place was jumping. "I'd never been to a church where you clapped your hands and kinda danced around a little bit," said Weatherly. "I tell you, he made it fun to go to church, and when he preached, you sat glued. There was an aura around him." The flock would go from the Sunday service to the parish hall and not want to leave.

The rector's personal life-style was also appealing. He enjoyed secular pleasures. He liked to eat well, openly enjoyed his drink, and smoked good cigars. There was no question of wantonness, but the way Tom sported these inoffensive frailties was eye-opening to those who had only known rectors cut from less human stuff. It made them feel good about him and therefore about his church.

Several parishioners pointed out that one of Tom's greatest strengths was his ability to inspire. "He got people so fired up that they could do something." His openness offered a fertile field in which to sow new programs. While the impetus was very much from Tom, the programs generated rarely originated with him. Nor did he get directly involved in them. "He never had the time to do that," said Patty Weatherly. He spent a lot of time preparing sermons, and although he never went out on Saturday nights, parishioners invited him and his wife to dinner almost every night of the week. "They hardly had any time to themselves. Everybody wanted to party with Tom and Margaret."

According to Brad Currey, Tom refocused the spiritual energy of the congregation. It began with changes in the service itself. One of the first things Bowers did was commandeer a table and set it between the pulpit and the lectern. It replaced the altar at the end of the apse, for when the priest stood there, his back was to the congregation. Everything about the new rector's service was directly connected to the congregation.

Tom included baptisms in the services in those days, something rare when he first came to Atlanta. Currey said he would never forget the first one. Tom held up a tiny infant and walked down the center aisle of the church saying, "Let us welcome the newly baptized," to a great roar of welcome and approval from the crowd.

Parishioners also remembered Tom Bowers as a social activist, interested in improving the quality of physical life in the city, just as he felt he was improving the quality of spiritual life in his parish. There was no "worshiping once a week" and then closing down the church, as Philip Alston put it. The church was put to work for the community.

Alston served on the search committee that picked Tom and was at St. Luke's for his entire ministry, except for the two years he served as Jimmy Carter's ambassador to Australia. When he was asked about the rector's best qualities, Alston paused a moment, then answered in a way that explains why Tom Bowers is controversial: "I think his concept of Christianity is different from that of most Episcopalians who are often willing to sit down, look at the Book of Common Prayer, and that's it—the beginning and end of everything." Alston admitted that he had been one of those Episcopalians before the rector convinced him passive Christianity wouldn't do. Tom had things to accomplish, people who needed attention, parts of Atlanta that needed looking after.

One subject for attention was the integration of St. Luke's. Since it was near the heart of downtown Atlanta, most of the people who lived around the church were black. During Mr. Tate's time "I would say we probably kept black people out of the church," admitted Alston. "[We] let 'em know, if they came to the door, that they weren't welcome." Tom "would not tolerate an all-white parish." A few years after he became rector, "it was no longer a surprise to see a black at St. Luke's." As he had in Washington, Tom wanted black clergy. He hired two, both African seminarians.

Hayes Clement's recollection of Tom's early years at St. Luke's are slightly different from Alston's. Although Bowers may have aimed for a more dramatic mixture in the congregation, according to his friend and former senior warden, there was not "significantly more" integration than under Tate. By 1985 five or ten times more blacks were attending than did in Bowers's time, largely the result, Clement believes, of the strength of a black clergyman who came after Tom left for New York, the Reverend Dr. Reynell Parkins. Like Ed Tate, it would seem, Tom Bowers paved the way for the next increment of change.

It was St. Luke's soup kitchen that made the church and its rector nationally known. The idea came from Jenny Pierson, a parishioner who approached Tom one day and told him she wanted to help feed the poor. Tom's job was to convince the vestry it was a good idea, and he did.

At first the soup kitchen was not a kitchen at all. Jenny and her husband made soup and sandwiches in their home and handed them out at the church. Only later was a kitchen set up on the premises. Some members objected to drunks using their church, even if they were hungry. "When you came in after they had gone, it could smell so bad you could barely stand it. But we got used to it," said Patty Weatherly. Tom overcame the opposition.

St. Luke's soup kitchen was (and still is) a volunteer operation, with fifty to sixty people of various denominations coming from all over the city to lend a hand each day. Volunteers opened the parish hall for meals from eleven o'clock till noon, then scrubbed it down and made it ready for more traditional church functions. Gifts from parishioners, other churches, and various secular sources paid for this large and complex operation.

William Milliken met Tom through a city-wide program called Leadership Atlanta. He came into the church because of Tom, who was also responsible for Milliken's wife's being one of the first women ordained as an Episcopal priest.

Milliken started out working as a Sunday school teacher at St. Luke's and ended up starting the Street Academy, a school for dropouts. It was conceived as a partnership between the city school system and St. Luke's, to provide uneducated youths with skills that would help them make their way in the world. Parishioners could get involved directly by tutoring and providing jobs for students and graduates.

Some members disliked the idea of the academy. Others simply felt put out by the inconvenience. A bunch of ragtag black street kids using the Sunday school classrooms during the week meant the rooms had to be completely rearranged each weekend. Whatever the objections, Bowers made it clear that you would share Jesus' concern and care for your neighbor if you chose to be a member of St. Luke's.

Eventually the difficulties brought about by the scheduling overlap were overcome, for the Street Academy grew too big to fit in the basement. Someone donated a neighboring building, and the congregation raised the money to renovate it and moved the school there. The church put up the money to pay the director's salary, and the Atlanta school system supplied three or four fully accredited teachers. By the mid-eighties about 100 sixteen- and seventeen-year-olds were enrolled.

The academy thrived only because of Tom's fund-raising abilities. "They raised a whole lot more money after he got things cranked up at St. Luke's," said Milliken. As he had in Washington, Tom convinced parishioners who hadn't been giving before to give. He also built a strong vestry and supplied the leadership needed to make these outreach programs possible.

Tom's Sunday morning "folk mass" caused a revolution in the way children thought about church. It brought them in, from college age down to toddlers, and Brad Currey called it an extraordinary experience for everyone.

"It was the first time in our life of raising children that we didn't have to kick them out of bed to get them to church," he marveled. The kids followed Tom and kept coming back. The music was contemporary (Currey's older son, then fifteen, was the jazz drummer), but there was "nothing in the least profane about it. It was truly religious. It had warmth and beauty and a sense of praise and thanksgiving."

Other programs also blossomed at St. Luke's, all self-funding. Time and Talent, which offered women seventy years old and up a chance to donate their skills to the church, proved that Tom's appeal went beyond the younger set. "Those little old ladies just loved him," said Patty Weatherly. "You know, he'd come in and pat 'em and hug 'em. He's a toucher. He hugs and touches a lot, which really rubbed off on the congregation at St. Luke's."

Tom was also involved in starting a television ministry at St. Luke's. Easterners tend to shove all religious television programming into a suspicious little bin called fundamentalism, which is another way of saying "southern" religion. But the appeal of the television ministry is determined less by regional differences than by denomination. There was little or no precedent for television programming among mainline Protestant sects in the South— Presbyterians, Methodists, Lutherans—and the southern branch of the Episcopal Church had no tradition of electronic ministering.

A young priest named Charles Sumners was the force behind

the television ministry at St. Luke's. Described as way ahead of his time for an Episcopalian, he had first worked for Tom as a seminarian at St. Patrick's, and they had hit it off well. When he was graduated and Tom's assistant left, Sumners got the job, and the rector asked him to come along when the call came from Atlanta. Sumners was to follow Bowers to St. Bartholomew's, where many assumed the television ministry was the real reason huge amounts of capital had to be generated through development.

Charles Sumners had dreamed of reaching out to people through television for some time and began to develop the idea of a TV ministry at St. Luke's in 1973. Bowers was a theological moderate but was willing to try new ideas and believed he could offer a temperate alternative to conservative television preachers.

When Sumners first suggested an electronic ministry for St. Luke's—with the rector's backing—it met with strong resistance in the vestry. St. Luke's had always been a conservative church (not unlike St. Bartholomew's in that respect), and the vestry was uncomfortable with the notion of TV ministering, not to speak of cluttering up the nave with the paraphernalia necessary for a television production. The electronic church raised some eyebrows in Atlanta, just as it would in New York. But Tom convinced them in Atlanta.

At first the programming was a simple affair. A commercial television station in Atlanta offered airtime from eleven to noon each Sunday. The time slot rotated among different denominations on a three-month cycle. There was no charge, but this kind of ministry was not for parishes strapped for funds, since each church provided its own equipment. St. Luke's received a gift of between $35,000 to $50,000 to cover the up-front cost, the result of Tom's gift for fund raising.

The response was phenomenal. Average attendance in the church was between 700 and 800, perhaps 1,000 on a good Sunday, said Brad Currey; it reached 20,000 via the airways. Hundreds of appreciative letters came in, mainly from the bedridden, who would not otherwise have been able to see a service. The programming continued for three years, but the station eventually found it too costly to donate that hour and began charging. St. Luke's could not afford commercial rates and switched over to cable transmission.

Whatever Tom Bowers had in mind when he came to New York praising the virtues of the electronic church, the Atlanta experience that whetted his appetite was never a money-maker. Unlike the PTL and other famous television ministries, St. Luke's made no brazen pleas for contributions. A few times, perhaps a dozen since transmissions began, a sign would flash on the screen saying the service was in memory of so-and-so, and you could send a check to support St. Luke's television if you wished, but nothing much ever came in that way.

Toward the end of Tom's Atlanta ministry, St. Luke's ran a large, capital-fund-raising campaign, which grew out of a meeting between Tom and two vestrymen. Bob Alston (Philip's brother) and Brad Currey met with Tom one afternoon to tell him some of the church's programs would have to be cut to increase the maintenance budget (the roof was leaking, parapets needed repair, windows were rotting, and so on, the standard litany of what goes wrong with old buildings). The cost of operating the church had also risen significantly, mainly because of the people hired to run the new programs.

"Tom is perfectly capable of getting in high dudgeon, putting it as politely as I can," Brad Currey said. "I've never seen a man angrier in my life, and we were close friends. He was absolutely furious, in a towering rage."

Tom chewed them up one side and down the other, and ended up saying, "You two so-and-sos didn't tell me when you got me to come down here that the damn roof leaked!" (It had been repeatedly patched by the time he came down and was already leaking again.) Tom did not suggest selling or developing St. Luke's property, however. He took the traditional path to solving a church's financial crisis. He ended his five-minute tirade by asking the two men if a million-dollar fund-raising drive would satisfy them. Currey doubted the rector could do it but was more than comfortable with the figure. "Then we'll raise a million dollars," said Tom. When the vestrymen asked him how, he said he didn't know. He would tell them later.

Patty Weatherly remembered the rector's coming into the office after that meeting and casually informing her about the fund raiser.

"What's the goal?" asked his secretary, in an equally offhand manner.

"A million five," he answered, whereupon his loyal secretary suggested he might be suffering from a weakness in the upper regions.

The capital campaign was to be run by the vestry, with the help of a professional fund raiser. The latter was Tom's idea, but when the fund raiser heard how high the church's sights were set, she was not encouraging. One and a half million dollars was an impossible figure for a church. Tom offered her a gracious way out, suggesting that people who didn't want to join what they thought was a losing battle should retreat now. She stayed, and they surpassed their goal. In four months the church raised $1.7 million, more than any Episcopal parish Currey ever heard of.

The money came from individuals, not large corporate donors. The parish was entirely caught up. "Little old ladies" who lived on Social Security wanted to give, even if they could afford only $1 a week. The rector was the most effective instrument in the drive; Currey credited him with raising $1 million on his own.

Others were equally awed by the rector's powers. Everette Doffermyre, a member of the fund-raising committee, considered Tom's performance just shy of miraculous. Doffermyre saw the rector take what everyone thought was an impossible situation and turn it into a triumph, "by virtue of sheer energy and magnetism, and authentic Christian power to communicate."

"If Tom went and did the talking," said Currey enthusiastically, "he could persuade anybody to give everything they had." The rector visited one widow who watched the televised services and explained to her that the church just couldn't continue doing that without serious funding. He left with a check for $150,000.

Currey also recalled that he and his wife agreed to the biggest financial commitment they had ever made—without knowing where the money was going to come from. That was the kind of giving Tom Bowers could inspire. "There's not another one like him anywhere."

Despite the programs that began while he was at St. Luke's, no one ever called Tom Bowers a superb administrator. His skills were political, rather than bureaucratic. Patty Weatherly called him a "people person first, an administrator second, or even third." Years later a vestryperson at St. Bartholomew's said offhandedly he would be stunned if anyone who had ever worked with Tom said he had any administrative talent. In general, the rector's managerial approach appears to have fallen nearer to a Reagan-like concern for the overview than to a Carteresque attention to detail. But whether Tom knew who was cutting up the celery for the soup or just stood back and told Jenny Pierson to "let 'er rip," the programs begun in his parish probably would not have happened without him.

One thing came through unambiguously in the recollections of his Atlanta parishioners. Tom was a dogged fighter. "He wouldn't pick a fight but wouldn't let anyone push him around either." Visions of Jimmy Stewart ambling down a dusty street. "He's gonna say what he thinks is right, and what he thinks is the Christian thing to be doin'," Hayes Clement said flatly. "He's not gonna stray from that, regardless of what people think."

Tom's feistiness came out in his handling of the parish. Politicking can take many different forms. One can feel one's way through a thicket of different opinions diplomatically. As the rector of one large New York church put it, you listen to all sides as they babble on, find out which pike they're on, and then gently move them over to where you want them to be. Or you can blow away dissenters by the sheer force of personality—Tom's approach. No smoldering fires of dissension clouded life in his parishes. If the differences were irreconcilable, the losing side—the one that opposed the rector—left the church. That was the way it had been in Washington, and that was the way it was in Atlanta. Malcontents were not actively evicted; they just had to decide "if they wanted to grow" with Tom and the parish, as William Milliken put it. If they did not, they moved on to a place more to their liking. Episcopalians traditionally vote with their feet.

It may have surprised Tom, but many who chose not to "grow" in New York also chose not to move on. From time to time during the Battle of St. Bart's, vestrymen and church wardens pointedly asked them to leave. They were even subjected to tongue-lashings by their own bishop. But the core of loyal opposition stayed at St. Bartholomew's.

II

ACCORDING to Bob Albergotti, who visited Tom from time to time in Atlanta, some church or other was always trying to lure him away from St. Luke's. How many offers he received in his seven years in Atlanta is not known. It is known that his work there—particularly the soup kitchen and his fund-raising abilities—turned him into a nationally known figure in the Episcopal Church. It is also known that it took St. Bartholomew's, one of the country's wealthiest and most prestigious Episcopal churches, three separate "courtin' " visits before it got Tom to say "I do." If ever a congregation was in love with its minister, it was St. Luke's, and the rector stunned his parishioners when he told them he was leaving.

St. Bartholomew's first approached Tom Bowers in late 1977, less than nine months after his amazingly successful capital drive.

He and Margaret made at least one inspection trip to New York, in December of that year. Tom told the vestry of St. Luke's about the visitors from up North but said he had turned them down.

After the fund-raising triumph of the previous spring the thought that the rector might leave was too farfetched for most people at St. Luke's to credit. Brad Currey had an inkling, however. "I knew that this rascal was comin' down from New York City to visit us," he said with a hearty laugh, "and I knew he wasn't here for his health. The little gentleman stood out in a crowd, although he was small." The "rascal" was Marc Haas (" 'Has,' as we call him down here"), who was then senior warden of St. Bartholomew's. "Some people in New York might have thought Tom Bowers was just another sweet-talkin' southern preacher. Not Marc Haas," commented Currey. "He's an astute judge of horse-flesh."

Marc Haas was born in Cincinnati, Ohio, in 1908, went to Horace Mann School, in New York, and Princeton. Like Disraeli and a few other famous Episcopalians, Haas came to the Anglican Communion from Judaism. Rumor at St. Bartholomew's had it that he had amassed a personal fortune of more than $100 million, and with it a reputation as a skillful politician and acute businessman. Even his hobby eventually turned into a lucrative pastime. He started collecting stamps when he was five, and in 1979 he sold 3,500 of them for more than $10 million. He said giving up the collection was like losing his children.

The process of getting Tom to New York became something of a religious experience for Marc Haas, according to Charles Sumners. The senior warden seemed to be convinced that his own calling was to bring this charismatic preacher to his church. "[Haas] is a man who was very used to power," said Sumners, but "he is a spiritually aware man, he's got a deep and meaningful relationship with God, and he was genuinely interested in the future of St. Bartholomew's."

Tom's congregation learned of his decision in late April, 1978, through St. Luke's weekly newsletter, the *Messenger*: "As I write this letter to each of you, my dear friends and fellow parishioners, my heart is filled with sadness and grief, for last night I offered my resignation to the vestry of the parish effective June 15 in order to accept a call to become the rector of St. Bartholomew's Church in New York City." With a flair for dramatic oratory that New Yorkers would soon get to know, Tom described the city to which he was being called as "'struggling for its life," and St. Bartholomew's as a dying church in desperate need of the "very gifts God has given me"—the ability to bring "new life, enthusiasm, joy, and love to parishes which are in need of regeneration." Age was also a consideration. He was fifty and did not expect to have the energy needed to regenerate a parish for too many more years. He saw St. Bartholomew's as his "last adventure of this kind."

Apparently not everyone read the *Messenger,* for there were audible gasps when he announced his departure in church the following Sunday. Years later the shock of that announcement was still clear in Patty Weatherly's mind. "He was so loved and nurtured by the people at St. Luke's that no one could believe he would leave."

She asked him about it at the time, and Tom simply said he had prayed about it, talked with Margaret again and again, and finally came to the conclusion that the Lord wanted him to do it. "I'm sure he has questioned the Lord many times since then," Weatherly added without hesitation.

Brad Currey, for one, tried to convince him not to leave. New York was a very different place from Atlanta, he advised, different from anyplace Tom had ever been. "Some of that was plain old sectional prejudice" on his part, admitted Currey, "but I just felt it was a mistake." Besides, there was a tremendous amount of productive work still left for Tom at St. Luke's.

In the end, St. Luke's parishioners could only take the parting as a fact of church life. In his open letter to the parish Bowers wrote of his early realization that the ministry was a nomadic calling and counseled that the pain and anger felt by the parish would soon pass. That was not enough to mollify some of his charges, obviously distressed that the rector could breach the bonds of parish life so easily. Among other parting gifts the rector received a bouquet of black flowers, carefully bound with a black ribbon.

Larry Lord, then Tom's senior warden, had apparently been told of the rector's decision beforehand, for he wrote an open letter in the same issue of the *Messenger*. Lord, too, used the word "anger" but went on to speak of the legacy Tom was leaving and the need to carry on the good works in other locations. In a curious choice of images, the final paragraph of Lord's letter quoted Zorba, the swaggering fictional Greek: "Life is trouble . . . to be alive is to undo your belt and look for trouble." He followed the earthy image with a prophetic closing sentence: "We know that St. Bartholomew's—rather all of New York City—better start preparing itself for your presence."

Tom Bowers and his parish felt he could take on the world and win.

Although Tom said his Lord called him to New York, he did not answer the call right away. On the vestrymen's first visit to Atlanta, the scrapper in Tom made him tell them that he was the wrong man for their church. I'll change everything at St. Bartholomew's, he said. He came anyway. However, there were hints that Currey's fears of possible problems in New York might be well founded.

In December 1977 Tom and his wife, Margaret, traveled to New York to scout St. Bartholomew's. John Chappell, then a warden of the associate vestry, took a call from Marc Haas's secretary a short time before the visit. A candidate for Dr. Finlay's position was going to be in town a few days before Christmas, and the senior warden wanted the associate vestry to have a luncheon for him on the twenty-third.

Like Bowers, John Chappell was born and raised in Virginia, growing up some fifteen miles from Tom's home. He is elegantly dressed and soft-spoken, with manners like a PR man's vision of the southern gentleman. His dark hair is never out of place, and on the hottest summer day he wears the banker's three-piece uniform as though it had a built-in air conditioner.

The associate vestry, of which Chappell was senior warden, did not occupy an official niche in the church hierarchy but advised the vestry informally on occasion and often functioned as a link between parishioners and the somewhat aloof body of church governors. The associate vestry was also a way station en route to greater power in the church, and some said John Chappell may have fancied that power.

After the call from Haas's secretary, Chappell noted that December 23 was "a very difficult date for Christians," a time when many people, particularly Manhattanites, were getting ready to leave town to see their families. Almost half the associate vestry was already gone, but that was the least of the problems. All the rental rooms in the Community House were booked for holiday parties. Chappell was a member of the prestigious Metropolitan Club, but it was also booked solid. Finally, through the intervention of some old and well-entrenched members, he managed to get the rules bent slightly and arranged to have luncheon served in the club's magnificent library.

It was a memorable event, as he remembered, fit more for an elder statesman than an Episcopal rector. The room was grand, with fine paneling, a graciously high ceiling, and rich carpeting underfoot. A fire blazed beneath an ornate mantelpiece at one end, while at the other, elegant place settings ringed a large dining table—round, so all would have equal access to the guest of honor. The luncheon consisted of fine prime rib, with all the trimmings.

There was a minimum of small talk. Elegant as the setting was, and although everyone assumed Marc Haas had already decided on Bowers, the luncheon was still seen as something of a job interview. Don Chappell, John's brother, asked a few questions to try to get an idea of how Bowers would run the church. Don, a Vietnam veteran with two bronze stars, was then an investment banker. Among other queries, he wondered how often and in what manner the rector intended to conduct holy communion. (The frequency of communion services is an indicator of low or high ecclesiastical style. The more frequent the communion service, the higher the church.) Don also asked about the Easter service. He had heard accounts of Atlantans wearing long-eared Easter bunny hats and wanted to know if Tom planned the same festivity for St. Bart's. It may have played on Peachtree Street, but he couldn't see it on Park Avenue.

Tom and Margaret left after dessert and coffee, and the church's contingent stayed on to talk things over. John said he thought the luncheon had gone beautifully, and everyone felt Tom would be a fine addition to the church. They could "work with him," as he put it.

Tom appeared to have had a different reaction; he was apparently offended by what he saw as fairly aggressive questioning. According to John Chappell, Bowers left the Metropolitan Club and later that day ran into Joe Shaw, also a member of the associate vestry. As the story went, he told Shaw that if the group he had just lunched with was a representative sample of what the church had to offer, he wanted no part of it.

John Chappell said word traveled quickly and accurately in the days before parish strife, and the grapevine soon hummed with news of how the would-be rector had excoriated the junior vestry. Those members of the junior vestry who had been at the luncheon were floored. According to Chappell, they felt they had received Tom and his wife in the finest possible way and thought things had gone flawlessly; there had even been genuine feelings of friendship around the table. Conversation was frank, but no one had presumed to tell the rector how to run his church. "It was a very social, civilized, talk-about-the-church-openly meeting." Just how accurately the grapevine reported Tom's reaction is uncertain, but resentment began to well up among some of the junior vestry.

One might expect the allegation of such scathing criticism of fellow parishioners to have ruffled some feathers on the real vestry, but they did not appear concerned. Maybe that was because it had become gospel—at least among those in power—that St. Bartholomew's needed reviving, and since Bowers had proved he had the "right stuff," was it not out of place for the vestry to question his methods?

As for the congregation, there was little precedent to encourage regular parishioners to poke their noses into vestry affairs—one of the few traditions Tom Bowers tried to perpetuate at St. Bart's. The vestry was a revered body; most ordinary souls barely knew the names of the vestrymen and were far from being privy to the details of how their church ran. Later on, as something of the church's inner workings came into public view, it was clear that even some members of the real vestry did not know certain details of the church's workings. When Ronald B. "Ron" Alexander was on the vestry, he recalled being asked to approve clergy salaries without knowing what they were. (He later played a featured role in the landmarks controversy.) H. Peers Brewer, the treasurer, would just present a paper saying clergy compensation would be split into taxable and tax-exempt, but no figures were given. Members were asked to sign it after being told the treasurer would fill the paper in later. "Brewer was a treasurer with an iron hand," said Diane Calvert, another vestryperson, "and a very secretive one. He let out only what he wanted the vestry to know."

When Tom came, the vestry of St. Bartholomew's numbered fourteen or fifteen. He eventually boosted that to seventeen. In times of parish peace, only candidates selected by the vestry nominating committee appeared on the annual ballot, to be elected for terms varying from one to three years. With that stamp of approval vestry elections were largely pro forma affairs. Other candidates could be put up by petition, however. That is what happened when the opposition to development formed within the parish.

The level of involvement in church activities varied depending upon the individual. Some turned up only at Sunday services; others worked as volunteers in various seasonal programs—the Lenten luncheons or the Christmas Bazaar, for example, fund-raising events run by the Women of St. Bartholomew's. But knowledge of the nuts-and-bolts operation of the church hardly seemed a pressing matter. While secular law required that the church make its annual financial statements available, few parishioners at St. Bart's asked for them. "Why bother?" said John Chappell. "The church ran so beautifully no one ever had to say anything but 'Ah, isn't this wonderful!' "

So, for various reasons, Tom Bowers's first foray into parish politics at St. Bartholomew's might have left him with the impression that these Park Avenue folks were pushovers. He had made his feelings known in no uncertain terms, and there had been not so much as a whimper in response. But the seeds of resentment were well sown. Tom Bowers had made his first tactical error on his newest battlefront.

Most priests would have welcomed the chance to move to Park Avenue. In that sense, the search committee's field of choice was as broad as the clerical spectrum of the Episcopal Church, which is broad indeed. And whatever the differences that surfaced within the parish over the real estate deal, almost everyone at St. Bart's agreed the church was looking for someone remarkable to replace Dr. Finlay. There was no other explanation for the way St. Bart's conducted its search.

A priest who followed the selection progress from outside felt its most remarkable characteristic was its apparent lack of rationale. Once the search committee had its short list, it talked to three different types of priests: a charismatic in Connecticut, a religious scholar from the Midwest, and an inner-city evangelist and public personality in Atlanta. Aside from their contrast with Terence Finlay, these three shared little except that each, in his own way, was famous. The most important characteristic of a new rector appeared to be the height of his profile, not its shape.

The "declining parish" scenario was the explanation offered most often for why the search committee settled on Bowers.

People had been deserting St. Bartholomew's over the decades, went the argument. The remedy was to have Dr. Finlay succeeded by a vibrant and attractive man. Even his most adamant opponents concede Tom is that. So it is clear why St. Bart's wanted the rector from Atlanta. But why did Tom want St. Bart's?

On the most superficial level, there was the attraction of the city itself. Tom and Margaret were not strangers to the bright northern lights. They loved the theater and visited New York a couple of times a year during their stay in Atlanta. Yet in spite of its lure, Tom twice fought off the temptation of the Big Apple. Why did he finally decide to leave a comfortable, "lovin' " parish, deep in his home country, for a place he himself said would be unsympathetic to him?

There is no question of the sincerity of his spiritual calling, but worldly considerations do appear to have entered into the decision. His dearest friends, from Virginia, Washington, and Atlanta, all mentioned one ingredient that did not find its way into Tom's own explanation of why he left Atlanta. In folksy but worldly terms, his close friends spoke openly of yielding to the sweetening of the pot, the perks, the secular goodies that have the power to entice when the spiritual pull is not enough. The true proportion of "pot sweetening" to "spiritual call" lies hidden in St. Bart's vestry minutes, and no one who was in charge of the sugar bowl at the time had anything to say publicly. To the outsider, however, the process of "stealing a rector," as Hayes Clement put it, appeared to be indistinguishable from the dickering one would expect between a Ford executive and a group of Chrysler suitors. The corporate whiz snatched from Ford surely does not make the move for metaphysical reasons. The enticement to leave a secure position must include offers of a greater challenge, more responsibility and power, and the material rewards that accompany such advances.

This appears to hold true for the ministry, too. While the details are hidden, certain facts are known. In the first four years

5 5

after his arrival, Tom's salary rose with the proverbial clockwork regularity. He received roughly $30,000 for his first full year at St. Bart's. In 1983 his salary was $58,300, with an additional $41,700 designated "housing allowance" and $2,300 for utilities. In 1985 his salary was $64,300, plus a $44,000 housing allowance. (To that the vestry added $3,600 for utilities and $24,000 in pension benefits, bringing the total to $136,000.) The purpose of the housing allowance was to help with taxes, said the vestry resolution of December 6, 1983:

> Whereas, under the Internal Revenue Code (IRS) of 1954 . . . a Minister of the Gospel may exclude, in reporting his income for income tax purposes, that portion of his salary or stipend designated by his employer to be used for utilities or other expenses in providing a home.
>
> BE IT THEREFORE RESOLVED, that the Rector, Church Wardens and Vestrymen of St. Bartholomew's Church do hereby designate as a housing allowance that portion of the total compensation to be paid in 1984 to each of the below-named individuals which is set forth next to his or her name.

In Tom's case, an unusual circumstance appeared to make the $44,000 housing allowance a double perk. The church owned its rectory, a twelve-room, four-bathroom co-op on upper Park Avenue, which it had always rented to its rectors. For reasons the vestry never chose to tell, it sold the apartment to Reverend Bowers, turning his tax-deductible housing allowance into a tax-deductible co-op maintenance as well. The church carried the apartment on its books at a value of $104,945. Bowers paid $250,000 for it, in the form of a demand note for $15,000 and a long-term note for $235,000. It was a very good price at the time, made even more attractive by the decidedly nonusurious 4 percent which the church charged him on the long-term note. (There were double-digit mortgage rates then.)

The rector's antagonists thought the circumstances of the sale were suspicious. Rob Morris, treasurer of the Committee to Oppose, said it had all the earmarks of "a tax [irregularity which included] the active involvement of the search committee and, at the very least, the acquiescence of the vestry." His suspicion hinged on a provision of the IRS code that says taxes need not be paid on a capital gain made from selling a primary residence if the money is reinvested in another one within two years. The rector sold his house in Atlanta and appeared to have purchased the rectory apartment in New York. If he had made money on the Atlanta house, the rectory purchase would have satisfied the reinvestment requirement for an exemption from the capital gains tax. Whether it did satisfy that requirement hinges on who actually owns the rectory, and that is not clear, as the rector has never paid anything on the principal.

The law says a property owner has certain rights (such as the capital gains exemption), but to own property legally, certain tests must be passed. A person must be able to make an economic gain from it, as well as be at risk to suffer loss from it. The arrangement between the rector and the vestry permits the church to buy the apartment back from Bowers at the original purchase price when he leaves the church. (The two notes will be canceled, and the rector will be paid $2,500 for each year he occupied the apartment, effectively reducing the interest rate to 3 percent per annum). As a result of this provision, the rector will neither gain nor lose when he sells his apartment. It is helpful in establishing ownership to have some equity in the property, although not absolutely necessary. As of 1987, the rector had yet to make an equity payment toward the $250,000 principal owed the church. (Interest payments were made, according to a spokesperson.) If the rector has no equity in the apartment and does not stand to gain or lose from its sale, is he the legal owner?

J. Sinclair Armstrong (or Sinc, as everyone calls him) echoed Morris's feelings about the rectory deal. "We wonder if the sale of the apartment was at a fictitious price in order to avoid his [Bowers] having to pay capital gains tax on his Atlanta real estate." If that were the case, he continued, "it seems to me there's a considerable question about his compliance with the Internal Revenue law." Even if the rector had made regular payments on the principal, he wondered whether the IRS would consider the apartment "sold"— for purposes of capital gains—when the seller can buy it back at the sale price. "We talk about it informally as a tax scam perpetuated by the rector and vestry."

"It is singularly grinding to me," said Rob Morris, "because I make my professional way having people pay me a hundred dollars plus an hour to tell them they can't do what this guy appears to have done."

This is all conjecture, of course. If there were no capital gain on the sale of the Atlanta house, for instance, there would be no tax problems. But if that had been the case, there would seem to have been no reason to do all the paper shuffling that was connected with buying and rebuying the rectory.

The possibility of a Park Avenue television ministry was another likely bargaining chip in the negotiations that brought Tom Bowers to New York. He had loved TV preaching in Atlanta, and although little has been said about it in recent years, he maintained his interest in the medium after coming North.

Bowers's installation ceremony was televised, as were a few other services during his first few years, including a Pentecost special for CBS. The vestry minutes of June 11, 1979, note: "The rector reported a most favorable national reaction to our CBS television broadcast of our 9 o'clock service on June 8th. He read a most complimentary letter from Billy Graham." The same minutes show that approval was given to move the organ pipes to accommodate a new speaker system, and an architectural plan was submitted by the junior warden, Anthony Marshall, for "a control room for [a] new sound system and the changes necessary . . . to install it," in anticipation of "regular television broadcasting where sound necessarily must be of broadcast quality." The vestry also recommended converting "the storeroom on the north side of the church to a broadcast control room according to the plan submitted."

A year later the fire still burned brightly when Tom spoke of his television ministry. In a March 1980 vestry meeting he spoke enthusiastically about "The Electric Church. Within the near future, this vestry must face the fact that electronic dissemination of religious expression is now the most critical factor in church life."

The Reverend Charles Sumners came from Atlanta with Tom "specifically to develop the television ministry" at St. Bartholomew's. Sumners said Bowers had been assured by the vestry that there would be enough money to continue his television ministry in New York. No one knew exactly what was meant by the "assurances," but both Sumners and Bowers assumed that if the resources to carry on the ministry were not already in hand, they would be found. But the ministry never materialized. A vestry committee met for some time trying to come up with a plan but never generated the interest or financing to get the Electric Church plugged into Park Avenue. In Sumners's experience, New Yorkers never thought of the television ministry as "an Episcopal thing to do." (The building scheme would have provided capital in the quantity needed to finance a New York television ministry, but the development idea was not conceived of for that purpose, according to Sumners. When the real estate scheme began to draw heavy public fire, and opponents began claiming the church was being sold for an electronic ministry, the rector and vestry stopped talking about TV altogether.)

The 100 percent-plus salary increases within the first seven years of his tenure, the rectory deal, outfitting the church for television sermonizing, were surely enticements that would have been difficult to ignore when Bowers listened to the call to New York. But there was something more. Old church hands had marked Bowers as a man of great talent, one whose record already placed him in line for the deanship of a cathedral or perhaps a bishop's chair. The eagerness of the search committee—its willingness to come after him again and again—surely promised the freewheeling power that accompanies a mandate, power to carry out grand plans, and presumably—at St. Bartholomew's—the financial wherewithal to do so with style. In sum, no one with

Tom's energy, enthusiasm, and ambition could have resisted this call. To stay in Atlanta would have been a sign of faltering professional inertia, a sign that the rising star had passed its zenith.

*   *   *

When Tom Bowers arrived at St. Bartholomew's, he found several things he expected (he had already made it plain he had no illusions about the character of the congregation), and a few he did not.

There are conflicting views about the finances of the church in the last years of Dr. Finlay's rectorate. There was little disagreement, however, about character and atmosphere. Old-time parishioners said Dr. Finlay, the man who had firmly, if naïvely, tried to fend off the landmarks commission, was in charge of a dignified, quiet-but-not-dull church, which ran without much scrutiny from the people in charge. To some extent that would have been due to the time of his tenure. Dr. Terence John Finlay took over the Park Avenue parish in 1955, and most of his tour of duty coincided with a time when critical self-examination was not the norm of the Episcopal Church. Traditional political and social values were rarely questioned, and the parishioners of St. Bart's assumed their church's financial future was secure.

"I love St. Bartholomew's very much," said Emmanuel de Olivera, displaying emotion in an uncharacteristic way for that parish, "and I'm proud to be an Episcopalian." A Brazilian refugee, de Olivera was Dr. Finlay's verger for a time and remembered him fondly and with some humor. To a Latin, the quiet Finlay was dreadfully reserved. "You had to be careful how you talked to him," because he was so restrained, "very English," de Olivera said, miming a ramrod posture, with chest thrown out and chin tucked in. (Finlay was Canadian.)

The rector retired after leaving St. Bartholomew's and now lives in Florida. He is a gentle man, graced with humor and liveliness; tall but not towering, on the thin side but not gangly. His forehead slopes back a bit, and the chin recedes ever so slightly, making the long, straight nose a prominent feature. The general impression is of someone rather good-looking.

Finlay's laugh is warm and robust, yet colored by what his former verger termed his "Englishness." One does not easily picture Terence Finlay rocking back on his chair in openmouthed laughter and slapping his neighbor on the back. This type of restraint is sometimes mistaken for politeness or good manners, whether it comes from a concern about imposing oneself on others or a fear of showing one's emotions. The impression with Dr. Finlay is that he is both sincere and accessible.

Some remembered the man Rob Morris called the "last grand Edwardian rector" as a brilliant speaker. His sermons were intelligent and anecdotal, but even people with the most congenial memories conceded that his message was less of our times than was that of his successor. The consensus was that Dr. Finlay was a dignified, stately gentleman with a gift for doing things appropriately, one who gave the appearance of leaving the church to run itself while he wrote his sermons and looked after his flock.

The great upheaval that pushed the Protestant Episcopal Church into the forefront of social and political change in the late 1960's did not reach Finlay's St. Bart's. There were signs of change (a woman on the associate vestry), but the movement toward more direct involvement in social causes did not come until Tom Bowers's arrival. That is not to say people were unconcerned, just that social and political feelings were private affairs in Terence Finlay's church. So while American policy in Southeast Asia precipitated divisive confrontations in towns and cities across the country, the aisles of St. Bartholomew's remained calm. "We never had any protests, never any untoward movements or happenings in the sanctuary," said John Chappell. "We never had any resistance or anyone speaking, even under their breath, about what should or shouldn't be done. We had absolute peace." Under the even hand of Terence J. Finlay, church was a place to be with God, not man.

Despite his eventual opposition to the development plan,

Chappell maintained he never opposed the new rector's outreach programs. Like most members of the Committee to Oppose, John Chappell was no stranger to church work. A parishioner for more than two decades by the time Tom came, Chappell had a substantial record of Christian involvement, but it was at the administrative level rather than the "down-and-dirty" labor that the rector from Atlanta appeared to find a more Christian concern—serving meals to the hungry or handing out clothes on Saturday mornings. Chappell served on the board of trustees of the Episcopal Camp and Conference Center and as his church's representative to the Interparish Council. He was a member of the board of trustees of the Church Club of New York, a social/religious organization whose only requirement for nomination is that a person be a baptized member of a church in the Anglican Communion, and had worked on the finance and stewardship committees of St. Bartholomew's for several years.

Although the social revolution did not reach Dr. Finlay's St. Bart's, the church did have outreach programs. Terry Grace is an energetic, take-charge woman, who recently went from sales and marketing for airlines into a career managing nonprofit corporations. She became a member of St. Bartholomew's back in 1974 through her work in its Community Club. Besides being a meeting place where young men and women "of character and similar taste may find opportunity for collective expression and companionship," the club offered a chance to participate in a variety of outreach programs. These were largely due to the energy and direction of Andrew Mullins, a sandy-haired young priest who ran the club in Dr. Finlay's later years. (Mullins was such a good administrator that Tom took him into the church as assistant rector.) By the mid-1970's the club had an extensive menu of "one-shot do-gooders" from which members could choose: parties for poor kids, packing gifts for the Seamen's Institute, big-brother, big-sister opportunities, and other activities for people whose active professional lives did not permit commitments to regularly scheduled programs.

*   *   *

Such was the general character of the parish Tom Bowers inherited. For its part, the congregation had no idea what to expect from the new rector. Only his reputation as a mover and shaker preceded him. No one outside the search committee had heard him preach, let alone met him face-to-face. (Dr. Finlay had given several sermons to his prospective parishioners while he was being considered.)

The reputation that preceded Mr. Bowers caused elation or apprehension, depending upon one's views about how a church should be run. (A rector is " Dr." only if he or she holds a doctorate in divine studies. Otherwise it is "Mr.," "Father," or "Mother.") His induction service did little to change either feeling. People remembered it differently, depending on which side they took later on, in the development dispute. According to vestryman Ed Finch, Jr., it was a perfectly normal affair. Low Churchers had a different perception. Anything beyond the liturgical minimum smacked of Romish influence, and they thought Tom Bowers's induction "made the crowning of the Pope look like a tea party."

Rob Morris called it a carnival, a major sideshow production that befuddled older parishioners. "Most of them sat dumbfounded, unable to fathom what on earth was happening before their eyes. 'Who was this guy? What planet did he come in from? And he's ours now?' "

The presence of a television crew, with its temporary lighting and bundles of draped cables, only increased the sense of unreality for the old-timers. Morris sat in the balcony of the south transept and just said to himself, "How 'bout that?" While it was not his cup of tea, he had no strong feelings about it at the time, believing, "It was just an item to marvel at." Different and unexpected? Yes. But not unchurchlike, he commented. Oddities and acrobats have been kicking around cathedrals for the past 1,000 or 2,000 years, so why not at St. Bart's?

What the ceremony did show, in his view, was the colossal

mismatch in expectations. Most of the congregation had anticipated—even looked forward to—an orderly, liturgical proceeding. Perhaps it would be a bit more ornate than the simplest rendering of the Book of Common Prayer, but at least within their ken: "And they were offered the Ringling Brothers Barnum and Bailey opening-day parade."

Morris described his rector as a "foot-washing Episcopalian," using a label usually reserved for Fundamentalists. "His real problem here is that in some ways he's a bug-eyed monster, an alien. He practices a kind of Episcopalianism that would pass muster if you traveled five hundred to a thousand miles south of here, but it doesn't make any sense to this conservative congregation."

Different expectations have led to a "War of the Worlds, innocently entered into by both parties." In Morris's estimation, Bowers had been so hotly pursued by the selection committee that he probably expected to be welcomed "with only slightly less fervor than the Second Coming." With that kind of preliminary, there would have been no way to anticipate the furor he and his ideas stirred up in parts of that genteel population.

Morris is a sharp-witted CPA, who looks ten years younger than his four and a half decades. Around six feet tall, with short, straight, sandy hair, he has the trim physique of an athlete and a self-described political stance placing him somewhere to the right of Louis XIV. Quick with gibe and jib, Morris, like Armstrong, is a Harvard graduate and an avid sailor. After youthful years of scoffing, it was at sea that the young accountant decided there was something to religion. Several days off the Maryland coast, en route to the Virgin Island, Morris found himself riding out a hurricane in a thirty-six-foot boat. For five days he and another passenger shared round-the-clock watches. On the fourth day he came off watch around 4:30 A.M. and collapsed into a sodden bunk. "As I stretched out, rather exhausted, some odd words began floating through my head: 'Now I lay me down to sleep, I pray the Lord my soul to keep. If I should die before I wake . . .' and somewhere around there my other side, being a good Gemini, said, 'What's that?' "

He could not recall having been through that formula in thirty years. "After I got over the novelty of it, I went back and said it through, end to end, with feeling, and followed it up by the Lord's Prayer as best I could recall, and have never ever since been disdainful of those who might do the like. 'Born again'? Nonsense! Grateful? No mistake! I have never cried my Lord for help, but I have never disdained it."

Marion McNeely said she knew at first glance Tom Bowers was the wrong person for her church. Wife of vestryman John McNeely, she first met Mr. Bowers at a get-acquainted party for members of the vestry and their spouses. Marion McNeely knew why the vestry had brought Tom to New York, and started grilling the new rector on the spot to find out how he planned to fill the church.

"As he was going on about St. Bart's not yet having touched the side streets" (Tom's way of getting a dig in about the "avenue" class of folks that traditionally attended the church), vestryman Jim Dunning came over and blasted her for her audacity. "Of course, Tom will fill this church," said Dunning.

Others in the parish, who now oppose the development project, claimed to have adopted a wait-and-see attitude. Some even declared a "resolve" to be open-minded, suggesting that some effort was necessary to maintain an impartial stance.

Even assuming that such avowals were sincere, a solid foundation for acrimony was already in place when Tom first took the pulpit. Apocryphal or not, the story of his remarks after the Metropolitan Club luncheon had provided as unpalatable foretaste, which would have to be cleared before some people could be objective about the new rector.

Life at St. Bartholomew's began to change soon after Tom arrived. One of the first things he introduced was an early-morning folk service, like the one that had been such a fabulous draw in Atlanta. One vestryman said the new rector thought of the nine-thirty family service as a way to bring in new members. The long-term strategy appeared flawed, however. The new faces were younger types, with small bank accounts. "He's bringing them in, but they ain't paying the freight," said the vestryman.

Barely a year after the rector's induction, E. Theodore "Ted" Lewis was nominated to complete the unexpired term of a retiring vestryman. Ted Lewis, a professional who searches out executive talent for large corporations, was the first black to serve on St. Bartholomew's vestry. A year later the parish elected him to a full three-year term.

In bringing a black onto the vestry, Tom was continuing along the path he had first trodden in his early parishes in the Virginia hinterland. But John Chappell saw the so-called integration of St. Bart's as a nonevent. "We've never had an enormous number of blacks at St. Bartholomew's—Harlem is fifty blocks to the north, after all—but we've always had some," he observed, "and I've never noticed anybody being uncomfortable or saying anything about it." There had been no fuss at all about electing Lewis to the vestry, Chappell added.

The first woman priest at St. Bartholomew's was also ordained in Tom's first years. That may have raised more eyebrows than the integration of a parish that in all likelihood never thought of itself as unintegrated.

The elimination of pew rents was perhaps Tom's most revolutionary move as far as longtime parishioners of St. Bartholomew's were concerned. "I told them they could sit there as long as they liked, but I wasn't going to take money from them."

English common law originally guaranteed any resident of an Anglican parish the right to sit in any seat in its church. (Nonparishioners were not automatically entitled to seats.) By the sixteenth century pew rental was common, however, and the practice came to America with the Anglican Church. England declared it illegal toward the end of the eighteenth century, but the custom continued in most American Episcopal churches for another 100 years or so after the Revolution. No definitive history catalogs its demise, but St. Bart's surely brought up the rear in that action.

Although it was hardly a bold liberal gesture, most people in the church appeared to think ending the antiquated practice of pew rental was the correct thing to do as they approached the twenty-first century. But Rob Morris thought it was an unfortunate "nonreform." No one could remember a time when only the renter could occupy a pew. The pews were held open until ten to fifteen minutes before the service, then freed for general seating. Renters usually came early—to fulfill the social obligation of churchgoing—but no one was ever left waiting at the back of the church while those pews stood empty. The only practical consequence of abolishing pew rentals was the loss of income, claimed Morris. The same people sit in the same pews now but the church does not take in the $25,000 in rents for giving them the privilege.

The revised version of the Book of Common Prayer also came with Tom. The original prayer book was written in the sixteenth century, when Henry VIII created the Anglican Church in breaking with the Pope. Besides reinforcing the schism, the Book of Common Prayer simplified and unified the complex Roman service, specifying among other things that Anglican priests and High Churchmen were to wear less ostentatious vestments. Several minor and major changes have been made to the liturgical manual of the Episcopal Church over the centuries, the last major one in 1662.

The Protestant Episcopal Church adopted its own prayer book in 1789. There was a major revision in 1928, and in the mid-1970's, after nearly a decade of stressful change within the church, the General Convention officially adopted yet another revision. Put into service in 1979, it is customarily called the " '79 Prayer Book." Although technically obligatory, many churches continue to use the old one, or at least portions of it.

The 1979 revision did two things to the traditional Episcopal service. It modernized the language and offered alternative forms to traditional rituals. As with haircuts and hemlines, preferences in the language of the prayer book are a matter of taste and therefore highly personal. At the heart of such choices lie the aesthetic and spiritual character of the worship service, which is important to people on both sides of the prayer book issue.

The differences in language are similar to the differences between the King James's translation of the Bible and the New World version. The following excerpts are from the old and new versions of the Nicene Creed. The differences in language are fine ones, the most glaring changes being the substitution of "we" for "I" and the removal of the gender-specific possessive pronoun "his":

1928 PRAYER BOOK	1979 PRAYER BOOK
I believe in one God the Father Almighty. . . . And in one Lord Jesus Christ, the only-begotten Son of God; Begotten of his Father before all worlds, God of God, Light of Light, Very God of very God; Begotten, not made; Being of one substance with the Father; By whom all things were made.	We believe in one God, the Father, the Almighty. . . . We believe in one Lord, Jesus Christ, the only Son of God, eternally begotten of the Father, God from God, Light from Light, true God from true God, begotten, not made, of one Being with the Father. Through him all things were made.

One might expect this skirmish in the battle at St. Bartholomew's to have divided on generational lines, but it did not. Each side had supporters from all age-groups. On one level, those who sided with Tom Bowers linked the "archaic" language of the 1928 book to the social elitism that was the anathema of the 1960's. Preferring the old book to the new, therefore, was symptomatic of an elitist lack of concern for the poor—a contemporary Marie Antoinette syndrome. Proponents of the old prayer book saw the new as a triumph of banality over beauty and considered its substitution of plural for singular and its elimination of masculine possessives to be a senseless aggression against traditional values.

The 1979 book went beyond language, to the form of the liturgy, offering alternative rituals to the traditional ceremonies. Thus the Sunday service, which under the old regime would have been the same, week after week, can have considerably more variety. Supporters of change reckoned this was freeing. Supporters of tradition mourned the destruction of the liturgical unity, where the unchanging ritual elements were combined like building blocks to form the magnificent and familiar edifice of the mass. They claimed liturgical continuity was critical to the refinement of the service and profoundly important to their personal religious experience.

With tongue only slightly in cheek, David Garrard Lowe, an art historian and parishioner of St. Bartholomew's, spoke of the old Episcopalian notion that it was better to have people obeying the laws than debating about what they should be. Behind Lowe's horn-rimmed glasses is a broad face punctuated by mischievous eyes, which twinkle as he makes mildly irreverent remarks about his church. "The Episcopal Church is not the church of folk masses and hymn sings," he quipped. "It is the church of T. S. Eliot and W. H. Auden. Episcopalians don't much care what you believe," he added, "it's what you do. Order. They take form as substance." Matthew Arnold, a famous nineteenth-century Anglican, put the same sentiment in starker terms: The choice is between culture and anarchy.

Once things began changing at St. Bartholomew's, there was some confusion about which of those changes should be ascribed to the new rector and which should not. Tom did not invent the 1979 prayer book, and although he may have been a pioneer in the 1960's, opening lay and clerical church hierarchies to blacks and women had been a policy of the national church for years before he came to Park Avenue. Only the elimination of pew rents came solely from the rector's initiative. While it may have shocked some old-timers, it did not qualify him for pole position in the race for ecclesiastical liberalization. As fervently as he may have believed in these changes, Tom Bowers was a vehicle for the policies of the national church. Had the search committee chosen a different rector, chances are similar changes would have been seen on Park Avenue at about the same time.

Tom Bowers was, however, solely responsible for the way he introduced those changes. There he showed a characteristically heavy hand, which did little to endear him to those who had held off on their final judgment.

Consider the way the new prayer book was introduced. Although it was officially adopted almost a decade ago, it is still a controversial subject in many parishes. Its introduction immediately provoked the creation of the Prayer Book Society, an organization whose purpose is to defend the 1928 book. In a pamphlet titled "Drastic Doctrinal Deviations," the society claims the new revision contains "serious doctrinal deficiencies and heresies" and that the 1928 Book of Common Prayer should continue in use until a satisfactory revision is made. For a staid Park Avenue church that had just given up renting pews, the new prayer book must have seemed fanatical. Everyone knew it was coming, however, it was just a question of when and how.

"How" had apparently been important enough that some parishioners asked a vestryman to speak to the rector-to-be while he was still in Atlanta. Would he introduce the new book "cold turkey"? The old would not be chucked out of the pews, and the new jammed into their hands, said Bowers. The changeover would be gradual.

Yet the first Sunday Tom took the pulpit he held up the 1979 book and declared it to be *the* book in his church. (Although officially adopted by the 1979 national convention, the revised prayer book had been available in virtually final form since it was introduced to the 1976 convention.) Several parishioners had kept their personal prayer books in the same pews for decades. Among them was J. Sinclair Armstrong's ninety-seven-year-old father. All the old books, including those personal copies, had been cleared out of the pews for that service.

Technically his actions were entirely legitimate. The rector was carrying out the stated policy of the Episcopal hierarchy. Strategically it was a blunder of enormous proportion, the repercussions of which still echo through the nave of St. Bartholomew's. The self-defeating nature of the gesture was apparent the instant it was made: Tom Bowers had created enemies where none had to be. But "growth" comes with confrontation, he likes to say. The rector made similarly challenging moves once he set about trying to secure the financial future of St. Bartholomew's Church through real estate speculation.

The tactlessness of the prayer book incident is particularly clear when compared with the way it was brought into other churches. John Andrews, rector of St. Thomas, was formerly chaplain to the archbishop of Canterbury. Andrews described himself as a "critical supporter" of the 1979 prayer book. He picks and chooses what of it he includes in his services. Although portions appear in almost every service, the new prayer book is not to be found in the pews at St. Thomas. The choice of which portions, of course, is an aesthetic one. "The language of the psalms [in the new prayer book] is not acceptable to me," Andrews stated flatly. "I think it's very poor quality. It simply is not memorable . . . and I'll defy anybody to argue with me on that." When the psalms are sung or recited at St. Thomas, they follow the old psalter, "and we shall continue to do that."

Andrews did feel the new book brought valuable insights into certain liturgies. The 1979 baptismal service is "infinitely more ancient and informed in content" than that of the 1928 book, for instance. The rewritten service is based upon a fourth-century precedent and, in Andrews's view, clarifies the meaning of that ceremony. Such discriminating acceptance was not practiced at St. Bart's.

Apart from the specific changes, some of the raised hackles at St. Bart's might be laid to culture shock. Any number of older parishioners, however, were decidedly uncomfortable with the new rector's insistence on informality. Many of the older women did not want to be called by their first names, nor were they comfortable calling the rector by his.

Marjorie Brown, the widow of an Episcopal clergyman, felt it was a sign of mutual disrespect. She had taught kindergarten for twenty-eight years; her students didn't call her by her first name, nor did she call the principal by his. Then a new rector came into her church of twenty-six years and started patting old ladies on the back and calling them by their familiar names.

The discomforted ladies were not fair-weather parishioners. Each had years of service in the Women of St. Bartholomew's, an organization that ran functions to raise money for church projects. At least two of them wrote polite letters to Mr. Bowers shortly after he took over, respectfully mentioning that some of the older parishioners felt uncomfortable with that form of address. No reply was on record, but Tom's down-home style did not change.

First-name calling is not a moral issue, of course, but a matter of tact. Courtesy, if not political savvy, might have dictated accommodation on the rector's part. Common sense makes one wonder why he did not respect his parishioners' wishes, given the animosity such small aggravations can create. But Tom did things Tom's way, even when compromise would cost nothing and stubborn persistence held great potential for trouble down the line.

His former parishioners, in Atlanta, were not surprised by the way Tom ran things in his new church or by the way some members of his new church reacted. The consensus in Atlanta was that Tom had a passionate and genuine conviction about how the church should serve the world and was willing to put himself on the line to see it happen.

Parishioners in Washington or Atlanta may have cussed Tom Bowers, tried to shout him down, or even disrupted a Sunday service to walk out. It didn't matter. Tom was on the Christian side of issues. If integrating a congregation wasn't as American as apple pie twenty years ago, there was a dim recognition—even by foot draggers—that it was the Christian thing to do. Painful as it may have been for some on Peachtree Street or Foxhall Road, to their credit they accepted the challenge and changed.

Feeding the poor was an equally unassailable mission. Who would play the fool by saying a Christian church should ignore the human beings starving on its doorstep? The same may be said of offering beds to the homeless, counseling the disturbed, giving clothing to those who have none, or schooling to kids who missed out the first time around.

Those were clear-cut issues, and Tom was always on the

honorable side. Is it not also morally repugnant to force a church to spend millions to repair its bricks and mortar when flesh and blood human beings are in need? As the Battle of St. Bart's unfolded, however, facts that led some to question the purity of that position came to the fore.

*   *   *

J. Sinclair Armstrong's family had a long history at St. Bartholomew's. Sinc's grandfather—the original James Sinclair—had joined the church in 1898, when it was on Madison Avenue and Forty-fourth Street. He contributed to the construction of the present St. Bart's, in which his grandson and namesake was christened and confirmed. One or more members of the Armstrong clan have been in constant attendance at St. Bartholomew's for almost a century.

The family's connection to the church came about accidentally. Sinc's grandparents were crossovers to the Episcopal faith, refugees from a vicious but long-forgotten intraparish conflict which had rent the Fifth Avenue Presbyterian Church. Eighty-two years after that, the grandson was in an identical circumstance in the church that had given sanctuary to the grandfather.

Like Tom Bowers, J. Sinclair Armstrong was not one to abandon a cause he believed in. Sinc grew up in St. Bart's, and his education was that of the model Episcopalian: Milton Academy, Harvard, and Harvard Law. Yet from the beginning he did not exactly fit the mold.

His parents taught him not to assume the conventional response was the correct one, but to decide what was right on the basis of a careful analysis of the problem. That tended to lead to liberal conclusions in Armstrong's case, conclusions not often shared by fellow Episcopalians. In a mock presidential election at Milton Academy, Armstrong and a handful of other heretical Miltonians voted for Roosevelt. "This isn't something you tell your classmates about in a select New England boarding school," he commented. The landslide majority went for Hoover.

While he said he never thought of himself as other than a

typically patriotic middle-class American, Armstrong belonged to the student union at Harvard and was on the left side of at least one highly charged political debate of the time, favoring the Spanish republic over Franco.

The tendency to side with liberal causes did not narrow this gregarious young man's spectrum of acquaintance. Armstrong formed a lifelong friendship with Caspar W. "Cap" Weinberger when Weinberger was president of the *Crimson* and Armstrong its editorial chairman. "Oh, we had a great time with Weinberger. He was impossible. He was a roaring conservative even then, and I was 'open-minded.' "

After law school Armstrong spent several decades away from New York and St. Bartholomew's, as a partner in a Chicago law firm. That was followed by government work in Washington, first as chairman of the Securities and Exchange Commission (1953–57), then as assistant secretary of the navy for financial management and comptroller of the Department of the Navy (1957–59).

Once back in New York, Armstrong returned to private life as an executive vice-president of the U.S. Trust Company, an investment banking firm. It was as a banker in the late 1960's that he organized the Wall Street Moratorium opposing the war in Vienam. That put 20,000 people in the streets in the heart of corporate and financial America. He also filled the nave of Trinity Church in late 1969, in a service opposing the same Southeast Asian venture, and was a sponsor of Business Executives Move for Vietnam Peace. Several times during those years Armstrong put his professional commitments aside to testify against the war before the U.S. Congress.

"I'm not trying to portray myself as a person who likes to put himself on the cross and get immolated," he said, "but I do say I've been pretty cheeky about expressing my own convictions on public issues of concern to the people of this country and trying to be on the side where the merit is, regardless of my own personal advantage. What you try to do in life is the right thing at any given moment. Sometimes doing what you think is right leads you into positions that are contrary to the general perception of the public at that given moment. But you hope you're right, and that the public [will come to] see it the other way." His outspoken opposition to the war bothered his parents deeply, for they were very patriotic and felt he was going against the decision of the nation.

The belief that principle should be served regardless of personal consideration informed many of Armstrong's judgments. He once supported his parents in a public fight over the rezoning of their Connecticut property although he privately disapproved of their position. That stand nearly cost him his job, for the opponent was a large investor at U.S. Trust. Sinc took a clear position nevertheless: "In a dispute between my parents and their neighbors, I was bound by the Fifth Commandment. If [U.S. Trust] wanted my job, they could have it, but I wasn't going to resign." A third of the board members asked for his dismissal, but the chairman refused to oblige them. For three and one-half years there were no promotions and no raises, although Armstrong believed a third to a half of the net profits of the bank came from business he developed and was administering.

Over the years church leaders have implied that Armstrong and others who oppose development are wealthy people who have no real concern about the poor. While that may be the case for some—just as it may be for some who favor development— members of both camps have participated energetically in a variety of service activities at the parish, diocesan, and national levels of the Episcopal Church. Armstrong's contributions have been particularly notable.

He lived in the Chelsea section of Manhattan in the 1960's, and rather than travel uptown to the family church, he joined St. Mark's in the Bowery, a modest parish in an ungentrified section known as the East (Greenwich) Village. Until 1979, when he returned to St. Bartholomew's, Armstrong's "great interest" was St. Mark's, and in that small parish he developed what he called a very rewarding life.

From 1968 to 1972 St. Marks had no rector, and Armstrong served as its senior warden at the request of Paul Moore, developing what he called a close working relationship with the bishop. One of Sinc's more important tasks was the orchestration of a delicate diplomatic minuet in which whites handed over the church government to the blacks and Hispanics. It was the time of student revolts and ghetto uprisings, not an easy moment in history for a white man to be a member of—let alone the guiding hand in— a predominantly black and Hispanic church. That went doubly for a man like Sinc Armstrong, an archetypical WASP who had come to the New York banking establishment via the classic educational route of the privileged.

But Sinclair Armstrong showed exceptional qualities. In that most unlikely circumstance he established a positive working relationship with people from dramatically different backgrounds from his own. He did so by showing a willingness to work for and with them. In turn, they showed their affection and trust; in open elections the parishioners of St. Mark's chose Armstrong to be senior warden over several black and Hispanic candidates. Sinc felt he was a member of a community of equals, although he acknowledged that perhaps half a dozen people at the church "had more money than most.

"I learned from my association with the blacks at St. Mark's what it's like to be a black in our society, and I made some of the most moving friendships I have had in my life there. In my opinion, that relationship between blacks and whites can't be experienced in a church like St. Bartholomew's. One or two prominent middle-class professional blacks have some status [in the church], and everybody thinks 'Oh, boy! We're an integrated community.' The only other blacks you see are the servants, the guards, the usher, the fellow that pushes the prayer books and hymnals back into place after the service and the people have left. That to me is not equality or 'black liberation.' Although I don't have experiences today of the kind I had with the blacks at St. Mark's, because I'm not associating with blacks in that way, I consider [my time at St. Mark's] one of the most important experience of my life."

One of Sinc's friends in that small parish invited him to a dinner of black accountants. It was absolutely amazing, he said, because they came from all over the United States and had their clients with them. "I don't believe there's another white man on Wall Street who has ever been received in a black professional group in which he was the only white. There were some very rich people there, men and women, and they were beautifully dressed. There were three hundred of them, and they had a whale of a party at a hotel. And I was the only white. There is no way that St. Bartholomew's can give to any of us the experience of what it's really like to be black in a civilization which is predominantly white."

Yet Armstrong refused to romanticize his experiences: "It doesn't solve any of the world's problems. It doesn't solve apartheid—I'd be scared as hell if I lived [as a white] in South Africa now; I'd be scared as hell if I lived in the Bronx, or the South Bronx, or north of Ninety-sixth Street. But I'm very fortunate to have had the experience with black people of love and friendship and trust. It amazed me, because it was the time when those people were terribly hostile. Yet they received me and loved me once they learned that I gave them the same respect and love. Bowers can preach till the cows come home," Armstrong went on with tears in his eyes, "and he'll never know what that experience is or know how to explain it to people."

Beyond the parish Armstrong has been an earnest and active supporter of the liberalization of his church, working to bring women and other minorities into its lay government and priesthood. He has served in a long list of respected positions: treasurer and trustee of the Cathedral of St. John the Divine, president and trustee of the Diocesan Investment Trust, vestryman and clerk of the vestry of St. George's Church, trustee of the Episcopal Church Pension Fund, and member of the Commission on the Observance of the 200th Anniversary of the Diocese of New York. Armstrong has also served outside the church, as trustee and treasurer of the New York University Medical Center and president of the Gunnery School in Washington, Connecticut (during the "difficult seventies," when drugs and alcohol plagued the prep school circuit). He is rarely involved in fewer than ten or twelve extracurricular activities at one time.

As chairman of the fund-raising committee for St. Mark's in the Bowery, he helped bring in more than $2 million for the restoration of the church after a fire had gutted it in July 1978. In that capacity he displayed a talent that Bowers could have made good use of had things turned out differently.

Armstrong was extraordinarily restrained about calling public attention to his credits. They showed up only in correspondence of the Committee to Oppose, where they might have a favorable bearing on the fund-raising efforts. "I don't need to be painted into an hereditary pew by the Rector," wrote Sinc to a potential supporter. "I've been out there. Tom Bowers has cleverly made me out to be a reactionary because my parents and grandparents were St. Bartholomew's people and paid pew rent, and my education has been Northern, and my associations [are] with business and government."

Joyce Matz, a public relations adviser who had donated her time to the Committee to Oppose, saw Sinc "as a man of a lot of courage and integrity, and a good amount of common sense and wisdom, who has really put his life on the line for this issue." Armstrong felt "done in" by the way the rector tried to detract from his liberal record and divert attention from the real issue: "the possible destruction of the greatest Anglican presence, a going concern in the heart of the greatest financial and business center in the West, just so the rector can have the wherewithal to finance a television ministry."

Sinc eventually left his beloved St. Mark's; his ninety-eight-year-old father, Howard S. Armstrong, could no longer walk to St. Bartholomew's communion rail alone, and asked his son to be there to accompany him. If Tom Bowers had not yet endeared himself to all his parishioners by the time Armstrong came on the scene, skeptics stubbornly clung to the olive branch, unwilling to criticize the rector openly, however close to the surface unrest lay. Newly returned to the church of his childhood, the younger Armstrong recalled supporting his new rector at virtually every turn. Sinc had been in regular attendance at St. Bart's for about a year when the $100 million real-estate offer became public in the fall of 1980.

III

By mid-September 1980 those parishioners of St. Bart's who had endured the heat of the New York summer were welcoming cooler weather. Those who had been fortunate enough to summer in the hills of Connecticut—or, like J. Sinclair Armstrong, on the shores of Martha's Vineyard—were just settling into the routine of the city once again when a surprise shattered their autumn calm. Sinc likened it to Pearl Harbor.

On September 19 parishioners of St. Bartholomew's unfolded their copies of *The New York Times* to discover that an unnamed corporation had offered to buy their church site—buildings and all—for $100 million! It set a new high for Manhattan real estate values, nearly three times the per-square-foot price paid for a nearby parcel only a year before. The church did not say it had accepted the offer but it was considering it. Some thought that alone showed an important new state of mind for the church. It had never occurred to anyone to sell or lease church property before. Rob Morris compared it to a loss of virginity.

One member of the congregation was not as stunned by the announcement as the others. The warning had come to John Chappell, senior warden of the associate vestry, on one of those days when nothing goes right, when the doomsday clarion seems at hand, as he put it. He had just left his wife at Kennedy Airport. She was catching a flight to France to visit a sick relative, and he had no idea when she would be back. On the return trip to Manhattan he picked one of New York's more reckless cabbies, who insisted on hurtling down the parkway as he leaned around to preach to his passenger about the imminent end of the world.

Chappell was recovering from that harrowing ride when the telephone disturbed the quiet of his apartment. He said it was the voice of Allan Sanford, a vestryman at St. Bart's, at the other end: "They've sold the church for $100 million." (Sanford denied ever having said such a thing but did say he was aware of the deal a few days before the story appeared in the *Times*. Years later he resigned from the Church Club in protest when John Chappell was elected an officer.)

Regardless of how the news came to him, Chappell did learn of the development offer before it became public and was consumed by an immediate and overwhelming opposition. "There are many office buildings on Park Avenue, and only one church. Why should my church be torn down?" It was all the more appalling because nothing in the rector's sermons or the church's publications had hinted at the need for such a radical step.

After the initial shock had dissipated, he telephoned his brother. Don was chairman of St. Bartholomew's usher's corps, a post that would be jeopardized by the position he eventually took on the real estate question. In the middle of the telephone call both men realized that they were probably the only ones outside the vestry who knew about what appeared to be a fait accompli. Flabbergasted, they wondered if anything could be done to stop the sale. The situation did not look encouraging, but someone had to try.

John's clearest recollection of those first few days before the offer became public knowledge was of a compelling sense of urgency. Since all appeared lost, there was nothing to risk in a last-ditch stand. The only peril lay in acting too swiftly, without first establishing a workable strategy and a proper organization to carry it out. The Chappells knew from the beginning that a couple of junior men in the church, relative upstarts, could not slay the real estate dragon by themselves. The success of an internal opposition would depend on who led it. The person would have to be well versed in legal matters and well connected at all levels of the conflict—the parish, the diocese, the city, and beyond, if possible. It would have to be someone whose integrity was as unquestioned as that of the rector and whose tenacity was equally intimidating. Once an organized internal opposition had surfaced, there could be no backing off or the cause would be lost.

While the Chappells pondered their options, news of the offer became public. The *Times* story contained snippets of interviews with various spokesmen for the parish and the diocese. Bishop Paul Moore, Jr., said he could barely begin to come to terms with the implications of such an offer. Marc Haas offered a rationale for considering the sale or lease of the church's property: "Monuments are very nice but they've got to be supported," implying the church could not maintain the buidings on its present income. He also hinted at a secondary motive. Nearby corporations thought of St. Bartholomew's as an asset to the neighborhood. The threat of selling the property might frighten them into offering substantial donations to the church, which, suggested Haas, "would make a difference in our considerations." No one said anything about imminent insolvency, just that the neighboring corporations might be willing to ante up to keep Park Avenue beautiful.

A few days after the announcement, the Women of St. Bartholomew's set up tables on Park Avenue and began gathering the first of nearly 12,000 signatures to save their church. Princess

Grace and her daughter Caroline were strolling by that day and were among the first to sign. Jacqueline Kennedy Onassis gave her support, as did Brooke Astor, one of New York's premier philanthropists.

By the time signatures were being gathered, John and Don Chappell had settled on the man they wanted to spearhead the opposition, and the younger brother approached Sinc Armstrong at a cocktail party just a few days after the *Times* article.

When Don asked what he thought of the rector, Sinc replied that Bowers seemed to be a great guy and a charismatic spirit with many good outreach ideas. He would be good news for St. Bart's, "he is a very dramatic fellow, and the church needs that."

Don phrased the question more precisely: What did Sinc think about the building proposal? Specifically, would Sinc consent to lead the opposition to that proposal within the church?

That was a different matter. (Don did not know that Howard Armstrong had already asked his son to look into the proposal.) Sinc said he needed time to think it over. He was leaving on a two-day business trip the next morning and would let Don know his answer when he returned.

It was not like Armstrong to shy away from confrontation, but he was prepared to tread with uncharacteristic restraint when it came to the building proposal. "I really wanted my father's permission before I became publicly involved. He was very old and very frail, and I knew that he and my mother were disturbed by the great deal of publicity I had had over the years, particularly when I was in public life. They were retiring, private people, brought up to regard it as wrong to have your name in the newspaper and wrong to be in the society page. With Father at ninety-eight I didn't want to disturb him by getting into another public controversy."

The building proposal proved a different matter for the elder Armstrong. Howard Armstrong thought saving St. Bartholomew's Church was the most important thing Sinc could do in his entire career. "It was the first time in my life my father had been enthusiastic for anything I did that involved personal publicity, danger, and expense." When Sinc returned from his trip, he phoned Don Chappell..

"Howard S. Armstrong is our patron saint," Rob Morris said years later. The elder Armstrong was not only the oldest but also the longest-standing member of St. Bartholomew's congregation. He had lived through five rectors and always said it was the church and the congregation that would stand and the rectors that would come and go, "and that has been our operating principle."

The juxtaposition of Armstrong and Bowers lent a curious twist to the Battle of St. Bart's. As rector of St. Mark's, David Garcia knew Armstrong well. He had also heard of the rector from Atlanta. When Garcia learned that Tom was coming to St. Bart's, he immediately assumed Sinc and the new rector would be teammates. He imagined that the energy and freewheeling style of the southern rector welded to the organizational powers and connections of the Wall Street banker would make an unbeatable combination. Both men felt deeply and sincerely for the less fortunate of our society, Garcia said emphatically. They saw eye-to-eye on 95 percent of the important social issues of our time. But that odd coincidence has been lost in the eddies and backwaters of the greater controversy surrounding St. Bartholomew's.

Because of his recent arrival at St. Bartholomew's only a few members of the opposition knew much about J. Sinclair Armstrong when he became their leader. Even fewer knew he had been courted by the rector as well as by the Chappells. On at least two occasions after the real estate offer became public, the rector invited Armstrong to join the prodevelopment faction. Tom Bowers even offered a vestry position; the rector would see to it that the nominating committee put Sinc on the ballot in the next election if he took Tom's side.

It was in one of those meetings that Armstrong posed an important question: Would Tom submit the development proposal to the parish for approval? "Sure I will," was the rector's answer, recalled Sinclair Armstrong.

Once the internal opposition had begun to take shape, Armstrong and the Chappells decided it would be wise to take out some legal insurance on the rector's casual response. Armstrong was not sure the law required polling the parish before making such a deal and had the question researched. (He had left U.S. Trust then and was a partner in the law firm of Whitman & Ransom.) The answer was negative. The law did not require parish approval before the vestry disposed of the church's property. It only had to obtain the permission of the civil court (a provision of the state's Religious Corporations Law) and the consent of the bishop and Standing Committee of the diocese (a provision of canon law). (The Standing Committee is a lay body whose duties include working with the bishop much as a vestry works with a rector.) Case law on the topic did suggest that the court might deny approval if a congregation strongly opposed the transaction, but it was too early to know where the congregation stood. It did not look good for the newly formed opposition.

The researcher did mention another possibility. The bylaws of a religious corporation could require a parish vote—but St. Bart's bylaws had no such provision. The Chappell/Armstrong group set out to rectify that omission.

Their chance came on the evening of October 9, during a special parish meeting to discuss the development question. The meeting was originally scheduled for the spacious parish hall of the Community House, but the turnout far exceeded expectations, and the crowd was redirected into the huge nave of the church. When the gathering was finally called to order, Peers Brewer, the treasurer of St. Bartholomew's, issued the first of many fearful predictions: "Sometime in 1981 we could be out in a blizzard . . . [and] a definite solution is necessary if the church is not to be held hostage, bound and gagged by the barbed wire of grim and brutal financial necessity." Brewer was a vice-president of the Manufacturers Hanover Trust Company and held a Bachelor of Divinity degree from Harvard. The annual deficit would rise to nearly

$750,000 by 1984, he continued. Fortunately, the church had received a pledge of nearly $1 million in 1980 from Mr. and Mrs. Marc Haas, but no other support had materialized. With a note of sarcasm Brewer remarked that the "deep concern" of parishioners and public over the possible sale of the church had not reached their pocketbooks. Since the announcement of the real estate offer, the church had received only $185 in donations.

The rector was equally pessimistic: "The physical beauty of the building is not enough to breathe life into the church." From the beginning the implication was that money could.

When it came time to hear parishioners' views, Armstrong introduced an amendment he himself had drafted, one which would play a key role in legal maneuvers of the church and its opposition over the next six years. He prefaced its reading by telling the congregation of the meetings with the rector and of the latter's decision to submit any deal to a parish vote. He then turned to the rector and asked if he might introduce an amendment to that effect. (To be official, it had to be read into the minutes.) The rector gave his approval. The intent of the amendment was simple. The vestry could not act alone in a matter as important as the sale of church property; the membership should also have a say.

Armstrong was en route to another engagement, and after reading the amendment into the record, he turned and headed toward the back of the church. A reporter stopped him to ask who he was and what he did for a living. Sinc offered his business card and a copy of the amendment and strode through the great bronze doors of St. Bartholomew's into the evening.

The next day the roof fell in, as he put it. His name was in the *Times*, and letters and checks began to pour in from people all over the country who wanted to "save" St. Bart's. That same day the Committee to Save St. Bartholomew's Church, Inc., was officially formed. In addition to the Chappell brothers and Sinc Armstrong, its founding members included Elizabeth Wigton Bristol, a twenty-nine-year-old nursery school teacher and member of the Junior League, and Marjorie V. Brown (the clergyman's widow). Its first letter to the parish sounded almost like a cry to rally behind the rector: "[L]oyal members of St. Bartholomew's . . . urged us to join hands and form ranks to save the Church." The only hint of rebellion was a reference to the committee's candidates, who would be fielded for the January vestry election—people who "share our loyal concern for the Church and [our] objective to save it."

Two weeks later a "new business memo" was filed in the records of Whitman & Ransom. The client: the Committee to Save St. Bartholomew's Church, Inc. Principal in charge of the account: J. Sinclair Armstrong.

The rector and vestry soon felt pressure from inside and outside the church to reject the notion of selling or leasing all or a portion of the property. One letter to the *Times* pointed to the fifty-five-year tax exemption St. Bartholomew's had enjoyed. If it now intended to cash in on the appreciated value of its land, should it not pay retroactive real estate taxes?

The architecture and preservation community decried the potential destruction of an outstanding example of American architecture. Ada Louise Huxtable, vicar of New York architecture critics, lambasted the church in an article titled "The Sell-Off at St. Bartholomew's." She pointed out that church officials had put the negotiations into the hands of outside real estate consultants "professionally adept at flushing the highest bidder." Was all church business now "Big Business"? queried the critic.

Huxtable also struck a disturbing chord that would resound throughout the struggle. The church, presumed champion of spiritual values, was cast as the greedy real estate speculator. The preservationists, archmaterialists, were playing guardian of the city's spiritual life: "Bricks and mortar are called secondary to human needs. It is said that cash will serve society better than beauty. And solvency has a beauty of its own. That the beauty of the St. Bartholomew block contributes to the spiritual welfare of the city and all of its people is not part of the reckoning."

Those outside the tight web of parish politics tended to be scandalized that a beautiful church might disappear simply because its governing board appeared bent on maximizing its income. The church had not yet made any public statements about financial difficulties, and the average citizen thought of St. Bartholomew's as a rich church that wanted to become richer. To do that, it was willing to cozy up to developers—a species many picture as cigar-chewing, money-hungry, wheeler-dealers whose concern for anything beyond their bank accounts is pure PR gimmickry. The unseemly communion between spirituality and speculation left a generally sour taste in the mouths of many New Yorkers.

Ron Alexander still thought the church could salvage its image. In his late thirties he is bright, personable, and gifted with the talent good lawyers have of cleanly categorizing and synopsizing events and bundling theories in ways that make the arcane seem eminently comprehensible.

Ron had favored the scheme from the start. He went to one of the early meetings of the Committee to Oppose and left feeling the financial danger to his church was too great to risk jeopardizing the project. Despite his preference for development, he thought the church's position would have been better served by a different opening strategy. Instead of blurting out the offer, it should have built a consensus within the church, then, slowly and carefully, in the surrounding community. The vestry should have openly acknowledged its wealth and the great value of its physical asset, then gone on to say that it naturally wanted to generate more funds for its good works. Much of the money would go to support the poorer parishes of the diocese, while some would be left over to do the kinds of humanitarian things churches do. In the course of this, continued the hypothetical press release, the church would be fortunate enough to acquire a new and efficient facility from which to carry on its good works. The Landmarks Law placed an obstacle in its way, and the rector and vestry would be pleased if the landmarks commission could be a bit more flexible.

But it hadn't happened that way. The church had dumped its decision on the parish and the city.

A year and a half later Ron was asked to join the vestry and later became chairman of the building committee. Although he continued to believe in the project, the church's methods eventually caused him to resign both positions.

By mid-October 1980 negative publicity had made the church leaders regroup. A few days after the October 9 meeting the rector sent a letter to the parish. After weeks of prayerful consideration the vestry had decided that "as a matter of policy, we will accept no offer, however big, enticing, or seeming to be the 'quick answer' to our growing financial needs, that would in anyway harm our world-renowned church or detract from its dedicated missions in God's name."

From then on, the rector and vestry denied they ever intended to sell the sanctuary itself, although evidence from several sources suggested otherwise. Anthony Marshall, the junior warden, had read a short essay at the October 9 meeting. It was titled "Good News." We must ask what it means to be a Christian, wrote Marshall. "As trustees of the Church's temporal wealth it would be irresponsible of the Vestry not to give serious consideration to the possibility of selling all or part of St. Bartholomew's." He went on to describe the tears that had welled up as he walked to the communion rail the Sunday after the news broke in the *Times*—tears prompted by the thought of losing the beautiful patterned marble paving between the choir stalls. The junior warden seemed to have had no doubt the whole church was on the auction block.

Vestryman John McNeely offered more direct evidence. He had been confirmed in St. Bartholomew's and could hardly recall having gone to another church. McNeely had been an usher for years and was deeply honored when elected to the vestry. As he told his wife, Marion, he thought it was only big shots with big names who got to be vestrymen at St. Bart's.

A member of the Committee to Oppose from the beginning, Marion McNeely vividly recalled the evening her husband came back from a vestry meeting "practically shaking and white as a sheet." His pallor came because the vestry had just voted to sell the church. Only he and one other vestryperson had abstained. Mrs. McNeely tearfully recalled her husband's anguish: "It was a very very difficult time for him."

The vestry's retreat came too late to quell the rebellion. It had blown the lid off Pandora's box, and forces over which the church fathers had no control entered the battle.

No one but the rector and vestry knew why a church with an $11 million endowment and a membership of more than 1,500 should suddenly decide it could not survive into the next decade without developing its property. The parish first heard of catastrophic financial problems in Peers Brewer's October 9 speech. The presumption was that the financial problems had preceded the real estate offer, but again, only the rector and vestry knew the details of how the $100 million offer had come about.

Rob Morris thought he might have gotten a glimpse into that genesis in a church meeting held at the prestigious Union Club in early November 1980. Marc Haas, the senior warden, presided. The audience consisted of a selection of younger parishioners of leadership mettle whom the vestry had invited to glimpse the church's future plans. Morris had not yet taken sides. Youthful, bright, and Harvard-educated, he found himself on the list of invitees.

"Marc Haas stood up with his hands on the back of a chair and made the major address," said Morris. He spoke of possible financial problems in years to come and said the auditors had told the vestry it was eating into the endowment. What was more, the senior warden continued, the parish was not raising enough money to do what it wanted to do. The combination of the auditor's anxiety and the church's desire to expand its programs led the vestry to look to development. In the process it had called in some real estate people to try to find out how much the Community House site was worth. Someone at that earlier meeting piped up with a question of his own, which Haas said had never occurred to anyone on the vestry. If the church could get X dollars for the Community House site, asked the questioner, how much could it expect for the whole block? Another voice then volunteered that if he could offer the whole block, he would go out of there and come back in ten days with a check for 100 million bucks. And that, as far as Morris knew, was the church's version of the $100 million offer.

What actually preceded the *Times* story is far from clear. If the "offer" was nothing more than a voice from the back of the room, why did the church bother to announce it formally—unless, perhaps, it was trying to stir up competitive interest? Two men viewed those events from a more privileged position than Morris. One was vestryman Tom Biallo, an importer of and expert on flavors and fragrances. The other was a priest. Both men concluded independently that a firm offer had been made, and that it had come from the First Boston Corporation.

Whether it was real or not, Morris and others among the opposition assumed Marc Haas's mental set and business interests would have led him toward such a decision. For years Haas was an associate of Allen & Company, a securities and investment banking firm, but his career also took him into the boardrooms of other corporations, and a portion of his reputed fortune came from real estate. He was on the board of the Tishman Realty & Construction Company at one point, he is a licensed real estate broker, and American Diversified Enterprises, Inc.—of which he is chairman— earns a quarter of its income from real estate dealings.

Morris's theory about St. Bart's and development revolved around Haas's remarkable accomplishments. The financier had been supremely successful in every business venture he touched during the twenty or so years he had been at St. Bart's. The thought that his church might eventually face financial difficulties made it the only part of his life that had not been a complete triumph (however minor those difficulties might seem to parishes with less generous endowments). "Ask a highway engineer how to solve the world's problems, and he is likely to say, 'Pave it.' "

What, then, would occur to someone who had made his fortune in and around real estate deals and who was a trustee of an institution which occupied a uniquely valuable piece of land? "Develop it." The possibility of a slow decline would be erased in a single masterstroke, and the author of that coup would have his portrait hung high in the gallery of senior wardens.

Morris did not think Haas would have suggested development for personal gain, but others were less generous. They pointed to his broker's license and his firm's real estate experience and noted that millions were to be made—legally—from the various fees connected with the deal.

How rapidly St. Bart's financial condition was deteriorating was a major point of debate. Over the years the rector and vestry released much information, some of it financial, explaining why they thought real estate development was the church's only option. Yet the statements that accompanied the original revelation gave no explanation of why the church needed such an enormous amount of money. There was only a remark by Marc Haas that St. Bart's had fewer members than it used to, a pitiable claim but one almost any Episcopal church in the diocese could have made.

Oddly enough, St. Bartholomew's fund-raising efforts went so well—in the years after the development scheme was announced—that the church never bothered to take advantage of a diocesan program to help financially faltering parishes. Reverend David Gordon, stewardship officer for the diocese of New York, has an impressive record for improving giving in the parishes he advises. Pledging has risen 30 percent in congregations using his strategies, only 15 percent in those that do not. He came to New York in 1983, and by 1985 he was talking to 139 of the 195 parishes in the diocese, and working closely with nearly 60. Despite the specter of doom foreseen by its treasurer, St. Bartholomew's never contacted Gordon.

Part of the difficulty in judging the church's future was that the state of its past finances—before Tom Bowers's arrival—depended upon the teller. The last bit of information from the church's side before the development bombshell was a November 1978 letter from the rector to the parish. It was written two months after Tom's induction, and in the midst of a stewardship campaign to cover the next year's operating budget. In it he said the church was in financial difficulty and had been running deficits since 1971. The Committee to Oppose disputed that in later years, but even assuming the worst, the rector's response to the situation showed that he thought the parish could avoid future difficulties by acting expeditiously. How? Tom gave a straightforward answer at the same time he announced the problem: "My experience over the years—within the life of a number of parishes—tells me that when the people know and understand the true situation, they will respond generously. St. Bartholomew's needs you!" The rector saw no obstacle so large it could not be overcome by traditional fund-raising tactics. Draw attention to the problem, hold a stewardship campaign, and count on the generosity of parishioners to support their church. It had worked phenomenally for him in the past, and he thought it could work at St. Bartholomew's, too, even if its parishioners were not accustomed to doing things that way.

The first every-member canvass was held in 1979 and came as a surprise to most parishioners. Some had been coming for more than half a century and had never been solicited directly. "It's not Christmas! It's not Easter! Why is the church asking me for money now?" The church always managed handsomely by relying on the weekly offering, the traditional Christmas and Easter appeals, and the rare solicitation from the pulpit for gifts to cover one-of-a-kind problems.

St. Bart's first every-member canvass may be taken as a sign that the rector thought his church was in trouble—as Tom Bowers and his followers claim—or as an indication that the rector and vestry decided to run their church the way most other churches are run in the latter half of the twentieth century—the opposition's view. In the light of later events the reason why he introduced the canvass is less interesting than the fact that he did. At the first hint of a problem Tom set about raising funds in a completely traditional way, just as he had done so successfully in Washington and Atlanta.

The canvass did not run perfectly the first year, but even those who eventually opposed the real estate plans thought it was a good move. Before a second one could get under way, the building scheme had surfaced and the vestry dropped the canvass, at least temporarily. Rob Morris was on the stewardship committee for the first canvass and felt the church fathers dropped it because they saw the potential for more income from the real estate deal. (The canvass was revived after a year's hiatus, once it was clear development would not come quickly or easily.)

For their part, members of the newly formed Committee to Oppose did not believe the church was in financial difficulty, at least not in the vivid colors painted by Peers Brewer. Marion McNeely had heard Tom talk about the church's poor financial state since shortly after he arrived. Sometime after the development option had surfaced, she looked closely at a set of financial statements issued by the church which showed deficits of several hundred thousand dollars during Dr. Finlay's last few years.

Marion McNeely is an attractive, slightly roundish elderly lady with the instincts of a good private eye. She decided to try to find out the facts of the pre-Bowers finances from General Luke W. Finlay (no relation to Dr. Finlay), the former treasurer, who had served under both rectors. McNeely was not sure where the general stood on the real estate question but knew from her husband that he had been "a stickler" for keeping tabs on the church's money and would not have let Dr. Finlay spend one cent more than he had to.

At a certain point in intraparish squabbles everyone begins behaving like a conspirator. Genteelly cagey, Mrs. McNeely did not ask about finances directly. Instead, she wrote an innocuous chatty note, in the course of which she mentioned that the rumor was Dr. Finlay had left the church in less than solid financial shape. Was that really the case? she inquired in passing.

McNeely said she received a letter telling her to ignore any talk about the poor financial shape of the church before Mr. Bowers arrived. Had the present rector continued along the path trod by his predecessor, the church would not be in any difficulties.

In other correspondence about the church's financial condition just before Tom came, the general stated categorically that he "did not regard St. Bartholomew's as being in danger of financial collapse at the time of Dr. Finlay's retirement early in 1978." He went on to say that there were ample unrestricted gifts to cover any operating deficits that might have been incurred: ". . . for the last two full fiscal years of Dr. Finlay's tenure as Rector the operating deficits of the church and the Community House were effectively offset by additions to the Unrestricted Gifts account in the Con solidated Church Fund that could, at the discretion of the Vestry, have been applied against the operating deficits." The general was, however, "fully conscious of some longer range problems facing the Church as a result of the combination of steadily escalating costs, *the expansion of the church's expenditures under Mr. Bowers,* and some unexpected mishaps, particularly two costly fires and heavy demands for building modifications emanating from the Fire Department as a consequence [emphasis added]." Development was the only solution to the church's long-term problems, concluded Luke Finlay.

Although detailed financial statements were rarely seen by anyone outside the vestry, no one thought of it as hiding things; it was just the custom. There was simply no need to scrutinize a well-running machine. The committee members wanted to change that custom. If the church was in the red, they wanted to see it in black and white.

Misunderstandings and misinformation abounded between church leaders and committee members, even at that early stage. Having fallen under the critical gun from the outset, the rector and vestry played a cautious hand when it came to publicizing details of the church's financial state. The committee approached the treasurer on two separate occasions and asked him to disclose the church's "true financial condition in recent years." The first time was the October 9 parish meeting. Brewer was circumspect then but agreed to meet with Armstrong the following week.

Sinc expected to see the financial figures when he convened with the treasurer. He was disappointed but did not yet feel things were out of hand. An amicable contact had been made with a fellow parishioner with a different point of view, and that was a start. In a follow-up letter he thanked the treasurer for his "fine work" in improving business procedures, introducing annual fund raising, and bringing the 1980 deficit down from the $650,000 predicted by the vestry (before capital additions). With only the barest hint of annoyance, he asked that the certified financial reports be made available as soon as possible, "consistent with the Senior Warden's and your statements at the Parish Meeting on October 9th. . . . As we believe we have a legal right to these, please consider this a formal demand."

The church made its offering a month later. It was too little too late for the committee. The report consisted of a single sheet (printed on both sides), accompanied by a one-page "glossary to financial statements." The third sheet was headed "How Is the Financial Management Process Handled at St. Bartholomew's?" and included a brief explanation of attempts to reduce expenses. Oddly enough, rather than a reduction, this showed that the annual deficit had risen by more than 200 percent since Dr. Finlay left, even by the most conservative estimate. The payroll had climbed from $337,500 in 1976 to $856,000 in 1980. Between Dr. Finlay's last full year and 1986, the rector's salary at St. Bartholomew's Church appears to have increased by 225 percent—excluding housing and utilities allowances. (The rector's total compensation for 1986 included a $66,500 salary and a $50,000 housing allowance.) Salaries for all other clergy at St. Bart's rose 260 percent during the same period, and parish expenses were up 443 percent.

*   *   *

The intensity of the committee's reaction to the development proposal provoked attacks by church officials, which brought counterattacks by the committee. The rector implied that people who were hostile to the building project were interested only in personal gain, rather than in the welfare of the church. That was a peculiar charge, since profit in development schemes normally accrues to those who favor, rather than to those who oppose. In a return salvo, the committee denounced the rector's remark as a slur and accused him of intimidation tactics more suited to an iron curtain country than to an Episcopal parish.

The rector then booted Don Chappell out of his post as chairman of the corps of ushers at St. Bartholomew's after four years' service. He accused him of deception, claiming Don had pledged his support for the project, then betrayed the promise a week later without having the courtesy to tell him of his change of heart. The rector closed his brief note of dismissal with a blessing.

Don claimed he had not deceived Father Bowers. "I did not pledge my loyalty to you individually at any point, but only to St. Bartholomew's. To the extent that its Rector's actions in regard to St. Bartholomew's are consistent with the Church's ministry and mission in New York I support him, but if they diverge I cannot. . . . I reciprocate your expression of blessing and faith." John Chappell got the ax around the same time. He was relieved of his duties on the finance committee. A few weeks later the names of Donald E. and John W. Chappell appeared on the slate of vestry candidates proposed by the Committee to Oppose, along with that of J. Sinclair Armstrong.

The first sounds of a major intraparish skirmish were heard in late November 1980. The church fired the initial rounds.

Public opinion about St. Bartholomew's development plans had been clear and hardly encouraging. Within the church an indeterminate number of parishioners were in open rebellion, trying to head off the deal. Unsure about the strength of the hostile insiders, church fathers began to wonder what was going to happen in the January vestry election. The committee had already circulated a petition and received more than enough signatures to put up its own slate—one of the few times in living memory the names put in play by the vestry's nominating committee would face an organized opposition.

The first overt sign of official concern came on Sunday, November 16. Among the announcements, the rector read the names of the vestry's candidates for the January election. In a minor breach of church bylaws—but a major breach of etiquette—he neglected to mention the names on the opposition slate.

The second indication of concern was more immediate and consisted of a two-pronged attack. The rector called J. Sinclair Armstrong into his study on December 2. He was handed a letter written by Marc Haas, the senior warden, which carried the threat of legal action. The gist was that the committee was infringing upon the church's territory by using its name. Because "St. Bartholomew's" appeared in its title, the committee appeared to be countenanced by the church. That could lead people to confuse the two, and funds meant for the needy church might end up in the committee's bank account.

The second prong of the assault involved the election. The rector hoped to head off the opposition by denying Armstrong's right to run. In the presence of the church's attorney, John Nelson, of Milbank, Tweed, Hadley & McCloy, the rector questioned Armstrong's bona fides. He claimed the opposition leader was ineligible to vote—and hence ineligible to run for the vestry—because he had not contributed to the church in the past twelve months as required by its bylaws.

Armstrong said he could show he had contributed.

After giving the letter to Armstrong, the rector shifted to an earlier tactic and tried to co-opt his errant parishioner. Despite objections to Sinc's candidacy on an opposition slate, the lawyer was once again offered a seat on the vestry, courtesy of the rector's intervention. "I would be welcome on the vestry," Armstrong wrote in a memo for committee files, "and will be recommended by the rector in due course." Sinc was the only one on the committee's slate to receive that honor.

Armstrong declined again. He could not submit to nomination by the present vestry because his supporters would not approve. On the contrary, Armstrong maintained, he and his fellow committee members "looked forward to the time when the rector would be on board" with them. He finished by pointing out that secular corporations were permitted to raise funds for preservation and, with a bit of boastful optimism, pledged that any money the committee might receive that exceeded their expenses would go toward endowing a fund to preserve the church.

The shepherd and his black sheep parted company with nothing resolved. A few days later the committee extended a thorned olive branch: It looked forward to working with the church leaders for "honest" elections.

Shortly after the December 2 meeting the church pressed its attack against Armstrong and made a serious tactical error for which it would pay in the future. In mid-December Armstrong received the first of several letters from the church's lawyer. Marc Haas had asked Nelson a series of questions about the voter qualification section of the bylaws. The pertinent paragraphs described qualified voters as baptized, eighteen years old or more on the day of the vote, and members of the parish. They also had to be in "regular attendance at worship services" and "contributors of record to [the church's] suppport for at least twelve months" before the meeting in which they wanted to vote.

Nelson advised Armstrong that he had reseached all readily available authorities regarding voter qualifications in church elections, to the point of consulting the senior legal officer of the diocese. With that preamble, he explained the rector's definition of "contributor of record": Anyone "who had contributed to the general support of the church in 1979 and 1980 would be deemed a 'contributor of record.'" Then came the punch line. Gifts made to the church for specific purposes (rather than general support) "did not evidence the kind of support of the Church which would make the person eligible to be a qualified voter."

Most charitable institutions rejoice if people give at all. Splitting hairs over how much is given for what purpose, and when it arrives, is rarely the custom in Episcopal churches. It is far too undignified, for one thing. Other priests in the diocese said their voters were rarely, if ever, questioned about contributions, and asking an attorney to pursue such a matter was unheard of. But other priests were not playing for the stakes St. Bart's was.

The rector's subtle definition of "support" appeared to be a Catch-22 designed to knock Sinc Armstrong out of the race. The lawyer responded with photocopies of two canceled checks and a letter from him to the rector, dated January 16, 1979. That year's annual parish dinner had been held in the Starlight Room of the Waldorf-Astoria. "That was a superb dinner dance, the 144th Anniversary Dinner, you gave for the Parish last evening. My experience as a past president of the Saint Andrew's Society (which had its 222nd Anniversary Banquet at the Waldorf this past year) leads me to believe that without the ability to change base metal to gold you could not have such a party for the price charged. So here is a modest contribution to help with it. Do not bother to acknowledge this." He enclosed a $100 check. He had also paid $42 for two dinner tickets, so contributions of record in the name of Sinclair Armstrong totaled $142 in 1979. (From the beginning of the controversy, Armstrong gave several hundred dollars a year to St. Bart's but made substantially greater annual contributions to other churches in the diocese, including Grace Church and St. Mark's.)

The church did not count contributions made by Sinc's father in the name of the Armstrong family, although Howard S. Armstrong wrote the following note:

> I am not quite sure you are acquainted with the charitable donations theory of a close-knit New York family. It is rather like the Three Musketeers, "All for One and One for all."
>
> I subscribe for two seats in Pew 50, one of which is for Sinclair, and also make a small annual donation. Sinclair, in

active aid of a poor parish, served as Senior Warden of St. Mark's in the Bowery, resigning from that missionary post only last year, but continuing his larger pecuniary aid [to St. Mark's].

Of course you could transfer the pew rental to Sinclair if it would make the lawyers feel any better and I would pay him to pay it.

In the meantime, the younger Armstrong had responded to Nelson's letter. He told the church's attorney that his own reading of the statute did not permit a parish to exclude an otherwise eligible voter simply because he had given to a specific program of the church rather than to its general support. Do St. Bartholomew's bylaws exclude from voting those who contribute only to its magnificent music program? he asked. Or to the Community Club, or other programs? "Supporting any program of the Church, I submit, is support of the Church."

Armstrong's refusal to be intimidated might well have triggered the unusual event which followed close on the heels of the exchange with Nelson. It was not customary for opposition to persist in Tom Bowers's parishes. If the committee did not crumble under the first fusillade, stronger measures were necessary. Judged from the quickness with which they came, they had been in the planning stage before Armstrong made it clear he would not back off.

On the evening of December 16, a scant nine days before the most joyful festival of the Christian year, the rector, churchwardens, and vestry of St. Bartholomew's Episcopal Church sued their own parishioners.

Summons serving has an important psychological element; it is usually done to intimidate, even when it is a rector and vestry suing members of their own congregation. The church chose a particularly harsh approach toward the one defendant most likely to be intimidated, the handsome and frail septuagenarian Mrs. Marjorie Brown.

On December 16 the clergyman's widow was about to leave her Queens home for some last-minute Christmas shopping in Manhattan. The phone rang just as she reached the door. A voice announced that the rector and vestrymen of her church were serving her a summons to appear in court on Monday, December 22. It demanded to know where she was going to be in the next hour. She was on her way out, came the timid answer, whereupon the summons server asked which store she was going to. He would meet her there. "If you don't accept this paper," added the voice, "you'll be in bad trouble with the court."

As a retired kindergarten teacher who had spent her private life in the society of churchmen, Marjorie Brown knew little about what a summons server could or could not do. The thought of being degraded in public terrified her. But she was equally afraid she would be a fugitive from justice if she didn't get this horrifying piece of paper. Mrs. Brown said she would not go Christmas shopping but would wait for the process server. He was at her door before she could begin to gather her wits about her.

She was appalled to see a legal document, signed by her rector, which said he was suing his own parishioners. The widow had known clergymen all her life and could not square that action with anything she had encountered in the past.

The stress that began with the call eventually affected Marjorie Brown's health. Despite her doctor's advice to distance herself as much as possible from her church, Mrs. Brown found that she was willing to put everything on the line. She decided she could not, and would not, retreat.

*   *   *

The ostensible purpose of the suit was to prevent the Committee to Save St. Bartholomew's Church, Inc. from using the church's name when soliciting funds. As Armstrong had learned from Haas's first letter, the church feared that an unauthorized committee could divert needed funds. (The lawyer for the church submitted inverse proof that this could happen, a few checks and letters intended for the committee that had come to the church.) The true purpose of the lawsuit appeared to have been to goad the malcontents into leaving the parish, thereby barring the committee from gaining representation on the vestry.

As it turned out, after having violated the scriptural admonition against suing a fellow Christian, the rector and vestry failed to take even the modest ground they had set out to capture. The suit did not scare opponents off, and while the court agreed that the committee's use of the church's name could cause confusion, for some unexplained reason the rector and vestry agreed to let the Armstrong's group call itself the Committee to Oppose the Sale of St. Bartholomew's Church, Inc.

The church had risked a great deal by entering the courts and received little apparent profit. Just what was at risk became apparent almost immediately. The targets of the suit had been at their wits' end. They had no $11 million endowment to draw on for their war chest and no pulpit from which to press their case each week. In short, they saw no way to block the project. Never in their wildest fantasies had they considered suing the rector. Once that psychological barrier had been removed, the opposition happily followed him through the courtroom doors and began filing countersuits. It proved a reasonably effective tactic for keeping the church on its toes in the coming years.

The committee's first counterclaim demanded that the rector honor the petition to place Armstrong's name on the ballot for the coming vestry election. He had filed it in plenty of time, but the rector ignored it long enough to let the ballots go out without his name. The court said Armstrong was a qualified candidate and directed the church to print another ballot.

Having two ballots for the same election created some confusion. The one without Armstrong's name was blue; the new one was yellow. In complying with the letter of the court order, the church managed to confuse the issue to its own advantage. In an explanation accompanying the second ballot, the rector said Armstrong's name had been left off the first one because the church did not consider him a "contributor of record." Buried farther down in the letter was a sentence about the court's having ruled otherwise, hence the new ballot.

Instead of voiding the original ballots, the rector muddied the issue further. He encouraged those who had voted before the Armstrong option became available, and who did not want to change their votes, to ignore the second ballot. In a left-handed sort of way, that bypassed the ruling that Armstrong's name should have been there in the first place.

Armstrong and his candidates lost the vestry election of 1981 in a landslide, and the rector took the outcome as a pro-develop-ment mandate. Looking for ways to mitigate defeat, the committee claimed a minor victory in the moral war just beginning to unfold before the public. The church had had its hand slapped for wrongly keeping Armstrong's name off the ballot. What was more, the committee pointed out, its candidates had captured 43 percent of the "yellow ballot" vote. (The highest polling church candidate, Anthony Marshall, received 484 votes. Don and John Chappell tied for top honors among the five opposition candidates, with 199 each.) The public face did not hint at the committee's private gloom. The most aggressive move it had been able to make was to fire another shot off into the courts, demanding that the vestry and rector consider the bylaw amendment Armstrong had submitted in October. With a bit of luck, they thought they might force the church to ask parish approval before a deal was struck. It was meager solace.

If the committee was on the ropes, the rector and vestry still considered it a dangerous foe and maintained an aggressive stance toward it. The classic strategy when facing internal opposition is to claim it survives because of outside agitators. Shortly after the 1981 vestry election a rumor circulated in the parish that the committee was the puppet of real estate interests bent on derailing the project. The name of Lewis Rudin, who owned the office tower directly behind the Community House, was mentioned in particular. Although the blanket allegation was never substantiated, as late as 1986 the bishop still called the opposition "outsiders."

A few weeks after the vestry election Armstrong wrote a memo to the committee outlining three possible legal tacks: (1) Try to overturn the election based on voting irregularities; (2) require the church to hand over its certified financial statements; (3) attempt to nullify the proceedings that took place at the annual meeting because the church had not voted on the bylaw amendment. He also suggested the committee members consider suing the church for libel or slander for circulating the rumor that they were supported by outside interests. "I am cautious about such [a suit]," he wrote, "but it might be fun to sue him who says we've been flung into the weeds, because it makes good headlines and reflects on him adversely." ("Flung into the weeds" refers to a remark Bowers had made about the committee's recent election loss.)

In the same memo Sinc put forth what he called a new "Armstrong Theory." It proposed suing the rector and vestry to stop them from wasting more of the church's assets "in pursuing a course which is likely to be held illegal." They would file an action as shareholders in the religious corporation to enjoin its directors (the vestry) from wasting corporate assets until they could show there was a chance the landmarks commission would approve the building.

The theory was only put to the test four years later. For the committee's own morale, and to show potential supporters they had not lost heart, Armstrong and his group needed an immediate and highly visible counterattack. That began in early March 1981; a blitz of letters went out to forty bishops, twenty rectors, and the members of nine diocesan standing committees around the country, designed at gaining ecclesiastical support for saving the landmark. Members of the Committee to Oppose knew it would be difficult to influence Tom Bowers through that kind of pressure but thought they might be able to make an inroad into the ecclesiastical camp. The effort was also aimed at trying to influence a far more formidable personality in the Episcopal Church, Bishop Paul Moore, Jr. Canon law says the bishop and the Standing Committee of the diocese must approve any lease involving church property, and some on the Committee to Oppose thought it might be easier to sway the bishop because of his greater distance from the project.

The "Clergy to Save St. Bart's" strategy never caught on. Like other professionals, clerics shy away from public criticism of their brethren. There would be no open rebellion against the rector or brotherly pressure on the bishop.

In spite of the political risks, a few priests did offer their support in private. The Very Reverend J. C. Michael Allen, dean of Christ Church Cathedral, St. Louis, expressed a view that lay at the heart of all arguments encouraging the preservation of ecclesiastical architecture: The physical church is a witness to the Christian God. The real issue was "whether the Church will continue to stand in the center of power and decision in New York or any other city as a constant witness to the claim of Jesus Christ on His city." Recalling the sack of Jerusalem by the Roman emperor Titus, A.D. 79, the dean of the St. Louis cathedral stressed that the Romans had not only dispersed the Jewish people but destroyed the Temple—the physical presence—to "remove God from His city." Sinc quoted that passage later in a letter to Moore.

A church historian from a neighboring diocese commended Armstrong on his stand. Baptized and ordained in the Cathedral of St. John the Divine, the Very Reverend David Rhinelander King wrote of his shock when he heard St. Bart's claim it was going out of business. Three decades in the ministry had taught him something of church finances, and he knew St. Bartholomew's could easily reduce "its extravagant life-style" and live within its means like every other church.

The same letter questioned the long-term wisdom of taking the easy financial road: "I feel it is spiritually destructive for the members of St. Bartholomew's to have the free ride which [the income from an office tower] will give them. Parishioners need to pay for their church, or it isn't their church. They need to give. Stewardship is, spiritually, vital."

But those were exceptions. Political realities held sway. Some simply chose not to venture an opinion one way or the other, saying it was clearly Bishop Moore's territory. Others said they supported Armstrong in spirit but questioned the propriety of a priest from another diocese interjecting himself into the affair. Several who answered the committee's plea sent courtesy copies of their replies to Moore. That brought on a heated correspondence between the bishop and Armstrong. The bishop flatly accused Sinc of embarrassing him by lobbying his fellow clergy to pressure him into vetoing the development project.

Perhaps ingenuously, Armstrong denied that claim. The bishop knew well that he could not be pressured by fellow clergy, wrote the lawyer. (Moore had a history of taking unpopular stands in the church.) Sinc informed his co-worker in Christ that, to a man, the other bishops said they would not interfere in another diocese. Which was not to say Armstrong had not tried.

Sinc also corresponded with the bishop on several other points regarding the parish. Perhaps it was the lawyer's penchant for precision and detail, or an equally lawyerlike interest in opening every possible avenue of approach, but Armstrong's letters were long, while the replies were brief and to the point.

The audited financial statements still headed Armstrong's list of desired information. He had to see the records to be certain the church's endowment was being cared for properly. Both the Not-for-Profit and Religious Corporation laws "call for financial reporting by an Episcopal Church to its members," he wrote. The committee had requested that information six months earlier and had not yet received it. Would the bishop please inquire of the rector and vestry on that point, to "bring them into compliance with law, civil and canon, by-laws, and proper practices and procedures of an Episcopal Church in your Diocese"?

The lawyer added that canon law required parishes to file certified financial reports with the diocese by September 1 of each year. If Moore had received what the committee had not, would he kindly pass it on to them and to the parish at large? (The committee received the 1980 financials from the church in January 1982.)

Armstrong also complained about the rector's efforts to restrict voter qualifications in the recent election. Keeping all avenues open for later court action, he pointed out that no law said a "contributor" to a church was one who pledged (by check) as opposed to putting cash in the weekly collection baskets or contributing to parish programs.

Leaving the tactical side roads, Armstrong returned to the main line of attack, the real estate proposal. The church needed the approval of both the bishop and the Standing Committee to lease its property. Would the decision be made before a parish vote? Or would the bishop stand by while the rector removed the "premiere [sic] Episcopal Church" in the heart of the city to finance his television ministry? (Armstrong took the preservationists' view that the whole complex was the "landmark.")

Moore accused Sinc of spreading untruths. The rector and vestry had already said they would not tear down the church itself. The prelate took the developer's position: The church was the landmark, and the Community House could be torn down without a significant loss to the city.

The lawyer and the bishop were not close to making significant contact on any of the issues.

Armstrong continued in a mildly threatening tone, saying that the financial future of the diocese would be deeply affected, that the bishop and Standing Committee had a significant stake in the St. Bartholomew's affair. The issue was not the perfunctory sale of a bit of church land or even the loss of a church of minor distinction, whose congregation had drifted away. "Our opposition, and the likelihood of our success, poses a financial risk to the church." Should the Committee to Oppose be forced into lengthy suits against the rector and vestry, it would have no choice but to assess its expenses against the church, and Sinc cited a case involving the Central Presbyterian Church of New York in which parishioners who successfully opposed its sale recovered their legal costs from the church.

Lastly in this long epistle, Armstrong called Moore's attention to a sermon titled "Seeking God's Will," which the rector had delivered just before the vestry election. In it Bowers had accused those who wanted to save the building of being "architectural idolaters." As far as Armstrong was concerned, the rector had as much as said "our Lord Jesus Christ . . . ordered . . . St. Bartholomew's [to] be sold, in whole or in part, and replaced by a skyscraper and a television ministry. We do not accept that as valid theology, but we are lay persons, not theologians."

*   *   *

Paul Moore, Jr., grew up as the son of wealthy New Yorkers, whose money came from various family companies, among them American Can and National Biscuit. He received a model Episcopalian education at St. Paul's School, in Concord, New Hampshire, and Yale University but did not follow his older brother into business. From his youth Moore felt called to the ministry and pursued that calling after college, in quiet defiance of his father's wishes.

He graduated from the New York City's General Theological Seminary in 1949 and asked to be posted to some "broken-down" city parish. Father Moore and his bride, Jenny McKean, spent their first years working together in a parish in Jersey City, across the Hudson River. Moore championed the causes of his downtrodden flock against a system that seemed to conspire to keep them poor. He and his fellow priest, Kilmer Myers, lobbied neighborhood politicians and the city and even ventured to Washington in defense of parishioners' rights. (Myers was also to become a bishop.)

In 1957 Moore left Jersey City for Indianapolis, to become dean of Christ Church Cathedral, then went on to Washington, D.C., and the post of suffragan, or assistant bishop. It was a meteoric rise, even for someone born to wealth. When he returned to New York in 1969, it was as heir to the bishopric. He took the pastoral crook from Horace Donegan four years later, to become the thirteenth bishop of New York.

From his first parish through his first decade and a half as bishop, Moore's record was impeccably liberal and marked by a harsh, almost puritanical sense of rightness of purpose. At each career plateau he won the love and respect of the liberal community, inside and outside the church, while incurring conservative wrath in equal measure. His unpopularity at the national level was even cause for comment at a St. Bartholomew's vestry meeting. Jim Dunning had gone into Episcopal churches across the country in the search that finally turned up Tom Bowers, and he returned after one of those trips to tell his colleagues how "impressed [he was] by the widespread negative opinions" of the bishop of New York.

The sixty-eight-year-old Moore is well over six feet tall, with a craggy visage. There is nothing yielding in his presence. He emanates confidence and complete ease with his power and the unbending hierarchy from which it derives. He served with distinction as a marine in World War II and retains much of the marine in his manner. The bishop gives the impression he is not accustomed to being questioned or contradicted.

Bishop Moore operates from deep personal conviction rather than from custom. His position on ordaining Episcopal clergy offers a clear illustration. In the late 1960's the Episcopal Church officially recognized certain inequities in American society, one of which was the unequal treatment of women. Factions within the church were suggesting it ordain the second sex, a proposition that flew in the face of 2,000 years of apostolic tradition and reduced conservative churchmen to apoplexy. Liberals thought it was a necessary step if the church was to retain its credibility. The issue came to a head in a single cathartic moment. In the summer of 1974, acting without the required approval of the episcopate, three priests ordained eleven women. The three were friends of Moore, and one of them, a former bishop of Pennsylvania, had written Moore of their intention.

Moore was "mad as hell" when he heard the news. He agreed that it had to be done but thought it should be done legally, with the approval of the necessary bishops and standing committees.

The ordinations did not have the predicted catastrophic consequences. The church handled the heresy in a calm and diplomatic manner befitting the spiritual sons (and now daughters) of the English Church. The women were outlaw priests for only two years. Despite old-guard bitterness among clergy and laity, in 1976 the General Convention passed a resolution decreeing that the canons of ordination be applied equally to men and women. With a minimum of visible trauma, the Episcopal Church leaped from the sixteenth into the twenty-first century in a single bound.

Bishop Moore took the inevitable next step. Among the women he ordained was Ellen Barrett, a self-declared lesbian. The ordination of an acknowledged homosexual outraged—and continues to outrage—many Episcopalians, leading Lester Kinsolving, the conservative religious columnist, to refer to the bishop as "one of the great frothing idiots of our time."

Moore's decision was not the logical consequence of the perverse pursuit of publicity, a motivation some detractors were quick to attribute to him. It was the act of a rationalist operating according to guidelines of conscience rather than convention— even when the convention was that of his own church. The bishop's argument was simple and compelling. The church had ordained male homosexuals for centuries; all the offenders had to do was avoid advertising their sexual preference. Here was a woman who chose to be honest rather than deceitful. Were Christians to punish honesty? There was an inexorable, pragmatic logic to that decision, which surfaced in the bishop's approach to the development of St. Bartholomew's.

*   *   *

Signs that inner strife was corroding the bonds of parish life had begun to show by the spring of 1981. Telephone threats were allegedly made against Father Bowers's life because of his pro-development stand, and a rumor—allegedly started by someone on the vestry—said someone from the Committee to Oppose had rung up the priest in the middle of the night and called him dirty names.

The notion that such shenanigans should be connected to the committee was a most unimaginable fiction, according to Rob Morris: "Anyone in the world could have dropped a dime in a phone and breathed heavy in Tom Bowers's ear, but our group, for the most part, is little old ladies of both sexes. You know, earnest old-fashioned sorts. An ex-president of the Women of St. Bartholomew's, an eighty-three-year-old member of the Altar Guild, and the widow of a man who was a parish member for fifty-seven years and a vestryman for twenty. Are these likely candidates to call the rector in the middle of the night and tell him dirty words?"

Some months later George Hayman, a stocky middle-aged supporter of the rector, wrote what Sinc Armstrong considered a threatening letter. Hayman suggested the lawyer and his compatriots give up their fight. No one wanted to push his face into the ground until it was thoroughly disfigured, he wrote, but that might be the only alternative if the opposition persisted. Two days later he realized the implication of what he had said and sent a second letter stressing the figurative nature of that colorful image, signed "Your pal in Christ." It apparently crossed Armstrong's reply to the first: "This threat to commit bodily harm to me, transmitted through the U.S. mails, in my opinion constitutes a criminal act under U.S. statutes."

"I suggest that you withdraw it at once and take your own counsel."

Sinc Armstrong contacted the U.S. attorney for the Southern District of New York and enclosed a copy of Hayman's letter with a note of his own. Armstrong's colleagues at Whitman & Ransom considered the threat a felony under U.S. Code, Title 18, Section 876. Armstrong asked that he and his wife be protected. "As far as I am concerned," he wrote to an adviser, "the third paragraph still fills me with a threat of physical attack."

Grand battles waged for large stakes are often accompanied by minor harassing actions. One such engagement took place far from the physical precincts of St. Bart's, but close to its spiritual and worldly roots. The Episcopal Church has a pension fund valued at nearly three-quarters of a billion dollars. It was founded around 1910 with $4 million in seed money from J. P. Morgan and has been augmented since then by assessments from clergy salaries. Bishops constitute the majority of the pension fund board, but the laity also serves. J. Sinclair Armstrong had been a board member for years as both secretary and trustee. He was first elected in 1967 and polled more votes than any other candidate in a later bid for reelection.

Two years after the storm clouds had gathered over St. Bart's, he again came up for reelection. Although the head of the fund gave Sinc his full support, heavy lobbying by a contingent from St. Bartholomew's did him in. J. Sinclair Armstrong was the only candidate put forth by the board of directors who was not reelected.

On a less dramatic stage, Armstrong loosed another volley in Moore's direction, complaining about the treatment of members of the Committee to Oppose at the hands of the clergy and lay leaders of St. Bartholomew's. They did not have to take communion or receive "pastoral care" from clergy who were "vigorous in the criticism of us," said the letter. They checked with a retired clergyman, and the committee believed it was within its rights in requesting the services of one of the two priests who had "not denounced us nor borne false witness against us" to act as a special chaplain.

Moore did not grant the committee's request for a special priest. Holy communion came from the Lord, he wrote, not from the priest who administered it.

It was very much a "them and us" situation in the parish by that time. Prodevelopment forces, including the clerical staff, believed the committee's actions could damage the church irreparably, while members of the opposition thought the clergy was actively hostile toward them. The wife of one committee member suffered a miscarriage but could not bring herself to call a priest from her own church to help her through that time. She genuinely believed the clergy hated her because of her husband's open opposition to the project.

Early in the affair the bishop had objected to the attempts of the Committee to Oppose to publicize the issue. Armstrong countered the request to keep it internal by pointing out that a debate over a major New York City landmark could hardly be kept within the parish. In truth, publicity was as much to Armstrong's advantage as it was to the disadvantage of the bishop, since the committee operated at a distinct strategic handicap. It had little money, compared with the massive resources of the church, and was constantly butting up against the overpowering advantage of an incumbent who held the high ground of the pulpit. The chances for a dialogue at St. Bartholomew's were slim to nil. There was no room for an opposing point of view in Tom Bowers's church, and Armstrong knew his best chance to gain support in the crucial landmarks battle to come was to place the affair squarely on public view.

The sure knowledge that they were facing a long battle, which had to be fought along several fronts, made the committee look for a variety of ways to fill its war chest. By the first few months of 1981 it had taken in a little less than $16,000 from nearly 300 supporters, most of them parishioners. It was not nearly enough to carry on a fight.

Letters went out to potential supporters, showing the committee's stiff, public upper lip. "We expect to win," wrote Sinc to one supporter, but he knew he and the other opponents had to keep the pressure on within the church and in the courts. Getting the documents they requested was not the most important part of the latter strategy. They wanted to depose the church leaders under oath, to ask them who, what, where, and when about the alleged real estate development offers.

Those fund-raising appeals also revealed the committee's broader strategy: "In the Diocese we are after Bishop Moore. If he resists, he will be part of the opposition. . . . If Paul Moore lets us down, as he likely will because [the diocese stands to profit from the development], we will need at least 100 grand. How can we raise it or assure it?" It was uncharacteristically tough talk for Armstrong and of a cut that rarely, if ever, surfaced in public statements. But it was the only way to convince outsiders that the committee was in the fight to win.

*　　*　　*

Later on stories about how things were handled in the church surfaced from people who had worked there and did not like what they saw. A few called attention to what appeared to be a discrepancy between the rector's rhetoric and his actions. Not that one who is concerned for the poor has to dig in himself—"Each person does his ministry in his own way," as priests often say—but Tom Bowers championed ministry to the downtrodden so vigorously that some of his fellow workers were disturbed when his actions appeared to belie the words.

Ann Nestor is a sweet, street-wise middle-aged woman who ran the Community House switchboard and front desk for several years after Tom came to St. Bartholomew's. "I don't see where he helps the people," she said. "He's a rich man and he's for the rich. He didn't help any of the people who were working there, in the low-paying jobs. Blacks and refugees, people who can't get jobs, he would take in, but only on minimum salaries, and that's where they stay."

Most of the staff were earning less than $200 a week when Nestor was there in the early 1980's, and they were afraid to open their mouths because they were working without green cards and feared a complaint would get them fired. "I was one of the low-paid workers. We had to fight and scream for increases. Tell me how you run a family on that."

She recollected having looked forward to the job: "I thought it was as safe as could be when I came there—a church, nice people, nice priests—wow!

"I was sitting at the board one day when a street person came in. They automatically came to me, and I sat them down and tried to get a social worker to talk with them. In the meantime, Mr. Bowers walked in. Naturally [the street person] jumped up, seeing a priest, [and] he said, 'Can you help me, can you help me?' I'm sitting there, and then Bowers said, 'Aw sure, just sit down,' then turned to me and said under his breath 'Get rid of him.' "

David Trovillion, an ex-verger of St. Bartholomew's, remembered a similar incident. (The verger is a kind of caretaker, who makes sure everything the priests need for the service is at hand. It was a part-time position at St. Bart's, and Trovillion also worked as a free-lance art director for a small trade journal.) The scene with the rector stuck in his mind because it happened just after Bowers had preached a stirring sermon about helping the poor.

The congregation had left, and an emotionally disturbed lady wandered into the church, carrying a notebook in which she was documenting all the attempts to kill her by radiation. She wanted to talk to Father Bowers, who was just coming out of his study, apparently on his way to lunch. A staffer told the rector about his visitor, but Bowers said he did not want to talk to her. He then hid behind a curtain at the side of the chancel and sent out an assistant priest to "try to get rid of her,"in Trovillion's words. Not that anything could have been done for her, said the ex-verger, but she wanted someone to talk to, someone to temper her fears. "It was the idea of [his] preaching the sermon in the morning and then repudiating it in the afternoon" that disturbed the shy Trovillion.

Tallish and thin, Trovillion seems the gentlest of souls, speaking with the hint of a soft drawl, the legacy of his youth in Fairfield, a small town in southern Illinois which describes itself in its civic slogan as the "Home of Friendly People." Trovillion found that friendliness too cloying. When he came to New York in the early 1970's, he was immediately drawn to St. Bartholomew's. There was a beauty and dignity in the restraint of the services under Terence Finlay. "To be exciting within the context of something very formal" provided a new and deeply satisfying aesthetic experience to the young man. Dr. Finlay conducted the worship services masterfully, and Trovillion made no bones about preferring the former rector's restraint to what he termed the "forced intimacy" of Tom's backslapping style.

Trovillion saw Tom Bowers as a product of southern culture, a breed he knew well from Fairfield—some fifty or sixty miles north of the Mason-Dixon line as the crow flies. He may have a certain "charm or mystery to native New Yorkers," conceded the midwesterner, but a northerner could not see it for what it really was. "We [midwesterners] kind of think of him as a snake-oil salesman," said Trovillion. "He's very skillful, and I admire some things about him, but I don't like him."

It was not only the rector's manner that offended Trovillion. The verger-cum-art director was scraping out a living in the big city, and while the rector continually spoke of the "poor," he had a well-known taste for the good life in food, drink, and cigars, lived in palatial splendor in the twelve-room Park Avenue rectory, and had a grand salary and an equally grand housing allowance.

Others felt little Christian understanding was shown when it came to the dissidents in the congregation. Several stories about his earlier parishes had come up from Atlanta with the rector. One involved a forceful dowager who approached Bowers at a coffee hour one Sunday, waggled a pudgy finger under his nose, and said, "This ministry for the homeless is ruining our parish house, and besides that, you aren't going to change one of them." Tom supposedly answered: "Madam, the point isn't to change them. The point is to change you."

Rob Morris recalled Marc Haas standing at the lectern one Sunday morning, about two months into the affair and extending a simple suggestion to everyone disenchanted with the church's intentions. In a city with so many Episcopal churches, said the senior warden, it would be a shame to keep coming to one that makes you unhappy.

The suggestion was reissued at a later meeting between leaders from the church and the Committee to Oppose, this time by the junior and senior church wardens. Marshall and Charles Scribner, Jr., (of the publishing Scribners) told Armstrong and Morris they wanted them and their followers to leave the church. Sinc asked the rector if he concurred, and Bowers backed off. "Jesus Christ was shepherd to all the flock," Armstrong recalled his saying, "and my welcoming arms, like Jesus', extend to you." Armstrong thought it a preposterous bit of hypocrisy, in view of the hostility of the church fathers. The suggestion that the dissidents move to "some other parish which is more attuned to their aesthetic sensibilities" has been repeated periodically over the years.

*   *   *

In the spring of 1981, with the building project over its first major hurdle (the implicit approval of the parish via the 1981 vestry election), the church set about trying to find a developer. To that end it retained John A. White, a development consultant and the chairman of Landauer Associates. White was in the right league for the church, having recently negotiated the sale of the Pan Am Building, just down the avenue from St. Bartholomew's.

Under White's orchestration, the church invited teams of developers and architects to submit proposals for the Community House site. The vestry retained Robert Geddes to help it choose from among the submissions. Dean of the Princeton School of Architecture, Marc Haas's alma mater, Geddes was to advise the church on the architectural merit of the schemes. Several well-known architects and developers submitted plans, but the public saw only the one that was finally chosen.

Geddes stressed the limitations of his role. He came to the affair long after the architects and developers had settled on their approaches and could give an opinion only on what was presented. He could not suggest changes. Geddes did not remember any discussions about the constitutional implications of the Landmarks Law or of the church's need to have a huge income for its mission work. It was a simple matter of which scheme offered the most, financially and architecturally. In his own words, his job was to pick the "lesser of the evils" from ready-made development packages. "You have to have seen Donald Trump's proposal to see what I saved the city from," said Dean Geddes.

A small group of parishioners received an early briefing on the details of the development project. A special Parish Leadership Conference was held on May 27 and 28, 1981, and "more than 80 church and [Community] Club committee coordinators, Vestry, staff members and others" gathered to "consider the real estate situation and its relationship to the future of St. Bartholomew's." It was a pep rally for the prodevelopment team. Although it was billed as a parish affair, attendance was by invitation. Known members of the opposition were not on the guest list.

The first session consisted of an explanation of the church's religious and secular circumstances. A later article in *St. Bartholo-News*, the parish newsletter, said some participants had shown concern over the project at the beginning, but their apprehension dissipated as soon as the rector explained the "theology of our problems and opportunities."

The theology Father Bowers presented was the first formal statement of the outreach ministry theme, which would become the centerpiece in later pleadings before the landmarks commission. "Christ is our example," the rector explained to the select group. Christ worshiped regularly, he went on, but most of his time was spent helping people. " 'The Spirit of the Lord is upon me, because he hath anointed me to preach the gospel to the poor; he hath sent me to heal the broken-hearted, to preach deliverance to the captives, and recovering of sight to the blind, to set at liberty them that are bruised. . . . [Luke 4:18]' We are called in Christ to use every resource to continue this ministry to people," he exhorted. The real cost of the church's buildings was borne by the poor, for maintaining them took money from the needy.

After providing a theological foundation for development, the rector offered his own version of how the idea had come about. It differed in detail, if not tenor, from what Marc Haas had told another group of parishioners at the Union Club six months before.

The architects who looked after the day-to-day maintenance of the church, Cain, Farrell & Bell, had done a study in the late 1970's which showed the need for major repairs. Its itemized list totaled approximately $2.4 million. That figure had now grown; $7 million in "essential repairs and improvements" were needed in the next ten years.

Cain, Farrell & Bell had also made suggestions for expanding the present Community House, at an estimated cost of $3 million. The rector did not explain what those plans entailed or how much additional space would have been provided (facts that surfaced only four years later, during the hardship hearings). The implication, however, was that $3 million was too much to spend for what they would gain.

Shortly after looking into the Community House expansion, "the church was approached by the real estate community and was told that it had a tremendous resource in the property. Soon very large offers put the church on the front page of *The New York Times*." Once they knew the potential, said the rector, the vestry began to think about what that meant for the church's mission. A speculative office building would cure any financial ills it might have in the future, plus provide the space and income to increase the outreach programs. (*St. BartholoNews* did not mention any questions from the floor about the church's need for more space or its financial difficulties.)

At the end of his presentation the rector said the legal power to decide to develop rested with the vestry. However, "any [vestry] vote would come only after parish input, such as this conference."

John White, the real estate adviser, spoke next. White had already reviewed several submissions, but the plans were preliminary. There was no hard information on construction cost or on critical issues like rents and where the Community House and its activities would be housed during the three- or four-year construction period. He outlined the three approaches then under consideration:

- Sell all the church's remaining development rights—that is, the air rights.
- Put up a building smaller than permitted by present zoning, and sell the remaining air rights. (White doubted the income from this option would be enough to make it worthwhile.)
- Build the biggest possible tower.

The third option would yield the greatest income but would also generate the most opposition, White pointed out. It was the one St. Bartholomew's finally chose. He thought the building could be finished by 1985.

On the financial side, Anthony Marshall, the junior warden, advised the gathering that the tower would bring in around $7 million a year. The church "would feel obliged to spend 50% of this income on outreach programs."

At the end of the two-day conference the select group of invitees cast secret ballots on whether negotiations with developers should proceed. "The vote to continue was almost unanimous," reported *St. BartholoNews*. It was not the full parish vote Armstrong had requested when he submitted his amendment, but it did have the appearance of "parish" approval.

The leadership conference proved a notable demonstration of how poorly church leaders appear to have grasped the problems they were to face. They told the gathering they expected the greatest opposition to come from owners of the three buildings surrounding St. Bartholomew's site: the General Electric Building (to the east and directly behind the main church), the Rudin Building (behind the Community House), and the Waldorf-Astoria (to the south, across Fiftieth Street). That may explain the rumors about Rudin's financing the Committee to Oppose, but as it turned out, little or nothing was ever heard from two of the predicted foes—the owners of the GE Building and the Waldorf-Astoria. Lewis Rudin was a slightly different case, but that, too, caused the church no serious problems.

Building in midtown Manhattan is never easy, and building

behind the landmarked Community House had been particularly exasperating and costly. Rudin's representatives had spent long hours before the preservation subcommittee at the local community planning board presenting detailed drawings and samples of materials. While community and city agencies examined the design, Rudin's architects worked with those of St. Bartholomew's to ensure that each detail of the new tower would be to the church's satisfaction, from the location of the loading dock to the height of the mortar joints in the brick veneer. Preservationists congratulated Rudin and his architect for a graceful building which complemented the landmark. The complement cost him about $4 million. Now, two years after the tower had been finished, St. Bartholomew's wanted to tear down the very Community House he had gone through so much trouble to accommodate.

That alone would have caused friction between the midtown neighbors, but other events also strained the relationship. St. Bartholomew's claimed Rudin was trying to scuttle its project because it would block the views from one side of his tower and force him to reduce rents. Father Bowers also said Rudin had threatened to run him out of town if the tower went up. Rudin denied threatening the rector, and his lawyer said none of the leases in his building contained guarantees about the view.

Perhaps the most remarkable misjudgment at the leadership conference was the suggestion that the church could easily shed its landmark designation by claiming financial hardship. It would spend almost four years and close to $2 million trying to convince the landmarks commission to remove the designation.

Curiously enough, if the church fathers were thinking about the Landmarks Law's curtailing their constitutional right of free exercise, they did not tell the invitees. The conference report did not even hint at possible constitutional implications, although that was the argument that eventually took them on a litigatory odyssey toward the U.S. Supreme Court.

Shortly after the close of the conference the church released the news the Committee to Oppose had been dreading for months. The rector and vestry had decided to lease the Community House site. For reasons no one understood at the time, no contract materialized, and no developer appeared on the steps of St. Bart's to offer the rector a handshake and a bag of cash. After a few months opponents began to wonder why.

The unexplained halt of the development juggernaut was offset by increased activity on the theological front. The first theological rationale for development was sent to parishioners in early June and appeared as a full-page ad on a back page of the Sunday *New York Times* three weeks later, beneath a banner headline announcing A THEOLOGY FOR THE MINISTRY OF ST. BART'S.

The purpose of religion, said the announcement, was to bring people into a relationship with God. In Christianity that was done by loving God and loving your neighbor. Love of God was expressed through worship; love of neighbor, through outreach ministries. The advertisement listed an impressive array of existing ministries at St. Bart's. Had plans for new ones spurred the desire to develop? It was silent on the topic of things to come, saying only that a portion of the development income would go to help the diocese, the national church, and victims of famine, pestilence, and war around the world.

Opponents surveyed the scope of that broad-brush vision and wondered where its boundaries lay. Everyone wants to have more money to do more things, but each involvement has its limits. The Roman Catholic Church sponsors many charities in New York City, but its elders have not suggested knocking down the outbuilding behind St. Patrick's Cathedral and leasing the land to put more muscle in its outreach. One cleric put it in more personal terms. A priest may care about the poor, and work to help the poor, but does not necessarily sell his clothing and household furnishings to benefit the poor.

In short, everyone draws the line somewhere. Before 1980 St.

Bart's had drawn it at the boundary of its site. What had stirred the church fathers to violate that line? The innocent answer to that question appeared in the last paragraph of the theological advertisement. The possibility presented itself, and "faithfulness to our Lord leads to a moral and Christian imperative to seize upon the extraordinary opportunity before us to consider the lease of the community house."

In the language of business, St. Bartholomew's was telling the world it wanted to enjoy the full value of a long-underutilized asset—a public reiteration of what Marc Haas had said privately, months before, at the Union Club meeting. When the opportunity fell into their laps, they were apparently overjoyed. The lag between the initial exultation and the realization that the dream was not universally shared may explain why a carefully constructed rationale for development began coming only months after the offer. St. Bartholomew's issued its first formal explanation of why real estate development was a theological obligation nine months after the *Times* article. Another four months passed before the rector and vestry produced a comparable document detailing its financial need for the tower. It would be five years before the final building block of the development argument was in place: professional studies showing that the Community House could not house the church's charitable purposes.

The awkward interval between the "solution" (development) and the statement of the problem led many to conclude that the lure of riches had so dazzled church leaders that they never imagined anyone would oppose the project, least of all their own parishioners.

A few days after the theological statement appeared, David Garcia, rector of St. Mark's, sent a personal note to his friend Sinc Armstrong. "The rector and vestry [of St. Bartholomew's] must have collectively touched the panic button. . . . Everyone at St. Mark's is stunned by the full page ad." He suggested that the committee's legal maneuvers, coupled with the uniformly negative public response, had provoked the church into placing the ad. "In all truth their fear and unease is [*sic*] transparent. My counsel is to keep up the pressure in the courts and begin to develop simultaneously an informal communication structure with your fellow Christians who are opposed to the sale."

The theological pronouncement also drove the first public crack in the clerical monolith supporting Father Bowers's position. The assumption that faithfulness to the Lord leads inexorably to religious real estate speculation—that beauty must be sacrificed to the demands of temporal mission—proved too much for one priest. In an anonymous broadside circulated in the religious community, the cleric spoke of "the task of safeguarding for our grandchildren every square foot surrounding historic buildings" as an almost sacred duty. Neither the artist nor the prophet was dispensable to the church. Although they spoke different languages, they had like roles. Monuments keep us human in ways only art can: "Similarly when we sit on our riches and neglect our brother or sister in need, we become sub-human and idolatrous, a blasphemy. Balance is required. We must learn how to keep both together, as Jesus showed when he permitted Mary Magdalene to pour costly perfume over his feet to the irritation of the Apostles who said the money should have been spent on the poor."

Support for preserving the church almost came from the cathedral itself. The dean of a cathedral looks after the fabric of the building as well as carries out normal priestly duties. Having studied under the famous Bauhaus master Walter Gropius, the Reverend James Parks Morton, dean of the Cathedral of St. John the Divine, is particularly well qualified for the former task. Morton's eyes sparkle when he talks about architecture, particularly when the conversation veers toward his present charge, St. John the Divine.

It was not surprising, then, that his sympathies should lie with the pro-architecture faction in this struggle. But Dean Morton is a close friend of the bishop's as well as the prelate's ecclesiastical subordinate. (He decided to enter the priesthood after hearing Moore speak and served with Moore in Jersey City.) Nonetheless,

Dean Morton was ready to venture a public opinion against development in an op-ed article for the *Times*. Shortly before it was submitted, however, the bishop asked that it be withdrawn. The cathedral is the flagship of the diocese, and the bishop, its captain, is an ex-marine. Moore did not want conflicting reports coming from his command center.

CHAPTER

IV

T H E Battle of St. Bart's was a seasonal affair over the years.
New York's Episcopalians tend to retire to the countryside or the
seashore during the hot summers, leaving all theaters of operation
quiet from late June through early September. Things picked up
again only after Labor Day.

In early September 1981 the Committee to Oppose fully
expected the rector and vestry to plunge ahead with the development plan. Hoping to slow it down, if not bring it to a halt, the
committee took to the courts once more. It asked for a restraining
order to prevent the church from signing a contract before the
membership voted on Armstrong's bylaw amendment of the
previous year.

The committee won in the short run. On September 10 New
York State Supreme Court Justice Charles S. Whitman ruled that

the congregation must vote on Armstrong's amendment. He granted an injunction to presevere the status quo for ninety days or until the membership had a chance to vote. The church's lawyers appealed, but the pace of the courts proved too slow to be of help.

A week after the injunction was issued, Sinclair Armstrong was at a social gathering with the bishop and passed him a business card with a brief plea inscribed in a small, neat hand around the engraved name: "Paul. Is it not time for you to put an end to this public controversy? . . . [T]he rector, churchwardens and vestry are bound to lose under New York Law. Respectfully, Sinc" There was no formal response from the bishop.

The rector and vestry marched on with their plans, apparently oblivious of the injunction. In late September *St. BartholoNews* carried a front-page message from the vestry real estate committee. It had met with advisers over the summer and learned a great deal about both real estate values and architectural principles. That fund of new information had helped it choose a parish-saving proposal for the Community House site: "[W]e can report with great excitement that it appears as if we will be able to find a solution to our present and long range financial difficulties which will enable our parish to carry forth the work of Christ in unprecedented ways, and, at the same time, build a structure which will be architecturally appropriate to our magnificent church and to our surrounding neighbors." The real estate committee was referring to the proposal submitted by a British real estate developer, Howard P. Ronson, to erect a fifty-nine-story, mirrored glass office tower on the land now occupied by St. Bartholomew's Community House. (The tower was designed by Peter Capone, of Edward Durell Stone, Architects.)

On October 16 the rector wrote to the parish, saying the entire vestry would soon see the proposal chosen by the real estate committee. (That committee consisted of Tom, Anthony Marshall, and the lawyer Paul Windels.) The same letter contained an inch-thick report, which must have been in preparation for months. Its formidable title, "Securing the Future of St. Bartholomew's Church and Its Ministry," reflected the vestry's sense of having found a final solution to the church's problems. It included a long section on the financial ills of St. Bartholomew's, which complemented the theological foundation for the building project. Budget deficits had been chronic after 1970 and had accelerated sharply after the arrival of Father Bowers. There had been "a substantial rise in the salaries of our employees . . . devoted men and women" whose pay was "embarrassingly low." In addition, old community service programs had been expanded and new ones added. Finally, inflation had increased annual operating costs across the board.

The report brought to light a new and interesting piece of information, which bore heavily on the church's later hardship case. While St. Bartholomew's was blessed with an endowment valued at $11 million in 1981, most of its enviable wealth was restricted by donors' requests. Only the interest income could be spent. The treasurer had researched the history of the endowment so carefully that he could calculate the availability of funds to the nearest half a percentage point. Only 4.5 percent was unrestricted, providing a meager cushion of some $500,000 to cover capital costs and budget deficits. (The latter were running hundreds of thousands of dollars a year in the early 1980's.) The state of the endowment offered scant comfort to anyone concerned about the future of the church.

Although nothing was said publicly, in the fall of 1981 the vestry was not of one mind about going ahead with the building project. The Committee to Oppose had a sympathetic ear on the vestry, who kept John Chappell informed. He told of one meeting, lasting late into the night of October 28, at which two people opposed the project. The rector scheduled an open-ended meeting for 2:00 P.M. the next day to try to force a unanimous vote. He convinced one holdout, but the other maintained his objections. With one abstention, the vestry voted on October 29 to accept the building proposal submitted by Howard P. Ronson.

Although all the developers had presumably had the same amount of time to prepare their submissions, Ronson's was by far the most impressive and complete; it included a scale model, perspective renderings, and plans, while the others showed the equivalent of back-of-the-envelope sketches.

The choice was surely influenced by the thoroughness of the presentation, yet there was one puzzling and persistent question. Why was the Englishman chosen over a hometown boy? Ronson had no knowledge of the challenging metropolis and presumably none of the connections that might help smooth out the rough development road. New York had a full complement of world-class developers who were more familiar with the territory. John Chappell suggested the local teams may have been less enthusiastic because they had a better idea of what could go wrong. "Considering the background, power and expertise of the withdrawing crowd," he wrote to Armstrong, "this should tell you something about the New York Real Estate community's feelings about who will win this fight. Poor Mr. Ronson is new to our city but he must learn too."

Ron Alexander's friends told him Ronson was chosen over the more seasoned competition because he offered the biggest building and therefore the greatest income. (Ronson's tower was larger than the zoning law permitted for the site and would require special approvals from the city.) Supporters of the real estate strategy saw the choice of Ronson's mammoth tower as the logical consequence of the vestry's enthusiasm to secure the future of St. Bart's by ensuring that its prime asset yield the largest possible return. Detractors characterized it as a choice based on greed, and shortsighted greed at that, considering the snares that await the real estate developer in New York.

On the same day the vestry approved Howard Ronson as its developer, and in apparent violation of the injunction maintaining the status quo, it sent a letter of intent to Ronson, signed by Tom Bowers and Anthony Marshall.

Once the developer was chosen, St. Bartholomew's public relations machine shifted into high gear. In a letter of November 3 1981, Father Bowers told his flock "You have in your hands the possibility to:

"Save this church from financial disaster.

"Create new and much needed space for our programs and activities. . . .

"Develop new forms of ministry in this parish and community only dreamed of in the past.

"Participate in the ministry and mission of Jesus Christ in this City and far beyond as we reach out to those in need. . . . The vote will be binding."

He scheduled a parish vote on the development project for November 17. Although the court had instructed the church to hold a vote first on Armstrong's bylaw amendment (which called for parish approval of any and all real estate deals), Bowers's announcement said nothing about the amendment. The November 17 balloting was "for the sole purpose of approving" the vestry's recommendation that St. Bartholomew's proceed with the development plan chosen by the real estate committee.

There was a speedy legal response from the Committee to Oppose. Four days before the balloting "to approve," State Supreme Court Justice Edward Greenfield granted an injunction blocking the November 17 meeting, the second for the church in three months. He ruthlessly rejected St. Bartholomew's justifications as "disingenuous to say the least." The purpose of the original order was " 'to preserve the status quo ante,' " which was precisely what the proposed meeting would upset.

> The argument of the church that "Constitutional principles of separation of church and state require this court to refrain from interfering from purely internal church affairs" is specious indeed! We have on the books an entire body of law denominated "The Religious Corporations Law." The "Not-for-Profit Corporation Law," also applies to religious bodies. . . . They in no way interfere with the operation of any church or religious body, in doctrinal affairs, or in the realm of theology. However, when it comes to temporal affairs, the church is obliged to "render unto Caesar the things that are Caesar's." Nothing could be more temporal and of this world

than a proposed multi-million dollar sale of a valuable parcel of New York realty.

Greenfield excoriated the church for its attempts to squash the internal opposition: "The court is . . . disturbed by what would appear to be 'steamroller tactics' employed by the church. If all the contentions of the Committee are true, tactics have been employed which would make the seasoned veterans of the old Tammany Hall blush."

The rector and vestry needed the November 17 vote. If the court accepted its outcome, the vestry would have carried off a double coup. It would have satisfied the injunction and sidestepped the bylaw amendment. Avoiding the latter was important because a bona fide amendment posed several obstacles. Without one, there was no way the opponents could enforce the outcome of a negative parish vote. The vestry could still pursue the project, as canon and civil law said it was in charge of the church's real property. With the amendment on the books, a negative vote would be binding. Even if the parish approved, an obstreperous opposition could claim a new vote was needed each time there was the slightest change in the original deal. That could be both time-consuming and dangerous, for with each new vote the opposition had another chance to scuttle the project.

Greenfield dashed any plan the church might have had of escaping the injunction and avoiding the encumbrance of the bylaw: "Unless and until the right of the majority of the membership to approve the sale of real property is embodied in the by-laws, the power remains with the Vestry." A vote on the real estate proposal before a vote on the amendment "would be a mere public opinion poll . . . to which the vestrymen could point as indicating support if the majority indicated approval, but which they could legally ignore if the vote were adverse."

Greenfield's opinion was handed down on November 13. St. Bart's gave no sign of calling off the vote as the seventeenth approached. On the evening of the sixteenth, Judge Greenfield's clerk called the church's lawyer to remind him of the injunction.

There was some confusion at the church the next morning—Gerald Fischer, lawyer to the Committee to Oppose, claimed the rector said he knew nothing about any injunction—but there was no vote.

Within days Father Bowers had sent another letter to the congregation. He had been "stunned" by the court's decision to cancel the November 17 vote. His honor and that of the vestry had been impugned. They would appeal the decision.

Despite the bluster, Tom and the vestry had adopted a bylaw amendment by the time his parishioners had a chance to read the letter. A week after the nonvote, John Nelson, the lawyer for St. Bartholomew's, requested a conference with Justice Greenfield. Sinc Armstrong and Gerry Fischer were there when Nelson said the injunction was no longer necessary. The rector and vestry had decided to submit the development proposal to a membership vote in December. It would not be binding, however, and therefore would not be in violation of the September 10 or November 13 injunctions.

The church appeared to have returned to square one. Greenfield asked what purpose the vote would serve if it were not binding. The attorney for the church then surprised the judge by reversing his field. He said the vestry was ready to adopt a bylaw amendment along the lines suggested by Armstrong. (Nelson had already exchanged letters with Gerry Fischer about its language.) The amendment was adopted by the end of November, and a certified copy sent to the Committee to Oppose. (A vestry can adopt a bylaw without a membership vote if it chooses.)

Why had the vestry's long-standing objection to an amendment evaporated so quickly? The explanation probably lies in the letter of intent between Ronson and Bowers, which said the developer would not go through with the deal unless the parish approved the project. Once the November 17 vote had been canceled, the vestry knew it could no longer try for parish approval on its own terms. It would have to call a vote on the amendment— which would take valuable time—or adopt one itself and get on to the development vote.

It proved a particularly bitter cross to bear. Shortly after the church adopted it voluntarily, the court of appeals ruled that Armstrong had introduced it improperly. The lower court should not have required the church to vote on it or enjoined it from consummating the deal. But the amendment was already law.

For better or worse, both injunctions were out of the way. Justice Greenfield set the real estate vote for December 18. He would supervise the balloting and rule on voter qualifications.

Information about the building proposal had been circulating in the parish since before the aborted mid-November meeting. One document, titled "A Summary of the Key Financial Terms of the Proposed Arrangement with the Developer of the New Building," clearly marked out each station on the road to financial salvation. The first was a nonrefundable preconstruction payment of $200,000, followed by $1 million when the lease was signed. Another $300,000 would come when the landmarks commission granted a certificate of appropriateness. There was a deadline, however. To get the $1 million, the church had to have parish approval and a signed lease by February 1, 1982.

In addition to $1.5 million in up-front, nonrefundable payments, the church expected to earn $3 million a year for the first two years after construction began, and $3.5 million a year thereafter, until completion. Once it moved into the tower, St. Bartholomew's would receive $9.5 million a year for the first ten years. Rents would escalate gradually after that, and by the end of the third decade its annual income would be $16.5 million.

St. Bartholomew's would occupy 75,000 gross square feet of unfinished space, "at no cost and rent-free," during the 100-year term of the lease to Ronson. (The existing Community House contained approximately 57,000 gross square feet.) The church had to pay for relocating Community House activites while the tower was going up and for finishing its own space in it. But those costs were minor compared with the potential income.

"Key Financial Terms" made the arrangement sound attractive, particularly in view of the desperate terms attached to the church's predicament. On December 3, Father Bowers told his flock that tragedy was unavoidable unless the project was approved: "Make no mistake, what is at issue here, hyperbole aside, is the survival of St. Bartholomew's. . . . Without this solution, it is possible that within the next 10 years the church building would have to be *abandoned, sold* and *destroyed* [his emphasis]."

Which parishioners would be allowed to vote to assure the future of St. Bartholomew's was problematic. The bylaws were clear on voter eligibility: One had to be a baptized adult, a member of St. Bartholomew's, a "contributor of record," and an active participant in church life. The first two requirements were easily agreed upon. "Active" participating in church life was open to uncomfortably broad interpretation. People worship in many ways, in public and private. As long as an occasional appearance is made at worship services, most churches hesitate to tie the voting privilege directly to the degree of participation. Such subtleties meant little at St. Bartholomew's, however. Even the church admitted its records were poorly kept. No one in recent memory had sorted out which parishioners had left town or, for that matter, which had left this world.

Appropriately enough, considering the object of the balloting, the final decision on voter eligibility depended on money—when and how much one had contributed to the church. Justice Greenfield had stated specifically: "No one will be ruled out on the basis of amount of contribution." He did, however, require that a contribution be made in the election year and "at some point more than 12 months prior to the annual meeting," that is, in the election year and in some year—any year—before. The size of the contribution did not matter; it could be $1 or $1,000. But the rector is the final arbiter of voter qualification in an Episcopal parish, and for reasons that were never explained, Tom decided that a parishioner had to have given $50 or more in order to qualify. (By 1987 he had raised the ante to $100.) The minimum requirement raised more hackles. Joel Rice, a theatrical producer, wrote the rector the following note when he learned there was to be a minimum gift, but before the amount had been set: "Surely you are old enough to remember that in the South the poll tax was uniform and published. Following your reasoning, I assume that you will eventually advocate that those Americans who pay little or no income tax be disenfranchised and prohibited from voting in Federal and Local elections. Tom, is it possible that you, and not Brooke Astor hate the poor? Feed 'em, but don't let 'em Vote!"

Despite their dislike of the real estate proposal, Armstrong and other members of the Committee to Oppose knew they had to maintain an active church membership if they were to remain a credible internal opposition. Armstrong supported several churches in the diocese, and others on the committee also gave money and volunteered time to other churches, but all maintained the minimum presence necessary to assure their right to vote at St. Bartholomew's.

Knowing voter qualifications proved easier than finding out who met them—at least for the opposition. To know who had contributed in previous years, you had to see the records from those years. The committee claimed to have asked for them but said it was denied access. It eventually took possession of the M–Z portion of the 1981 voters' list just a few hours before the election. A–L came four days after it. The assistant rector, Andrew Mullins, claimed the opposition had been given lists as soon as they were available but said it had not asked for them until a few days before the balloting.

It is difficult to tell where the truth lies or whether each side is telling the truth. St. Bart's was computerizing its membership list around that time, and the lists were apparently not yet in good order. At one point in the proceedings Mullins, who was supposed to pass the voter information along to the committee, told Greenfield outright that some of the church's information about who was eligible to vote was probably wrong. He later thanked the Committee to Oppose "because they have more accurate parish lists than we have." (It took years for St. Bartholomew's to get its voters' list in order. As late as the 1986 vestry election, it was still relying on a data base of church members compiled by Rob Morris. If a prospective voter's name was not on the church's list but Rob Morris had it on his data base, that was enough proof of eligibility.)

In the judiciary's view, parish elections were subject to the same shenanigans and misrepresentations that plagued their secular counterparts. Greenfield told both sides that if he got involved in every little squabble over the way this one or that one complied with this or that detail, there would never be an election.

One aspect of the electioneering never came to Justice Greenfield's attention. Tom Bowers did everything he could to ensure the loyalty of all his troops. A few days after the $100 million offer had surfaced back in 1980, Father Bowers called a meeting of the clergy of St. Bartholomew's. He was succinct and to the point, according to a priest who was there.

"Gentlemen, I want you to understand one thing: We are now playing hardball. If I can't have a hundred percent backing and cooperation on this, I want your resignation in twenty-four hours."

There were some startled faces above the white collars, but the maneuver assured Tom of the loyalty—or at least the noninterference—of the six or seven clergy and their families. That could mean as many as ten or twelve votes in the coming election.

He took a similar approach with the nonclerical staff. It numbered around 70 then, many of whom—with their families—were qualified voters. Securing the loyalty of the staff would guarantee a substantial block of 60 to 100 votes.

A few weeks before December 18 the rector held a meeting. It was in the afternoon, so not everyone could attend, but David Trovillion, the young verger of St. Bartholomew's, was there, and he was certain the rector's message quickly made the rounds.

There was no fist pounding or direct threats, only an enticement and a statement. Bowers implied that if the project went through, salaries would go up. "I expect all of you to support the project." He did not add, "If you don't, you'll lose your job," but Trovillion thought it was the obvious inference. A week or so later the rector confirmed that suspicion.

A few days after the staff meeting Trovillion came upon a *New*

Yorker cartoon showing four portly businessmen congratulating one another. He changed the text to speak to the recent events at St. Bart's. The altered caption read: "So the other Indian says: Yeah, but think of all the things we could do with $24 worth of beads." Trovillion ran off a few photocopies, which quietly made the rounds of the staff.

The next Sunday Trovillion was preparing for the services in a small room off the chancel. The rector came in, and for a moment he and the verger were alone.

"I saw that little cartoon you made," said Father Bowers. "I expect you to support our program, or I think you know where you'll be going."

"There are no shades of gray with the rector," said Trovillion. "You're either with him or against him."

On the morning of December 18, 1981, the ballots of St. Bartholomew's first referendum on the building project were collected from the rector's office and carried, unopened, to Judge Greenfield's chambers downtown. Under Greenfield's and Bowers's restrictions, 729 voters had been declared eligible out of a parish list of between 1,500 and 2,000. The resolution to pursue development passed by 21 votes, 375 to 354.

Both sides claimed victory. The church had its mandate to proceed. The opposition cited the slim margin as proof of a healthy internal opposition.

Off the record, priests outside the parish questioned the wisdom of pursuing a project so rife with dangers based on a hairsbreadth victory. "We at St. Mark's are very proud of you," wrote its rector to Sinc Armstrong. "Keep up the good fight. I can't imagine Fr. Bowers claiming a victory on such a close vote. . . Your pledge to St. Mark's is deeply appreciated."

From the bishop's seat came a gibe from one who asked to have his anonymity protected. It was a small sketch, which he described as an important gift to the cathedral from a poor but talented young artist whose heart was in the right place. It showed the back of a ten-dollar bill, with St. Bartholomew's Church where the Treasury Building should have been. Above it, on a floating scroll, was the motto "In God We Trust."

The annual vestry election came hard on the heels of the building vote. The rector's candidates ran away with it. Why were the two votes, held within weeks of each other, so dissimilar? Minds rarely change that rapidly, so the explanation must be sought in the nature of the vote. The average parishioner seems to see the relationship between the rector and vestry as similar to that between the President and his Cabinet. Therefore, the makeup of the vestry should be left to the rector, a belief that may be what makes parish elections as predictable as the phases of the moon. People are jarred into thought only when something extraordinary is interjected into otherwise humdrum parish life, such as the leasing of half the church's property. If the theory is correct, the close building proposal vote suggests that the issue was important enough to shake parishioners out of a knee-jerk, back-the-rector reflex and into a thoughtful and substantial opposition.

Although twice defeated, the Committee to Oppose took some consolation in having placed on public view what the judge called the Tammany Hall tactics of the church. One such tactic surfaced only later, however: the decision not to tell parishioners certain of the less appealing details about the arrangement with the developer.

The information sent out to the parish before the December 18 vote led the members to believe that if they approved the project, Ronson would sign the lease and make an additional $1 million payment (refundable only in the unlikely case that the New York State Supreme Court failed to approve the lease). But Ronson did not have to sign, even if the parish approved the deal before the deadline. The letter of intent gave him two choices. He could sign the lease and pay the $1 million or not sign it and pay only the first $100,000 in professional fees accumulated by the church when it applied to Landmarks.

February 1, 1982, passed, and Howard Ronson did not sign.

*   *   *

The discrepancy between the facts and what the rector and vestry told their parishioners would soon cause the first visible breach in a solid wall of vestry support. But that was still six months away. In the meantime, the Committee to Oppose had lost both elections and faced an uncertain future in January 1982. Sinc and the others assumed the church would produce a lease agreement any day. The rector and vestry would not have rushed to adopt the bylaw amendment unless a contract was waiting. Contract or not, a confidant of Armstrong's at the Municipal Art Society doubted that the landmarks commission would ever approve the tower the parish had voted on in December. Even if the tower did manage to squeeze by, it violated existing zoning ordinances and therefore needed special permissions from several agencies, all of which would take time and money.

To deflect St. Bartholomew's from what the members of the Committee to Oppose thought was a costly and ultimately hopeless course, they decided to propose a compromise: The church should try to sell its unused development rights. Such a sale promised a respectable income and would not drag the parish into a long and costly battle with the city.

Each site in Manhattan has a zoning envelope, which defines the maximum volume a building on that site can occupy. Development rights, or air rights, are the part of the envelope that is not filled by the existing building (or buildings, in St. Bartholomew's case). New structures generally fill their envelopes; bigger buildings yield bigger returns. Zoning codes have changed over the years, however, and the envelopes have increased in volume. That means existing buildings are often smaller than they could be under present regulations. Normally that would present no problem. An owner who wants to profit from the increased potential of the site simply adds floors or puts up a new building that uses all the envelope. However, that option does not exist for landmark owners, and this inequity was a frequent topic of discussion at the landmarks commission in the late 1960's. Harmon Goldstone, then chairman, was sincerely concerned about the penalties imposed on landmarks owners and was pleased when the city settled on a way to help them: "What grew out of [these discussions] was the transfer of development rights, which would give a landmarked, nonprofit organization some financial relief."

Transferring development rights involves adding the unused portion of a landmark's zoning envelope to the envelope of a contiguous site. St. Bartholomew's had almost 600,000 square feet of transferable air rights. There were many versions of what the church wanted to do with that particular asset.

George Hayman (author of what Armstrong had taken to be a threatening letter) claimed St. Bart's had tried to sell its air rights to Lewis Rudin but was turned down. A representative of Rudin's said the church had made an offer, but too late. The developer already had his approvals from the city.

Herndon Werth heard several different stories about St. Bart's and its air rights. Werth, a quick-talking parishioner who loves the minutiae of the battle, makes his living advising people on how to use their money, and air rights immediately popped into his head when talk at the church turned toward financial difficulties. He claimed to have broached the topic to vestrymen on three separate occasions in the late 1970's and to have received three different responses: (1) Selling the air rights could tie down future vestries; (2) the church was in the midst of changing rectors, and could not pay attention to the disposition of air rights at the time; (3) Rudin never asked the vestry if it wanted to sell. Mulling over the replies, Werth began to think that perhaps the vestry was asleep at the helm. If not, why had it not pursued the sale of its air rights—to Rudin or someone else—more vigorously?

One explanation may be that the church did not need the money. Contrary to what the parish and public were told, a priest who worked at St. Bartholomew's in the early 1980s recalled a vestryman's saying the church's biggest financial problem up to the mid-1970's had been figuring out where to hide the surpluses. (That good fortune may also explain why the vestry passed up an opportunity to buy the lot behind the Community House on which Rudin's building now stands. The Roman Catholic archdiocese offered it to St. Bart's in the mid-1970's, but the vestry said it was not interested.)

Once Tom Bowers moved in, and spending took off on an exponential curve, there was an incentive to look for more income, but soon there was also a potential new source, which was far more lucrative than air rights. Once the development option existed, with its promise of a royal income in perpetuity, the church said little about its air rights. One vestryperson mentioned them in an affidavit, but only to say that selling them would amount to handing over the church's "God-given birthrights for a relatively small bowl of pottage."

Not knowing what, if anything, the church planned to do with this resource, the Committee to Oppose had asked its real estate adviser to prepare an air rights analysis in the fall of 1981. In mid-January 1982 the Standing Committee of the diocese invited Armstrong and his group to suggest alternatives to development that might ensure St. Bartholomew's financial future. The air rights report of Jonathan Morse (president of the Cowperwood Interests) went to the Standing Committee on February 1, 1982. The church could sell its air rights for between $54 and $81 million, according to Morse's calculations. With interest rates then near 10 percent, the air rights sale would have added between $5 and $8 million a year to the church's investment income. The Standing Committee did not comment on the report, and the church never applied to the landmarks commission for permission to transfer its air rights, although no application for a special permit to transfer air rights from a landmark has ever been denied.

Meanwhile, everyone was waiting to see what the bishop would do. Months before the parish voted, Sinc had written the bishop asking him to take sides, hoping he would kill the project before it gained momentum:

If you approve the proposal, there will be two or three more years of litigation in which you as Diocesan [leader] will be central. You will find yourself defending an illegal project against which all press, radio and TV editorial opinion and architectural professional opinion are arrayed, and will be fighting not just our little band of parishioners but a wide array of civic and cultural organizations and governmental authorities such as the Landmarks Commission. What a waste that will be of your valuable time, leadership positions on vital issues, and resources! . . . The last thing I want to do with my time at 66 [years of age] is fuss about a church building. I would much rather collaborate with you, as I have in years past, on issues of peace, civil rights, social justice and freedom under law, with emphasis on peace in the nuclear age as we discussed on Saturday morning. St. Bart's is a terrible and wasteful burden. Please get Tom Bowers' [sic] Golden Calf out of our church! . . . I urge you to tell the rector to quit this deal. . . . Recently I mentioned to you that you and I are sailors. A sailor needs a port in a storm. You're that port for Tom Bowers. If you don't give it to him, he may founder in the storm.

The bishop chose not to intervene. It was too early, he told his friend. He would gladly listen to disgruntled parishioners but would not join the fray. If he started meddling in the St. Bart's affair, every parish in the diocese would ask him to settle this or that minor quarrel.

Moore was not obligated to step in, but the church does permit a bishop some latitude when it comes to interfering in parish affairs. The canon places "[c]ontrol of the worship and the spiritual jurisdiction of the Parish" in the rector, but it also says each parish is "subject to . . . the godly counsel of the Bishop." In St. Bart's case the bishop later said he had offered no counsel because he thought the rector and vestry were doing the right thing.

Critics wondered if it was only shared theological principles that kept the bishop out of this parish affair. He had long been known for the élan with which he pursued the underdog's causes— no one, supporter or not, denied that quality—but critics thought the bishop was too willing to let his enthusiasm for the end excuse what appeared to be an impropriety of means. Two months before the project vote, Tom Bowers and the vestry announced that St. Bartholomew's would spend "at least fifty percent" of its skyscraper income outside the parish. That amounted to about $4.25 million, or more than twice the diocesan budget. No one said how much of that would go directly to the diocese, but observers on both sides of the battle line assumed it would be a substantial percentage, if not the entire sum.

Sinc feared the promise of a threefold increase in spending power might encourage the bishop to favor development. "When one party to a controversy offers the tribunal or judge half the value of a judgment in its favor," he wrote his bishop, the tribunal or judge is no longer able to make an unbiased judgment. Rather than decide the issue himself, Armstrong suggested the bishop ask the head of the national church (the presiding bishop) to appoint a panel of bishops from nearby dioceses to determine St. Bart's fate.

Armstrong's letters spoke figuratively of money from St. Bart's going to the "bishop," meaning the "diocese." Moore took it personally, as though the lawyer expected the already wealthy prelate to profit from the arrangement. He assured his friend that he would not. Furthermore, it was his duty as diocesan leader to make the decision. Moore also asked if the conflict-of-interest accusation was meant as a threat. Sinc answered with a sailor's metaphor: Should the buoy that sounds a warning in the fog be considered a threat?

Armstrong had seen the bishop operate in a somewhat similar situation years before and had been uncomfortable even then. "I had a run-in with him when I was treasurer of the cathedral," Armstrong recounted. "He's a person who tries to do what he wants. . . . [He] doesn't necessarily do the right thing but tries to make it seem to be the right thing." The affair Armstrong referred to involved a transaction he characterized as devastating to the cathedral's endowment. Stocks were down and interest rates had risen at the time, so the bonds in the cathedral portfolio were low. According to Armstrong, "Paul listened to an adviser he brought on from Citibank" and decided to sell the whole portfolio and put it in certificates of deposit (CDs), then yielding 10 percent. The portfolio was part of the Diocesan Trust, of which Armstrong was a custodian and Moore the president. The trust included funds from some fifty other churches, and when the cathedral withdrew, the trust was reduced by about 50 percent.

As a trustee, said Armstrong, "you don't sell stocks when the market is low, and you don't sell bonds when they're underwater if they're good-quality investment securities and yielding the income for which you bought them." The diocese was simply spending more money than it had coming in and did not want to cut back—hence the attraction of a quick return on CDs.

Armstrong wrote Moore his views on the proposed transaction but first asked his financial colleagues to review the letter. Senior officers at U.S. Trust considered it sound investment advice. According to Armstrong, the bishop said the diocese needed the extra income; he would try to bring down the budget but did not want Armstrong disagreeing with him openly in the boardroom.

The resolution to sell passed with two nays, one from Armstrong, the other from a Union Carbide pension fund manager. The entire endowment fund of the cathedral, about $12 million, was taken out of the Diocesan Trust. The bonds lost about $2.5 million, as Armstrong recalled; the stocks, between $200,000 and $300,000. When the bank asked for a signature to approve the transaction, Sinc, who was also treasurer of the cathedral, refused to sign: "Why the hell should my signature be on that piece of paper telling the Bank of New York to do that?"

Again, he told Moore he thought the move was a mistake, partly because of the losses the cathedral would incur and partly because of the small gain in income. The bishop called a special meeting of the board, appointed a new treasurer, and proceeded to give a speech about what a great one Armstrong had been. He did not say why Armstrong was stepping down.

"Well, you know, this guy was covering his tracks. Everything was nice. I didn't make a fuss. Nobody knew, nobody gave a damn. And three million dollars was gone forever. You don't get three million dollars into a church endowment fund easily. You try to protect it. Clergy have a tendency to be very sure of their own judgment," Armstrong mused. "I hope I'm right in my judgments, but I think you'll notice that I'm not *sure.*"

Although Moore tried to maintain a neutral public stance toward St. Bartholomew's development plans, it was difficult for him to be dispassionate in private, for many smaller and poorer parishes in his spiritual care stood to profit from St. Bartholomew's good fortune. It was common knowledge among churchmen that the New York diocese was in decline. By its own calculation, its membership had fallen from more than 100,000 to around 42,000 in the last two to three decades. Conservatives claimed the bishop drove them off with his rabid liberalism, but statistics belie that assertion. Presbyterians lost about as many members as Episcopalians during that time, although other sects did somewhat better. Depleted congregations meant reduced revenues, even for wealthy parishes, which translated into fewer dollars for the diocese, which is financed by assessments levied on each parish according to its income.

Whatever the cause, the bishop was aware of the trend when St. Bartholomew's offered him a portion of the income from its tower-to-be. A cleric who talked at length with him, some months after the development vote, said the bishop spoke about the St. Bartholomew's project as something of a godsend. The thought of having to shut down as many as forty of the poorer parishes within the decade haunted him.

The bishop approved St. Bart's development plan a few weeks after the parish vote. The Standing Committee followed suit a few days later.

With a vested interest in sanctioning St. Bart's development plan, the bishop had to handle the approval delicately. He needed impartial confirmation that the rector and vestry had accurately represented the church's circumstances. "I had a separate investigation," the bishop said later, "and was told by people who know about such things that indeed, there was the amount of deferred maintenance the church had projected. . . . I did not have an elaborate engineer's report, but someone who was conversant with church maintenance" looked over the church itself and the vestry report and said it "was a fair estimate." Moore could not recall if the engineer had made a written report on the condition of the church. The bishop's financial advisers, the accounting firm of Davies and Davies, had not examined St. Bartholomew's books or talked with its accountants. At the request of the bishop, they had looked only at the church's own figures, as set forth in "Securing the Future of St. Bartholomew's Church," calculations that had been made by the treasurer. While they agreed with the church's conclusion—that bankruptcy was inevitable based on the figures it had put out—they qualified their report by saying the firm was not expert in financial projection (a reference to the church's projected deficits), nor had it inspected the endowment to verify the treasurer's contention that only a small portion was unrestricted. The bishop did not ask parishioners who opposed the rector's plan for their views on the physical and financial state of the church.

Both direct and indirect pressure had failed to convince the church hierarchy to steer clear of the Park Avenue shoal. Armstrong prepared for combat. "The Bishop approved the deal," he wrote to a sympathizer. "That was to be expected. Now we can take our gloves off in the courts and landmarks commission. We don't have to be so polite to the gentlemen with the clerical collars any longer."

While some skeptics thought the bishop had stopped looking for the facts too soon, others found it difficult to understand his willingness to sacrifice the architectural ensemble of St. Bartholomew's in light of his approach to the cathedral's problems. Over the years Bishop Moore has never publicly doubted St. Bart's claims that it could not survive if it had to rely on traditional fund-raising methods, yet his pessimism did not stop him from thinking his cathedral could. Within months of approving the St. Bart's development deal, the cathedral newspaper heralded the beginning of the largest fund-raising campaign ever held for a single church. Bishop Moore set his sights on $35 million, $20 million of which was to go toward completing the cathedral. The previous bishop had said no money should be spent on completing the cathedral as long as there were poor people within sight of it. Armstrong brazenly asked if the bishop himself was not guity of architectural idolatry. While Moore acknowledged that fund raising was sometimes hard going, even for a bishop, he never suggested that his cathedral follow the course he so wholeheartedly endorsed for St. Bartholomew's: that it open its own spacious site to commercial developers.

The cavernous Cathedral Church of St. John the Divine is an odd mixture of styles, mainly ersatz Gothic and Byzantine. Although its construction was begun in 1892, the towers and crossing are still unfinished. Its entrance is on Amsterdam Avenue, between 110th and 113th streets. Its apse looks over Harlem from the top of Morningside Heights. To the south is a large close, or cathedral grounds, on the far side of which is a collection of administrative buildings. While the unbuilt close would never command midtown prices, venerable neighborhood anchors like Columbia University and St. Luke's Hospital make it a solid real estate investment. A low wraparound condominium would not compete with the mass of the cathedral and could provide a fair income. Should the bishop be willing to part with the unassuming revival buildings now housing diocesan offices, there would be room for even more condos. The diocesan buildings are architecturally and functionally comparable with St. Bartholomew's Community House, and the activities they contain would easily fit into the new structure. If the income stream was still too sluggish, a slender tower could be added and leased to the university for scholars seeking a monkish setting. The top, of course, would be saved for commerce. What developer would not leap at the chance to operate a concession like Dining at the Top of the Close? Yet the bishop chose the difficult, traditional route to raise money for his cathedral.

James Sargent, an old friend of Sinc Armstrong's and a fellow attorney at Whitman & Ransom, marveled at "Bishop Moore's outrageous stand of permitting a rebuilding of the cathedral to further the principles of building construction idolatry [while he can expect to benefit from] the proceeds of the destruction of the beautiful Byzantine church on Park Avenue and 50th Street."

But a bishop must consider his diocese. Painful as it might be to bleed the Park Avenue landmark, the result would be a lifesaving transfusion for the larger flock.

*   *   *

Many on the Committee to Oppose thought the approvals of the bishop and Standing Committee sounded the death knell for their efforts. Nothing appeared to stand between the church and a final contract with Ronson, yet no visible move was made, by the church or the developer, for nearly eighteen months. There were as many theories about why as there were people willing to speculate. High on the charts was the thought that perhaps the developer was not cooperating. Shortly before the building vote, the committee had received some interesting information about the developer.

Howard P. Ronson was British and had been in America only a short time when St. Bartholomew's chose his scheme. One of Sinclair Armstrong's many extracurricular activities is the English-Speaking Union, an organization fostering ties between the United States and England. His English connections provided him with preliminary intelligence on Ronson's activites before he came to America. One piece of news came about the same time Ronson became the developer of choice. It was a *Financial Times* article, headlined UK NOTORIETY TO NEW YORK "PHILANTHROPY," which cast a shadow over Mr. Ronson's methods as a developer. Shortly thereafter three hefty volumes totaling several thousand pages came to rest among the neatly piled books and papers on Armstrong's crowded desk. They were the fruit of a seven-year investigation by the British Department of Trade of two development companies run by Gerald I. Ronson and his son, Howard P.

1 5 1

The title read "Investigation of Dwell Constructions, Ltd. Yorks and Lancs Construction Company Ltd., under Section 165(b) of the Companies Act, 1948," and the byline read "by RG Waterhouse QC and JC Steare FCA (inspectors of the Dept. of Trade)." The conclusions were more colorful.

The Department of Trade undertook the investigation because subcontractors complained that the Ronsons had not paid for goods delivered and work completed. Some thought they had been deliberately defrauded. The report clearly assigned accountability: "There can be no doubt that the overall responsibility for the conduct and management of these companies rests upon Mr. Gerald Ronson and Mr. Howard Ronson . . . the latter was a director of all the companies [under investigation] except Ronwood Investments Ltd and Ronson (Furniture) Ltd." Then the inquiry moved on to detailed allegations.

Testimony by men who had had firsthand contacts with Howard was quoted in the Department of Trade report:

> Mr. P. J. Smith, who was intimately involved in the building work on all the sites, reached the conclusion that the Ronsons were adopting a deliberate policy of withholding payments without justification. He recalls one occasion when he asked Mr. Howard Ronson point blank whether the Ronsons intended to pay the subcontractor creditors of the building companies. Mr. Ronson replied in words to this effect[:] "You don't think that we are going to give away to subcontractors all the money that we have now made at Grassmeade." Later, Howard said to Smith: "You know we don't intend to pay the bastards."

The report said the Ronson companies were gravely and persistently mismanaged in part because of "[g]rossly inadequate estimates of the interest charges likely to be incurred in respect of moneys borrowed to finance purchases of land and the building work." The "[o]verwhelming preponderance of blame" rested on the father, who, in a juicily Dickensian image, had been "misled by avarice and overoptimism." Therefore, continued the report, it

J. Sinclair Armstrong, head of the Committee to Oppose the Sale of St. Bartholomew's Church BRENT C. BROLIN © 1987

Reverend Thomas Dix Bowers, greeting parishioners on the steps of St. Bartholomew's Episcopal Church   BRENT C. BROLIN © 1987

*Robert Morris, treasurer of the
Committee to Oppose the Sale of
St. Bartholomew's Church*
BRENT C. BROLIN © 1987

Ronald B. Alexander
COURTESY RONALD B. ALEXANDER

*Sketch of ballot-counting, December 18, 1981. Left to right: John C. Nelson, law-
yer for St. Bartholomew's; Gerald Fischer, lawyer for the Committee to Oppose;
James Sinclair Armstrong; Reverend Thomas Bowers.* IDA LIBBY DENGROVE

Gerald Fischer, lawyer for the Committee to Oppose the Sale of St. Bartholomew's Church
BRENT C. BROLIN © 1987

John Chappell, one of the founders of the Committee to Oppose the Sale of St. Bartholomew's Church
D'ARLENE STUDIOS

Donald Chappell, one of the founders of the Committee to Oppose the Sale of St. Bartholomew's Church D'ARLENE STUDIOS

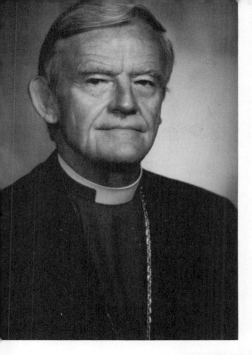

First skyscraper proposal (photo of model):
fifty-nine stories, mirrored glass. The
caption of the press photo handed out by the
architect read: "In harmonious composition
with the Church and surrounding buildings."
COURTESY EDWARD DURELL STONE, ASSOCIATES, P.C.

*Second skyscraper proposal (photo of model): forty-nine stories, cast stone and
brick lower stories, glass upper stories* COURTESY EDWARD DURELL STONE,
ASSOCIATES, P.C.

Second skyscraper proposal (rendering of proposed building superimposed on a photo of the existing church): forty-nine stories, cast stone and brick lower stories, glass upper stories COURTESY EDWARD DURELL STONE, ASSOCIATES, P.C.

St. Bartholomew's Episcopal Church, terrace, garden, and Community House
BRENT C. BROLIN © 1987

would be wrong to attribute responsibility for overall financial strategy to Howard, who was only nineteen. But the investigators did not let him any farther off the hook. "Our conclusion is that the failure of both companies is directly attributable to gross mismanagement on the part of their two effective directors, Mr. Gerald Ronson (the chairman) and Mr. Howard Ronson (the managing director). . . . Mr. Howard Ronson played an important part in the day to day conduct of the companies and must bear a full share of the blame for the other management failures. . . .

"After careful and anxious consideration of this question," the investigators concluded, evidence existed "from which a court might infer that . . . Mr. Gerald Ronson and Mr. Howard Ronson were knowingly parties to the carrying on of the business of both companies with intent to defraud the companies' creditors."

The Committee to Oppose was particularly interested in the estimates of Ronson's worth just a few years before he arrived in New York. "The evidence before us . . . does not suggest that either [Gerald or Howard] has any substantial assets at the present time. We cannot be certain, however, that the account of their resources that we have been able to obtain is complete."

Parishioners had known nothing about this report when they voted on the project. Their knowledge of the church's man was based on a few pages the church put out titled "About Howard P. Ronson." They were informative on a public relations level: The church's man was a British-born real estate developer and investor who, until recently, had limited his business interests to Europe. He had toured forty-seven U.S. cities before deciding to settle in New York and had been in the city about three years by 1981, when he became St. Bart's developer.

The release quoted Ronson's obvious delight with the opportunity: "The development of St. Bartholomew's is a great and wonderful challenge. It is not merely a commercial project but one which enables the church to continue its excellent community work, provides new and increased church and community facilities, and creates a magnificent aesthetic addition to the City of New York while preserving the beauty and uniqueness of a church. Thus it embodies the true objective of real estate development which is to serve the population at large while justifying its existence in financial terms."

When rumors based on the *Financial Times* article began circulating, the rector's office issued a few more sheets, titled "Setting the Record Straight on Ronson." The church warned that the Committee to Oppose was circulating "willful misinformation" about Ronson, to cast doubt on the proposal. "Setting the Record Straight" attributed his troubles to enthusiasm, the desire to get things done quickly, and "lack of experience in the contracting business." When the seven-year investigation came to a close, "having become one of Europe's most successful office building developers, [Howard Ronson] put the matter to final rest by voluntarily and personally paying approximately $45,000 to settle all claims although he had absolutely no personal responsibility or liability for these corporate debts," refusing to accept "damaging allegations made by the inspectors or made to them by some of the witnesses."

The church also questioned the investigative procedures of the Department of Trade and declared them unfair. It claimed that the investigators, "finding no intent to do wrong, did not recommend that the Department of Trade move to prosecute, and no judicial charges of any kind were ever filed against the Ronsons."

This was partly true. According to the report, the substance of the case against the Ronsons rested upon a "pattern of conduct," rather than upon individual transactions, and for that reason, "[a]ny proceedings against them would be highly complex because they would involve consideration of the financial structure and results of at least 13 of the companies under investigation and a huge volume of contracts and subcontracts." The Department of Trade did say the Ronsons had vehemently denied any intention of defrauding creditors, but despite their protestations, it concluded that "neither of them is a suitable person at the present time to act as a director of a company."

The next communication between the rector and the parish about Howard Ronson came two years later, in early December

1983: "This is just a note to let you know that we have completed our development arrangements with Mr. Howard Ronson, who is to be the developer of the Community House site, and we plan to file with the Landmarks Commission on Monday, December 12th."

By the time that letter reached parishioners, the rector and vestry had defused the first of several land mines they would come across along the road to development: the first defection from the vestry.

On a Monday morning in late August 1982 J. Sinclair Armstrong returned from Martha's Vineyard, expecting to find the usual stack of new correspondence on his desk at Whitman & Ransom. What he found was anything but normal. On his desk were three typed pages, on plain white paper. No one knew who had put them there. Sinc knew one thing, however. They had not been meant for his eyes—at least originally. The only identifying mark was the heading on the first page:

July 19, 1982
TO: The Vestry
FROM: Mark Green (on vacation)

Mark Green was a vestryman at St. Bartholomew's.

Armstrong read it quickly and sent a copy to the committee's lawyer, Gerald Fischer. The business card clipped to it said: "The attached was hand delivered to my office on July 30, 1982, I know not by or from whom. If authentic, would it not be the basis for a new vote now whatever deal the church may make? Sinc"

The "first point" of the confidential memo was "one of ethics." Green thought the rector had intentionally deceived the parish about the agreement with the developer. "The Rector's correspondence of December 3, 1981 . . . willfully mis-stated the facts of the deal," he wrote. "The original press releases contained misstatements of the deal. The documents sent out for the first vote contained misstatements." (The "first vote" was the one scheduled for November 17, which was enjoined.)

Green had become uneasy months before the December vote. When he read the church's flyer about the November 17 vote, he and others on the vestry told the rector and the junior warden it was not accurate. "When some of the members of the vestry found out we should have a second vote because of J. Sinclair Armstrong's delay of the [November 17] vote I appealed to Tom and Tony [Marshall] to state the facts correctly." One vestryperson even wrote to Bowers and Marshall, explaining what to say in order to tell the truth. "Much to the amazement of several of us, the correspondence of December 3 remained silent of full disclosure. So my first point is one of ethics. We told the parish one thing and we must live by it. Otherwise, the foundation of the building will be nothing but quicksand."

Green also had doubts about the financial arrangements. He feared the parish would end up with a smaller building than the one it voted for, and he was leery of loopholes favoring Ronson. There was a maximum size for the building, for example, but no minimum. Ronson could whittle it down, making it more acceptable to the landmarks commission, but at the same time reducing the church's income and space allotment (which was tied to gross square footage). "Any deal with Ronson as described in the proposed negotiating position is *irresponsible* because it does not fix a deal on which we can depend [Green's emphasis]."

Sinc thought the memo proved the congregation had been misinformed before the previous December's building vote, a fact that might be enough to have that decision overturned in the courts. The committee issued a press release to that effect, saying the parishioners had made up their minds on the basis of fraudulent information. It wanted to set aside the building vote and block the church from going ahead with its plans until a new vote was held.

What stopped Armstrong and the committee in their tracks was Green's surprising recantation of the memo. It was as surprising for what it did not say as for what it did. In an affidavit dated September 16, 1982, he said he had originally thought the rector and junior warden (Anthony Marshall) were "moving in the direction of support for a building that could have been substantially less than that voted by the Parish," which was "contrary to the interests of the Church and inconsistent with what the Parish had been told in connection with its vote last December." In the two months since his July memo he had found that was not the case. "Accordingly, I want, emphatically, to remove any implication that I entertain any question as to the integrity of the Rector or the Junior Warden or any of my fellow Vestrymen or that there was any impropriety in the Parish vote."

The interesting thing about Green's affidavit—and one filed by vestryman Jim Dunning on the same date—was that neither disputed the original charge that the rector "willfully" misinformed his parishioners on several occasions. One cleric at St. Bartholomew's vouched for Green's integrity: "He was scrupulously honest." He was also the largest pledger in the parish, except for multimillionaire Marc Haas. "Even though his income was a fraction of what Marc Haas's was at that time, he still gave a huge amount of money. That's the kind of person he was."

When the affair of the mysterious memo was over, Mark Green quietly resigned from the vestry, the first of several departures.

It was more than a year later that the rector and vestry finally came to an agreement with the developer, Howard Ronson. They renegotiated the terms of the original letter of intent, in a number of cases responding to the criticisms in Mark Green's memo. Only then, in the winter of 1983, were they ready to go before the Landmarks Preservation Commission.

CHAPTER

V

A building must pass several tests before becoming a landmark. The staff of the Landmarks Preservation Commission first
singles it out as a likely candidate because of its beauty, its stylistic
importance, or some special historical event that took place within
its walls. It may designate exteriors or interiors, but not the
interiors of religious buildings. These are exempted because the
authors of the legislation thought regulating them might be a
constitutionally unacceptable interference in church affairs.

Once the commission has declared a building worthy of
landmarking, it listens to arguments for and against designation in
public hearings. When those are over, the commissioners meet in
executive session to examine the testimony. If they vote to
designate, the recommendation is forwarded to the City Board of
Estimate, which makes the final decision.

Once the shield of the Landmarks Law has been affixed, an owner may change a protected structure only if the commission approves the modification. Requests to alter are made to the commission and are accompanied by plans, facade drawings, and perspectives, along with samples of materials in an effort to show that the proposed changes would be appropriate to the landmark. If the commission approves, it issues a certificate of appropriateness and the owner goes ahead with the work. In judging appropriateness, commissioners must consider the effect of the changes on the aesthetic, historical, and architectural value of the landmark and its neighbors. In short, they must exercise what eighteenth-century essayists called the "faculty of taste."

There is a way to alter a landmark that does not involve taste. An owner may apply for a certificate of appropriateness on the basis of "insufficient return"—"hardship," in popular parlance. Generally the commission returns a finding of hardship if the owner shows the property cannot earn a "reasonable return," defined by the Landmarks Law as 6 percent of the assessed value of the property. "About eight" hardship applications have been heard during the commission's twenty-year history, and findings of insufficient were returned on all but one, said Dorothy Miner, the no-nonsense counsel for the landmarks commission.

When an owner wants to change only a portion of a protected building (as in St. Bart's case), the commissioners must take an optimistic view. They cannot say it is impossible to make an appropriate addition; they must assume it can be done. That logic works for the landmark owner; there is no reason to prepare a hardship application if there is a chance the commission will decide the changes are not harmful to the qualities that made the building a landmark in the first place. As a result, the first thing an owner does is to apply for a certificate of appropriateness. If rejected, the owner can apply, under the hardship provision, to make the same changes. (The obvious exception to this sequence occurs when the entire landmark is to be destroyed, an alteration the commission automatically considers inappropriate. In that case, one would apply directly under hardship.)

Thus it was that St. Bartholomew's filed first for a certificate of appropriateness. That decision had not come easily. Throughout the summer and into the fall of 1983, church leaders discussed how they should approach the commission. Anthony Marshall, the junior warden, compiled an informal history of those months which tells something of the players involved and of the views they brought to the vestry room.

John Zuccotti, one of two lawyers retained by the church at that time, was eventually chosen to spearhead the church's presentation to the commission. He was intimately acquainted with the process, having gone from "our side" to "their side," in the words of the former chairman of the commission Harmon Goldstone. Zuccotti was deputy mayor of New York City before he became chairman of the City Planning Commission, the administrative elder brother of the landmarks commission. He later retired to practice law, where he puts his knowledge of city government to work for private clients.

Zuccotti apparently doubted that the commission would ever approve the fifty-nine-story tower. According to Marshall, the former city planning commissioner "wished we could find a way to get a decision from the Landmarks Commission without [showing them] the building because he knew that the building would attract negative reaction and possibly overwhelm our other issues."

At one point the vestry considered applying for "demolition [of the Community House] only, based on no protected architectural features." (That was consistent with the prodevelopment claim that the church, rather than the Community House, was the "landmark" but ignored the designation report itself, which said the church, terrace, garden, and Community House were the "landmark.") If the church gained a favorable ruling with that gambit, it planned to demolish the Community House immediately "on the hope that Landmarks Commission faced with hole in the ground next to church would be more amenable to new building."

Church leaders also considered bypassing the commission entirely and challenging the original designation in court. That idea was abandoned when they decided a challenge raised fifteen years after the fact would carry little weight in the courts, and the church was likely to find itself sent back to the commission to apply under the standard procedure specified by the Landmarks Law. Courts hesitate to upset a law if a less drastic remedy is available.

After much discussion the vestry rejected all those options and decided to take the most conservative route. It would file for a certificate of appropriateness to alter the landmark by removing the Community House and putting up Ronson's tower. Given the "strong public opposition to our case and the prominence of our Landmark," it doubted the commission would permit any short-cuts.

In December 1983 St. Bartholomew's filed its application for a certificate of appropriateness. In addition to plans, elevations, and perspectives, the package included a piggyback application for hardship, under a heading titled "Incidental Relief." That was the result of a compromise between John Zuccotti and Paul Windels, another lawyer working for the church. Windels insisted the church apply for hardship first, wrote Marshall. He "did not want the LC to be considering architectural features only for six months without our being able to present our hardship, which is the reason we are requesting the architectural changes." But most on the vestry thought the commission would first want to decide if the building they were presenting was an appropriate alteration. "If the LC rejected our application," said Marshall, "we planned to appeal directly to the federal courts," where the church would claim the Landmarks Law was an unconstitutional intrusion of the state into church affairs.

Dorothy Miner said it was a muddy application. Reams of paper, all of which were irrelevant to the certificate of appropriateness application, were aimed at proving the church's hardship claim. Her opinion concurred with the private speculations of St. Bartholomew's own advisers: As long as the church presented a building, its appropriateness to the landmark would have to be considered first.

*   *   *

Father Bowers had publicly pleaded his case since the fall of 1980. Now the public, in the form of the Landmarks Preservation Commission, was an official party to the Battle of St. Bart's.

The hearings were crowded. Some people came because of the prominence of the landmark; it was the most publicized case since Penn Central's attempt to build over Grand Central Station, a decade before. Others stayed through the day to get a chance to speak for or against the proposal.

Public hearings on landmarks issues are usually held in the commission's conference room on Vesey Street (named after the Reverend William Vesey, first rector of Trinity Episcopal Church, Wall Street). The commissioners expected an overflow crowd, however, so the hearing was moved to the Board of Estimate chamber in City Hall, a large, elegantly ornamented room with refined proportions which could have been deemed almost church-like as the public gathered to hear the story of St. Bartholomew's. Its classical ornament defines the space with uncompromising clarity, recalling the rationalism of eighteenth-century deism, not the mysticism of the East, the architectural birthright of Byzantine St. Bartholomew's.

There are two banks of shiny wooden pews in the Board of Estimate chamber. A center aisle divides them and leads to a low railing whose delicate white balusters lend a homey touch, like a front yard fence or perhaps the communion rail of a New England church. Witnesses testified at a lectern before that railing. Beyond it sat the commissioners, behind a mahogany desk almost as wide as the room itself, whose semicircular arms reached out to embrace the lectern. Without any prompting, prodevelopment supporters lined up on the right side of the aisle, those opposed on the left, according to some obscure law of social gravity that binds like thinkers together.

People wandered in and out throughout the day, as the commissioners listened to the testimony. Small knots of two or three would gather in the aisle from time to time, then move toward one of the side doors and disappear into the hallway. Outside, huge portraits of former governors looked down indifferently as witnesses reworked testimony, revised strategy, or tried to break up the boredom of hour upon hour of mostly repetitious testimony.

Thomas Dix Bowers made his opening statement in midmorning on January 30, 1984. St. Bart's had always had a broad definition of its religious mission, he told the commissioners, then recounted the many outreach achievements of his church under previous rectors. Its basic tenet, which is that of the Episcopal Church, is "Love thy neighbor as thyself." The New Testament uses a special Greek word to describe that kind of love: *agape,* an emotion involving self-sacrifice and self-giving. It is the cross; it is the meaning of Jesus Christ. Father Bowers then reiterated the argument church leaders had been making for nearly three and a half years: "At present the Church's ability to serve God and the World is stymied by the temporal realities of lack of money and lack of space. The Commission's Report [which landmarked the building on March 16, 1967] specifically recognized the interaction between the viability of the Church and its structures."

Dr. Finlay and his vestry had accepted the commission's designation in good faith because they were given what they thought was an assurance that changes in the building could be accommodated if the life of the church demanded it. Repeating a claim he made to the parish before the first vote on the building proposal, Tom Bowers assured everyone there that without the additional income, the present church would "have to be abandoned, sold and destroyed" within the decade.

The building that St. Bartholomew's showed to the commission was the same one the parish had seen before the December 1981 vote. According to Peter Capone, its architect, the church had had nothing to do with the design of the tower beyond the original charge, given to the developers and their architects, to "produce the maximum allowable" building for the site. Capone himself explained the building to the commission.

Architectural presentations often demand some exercise of the intellect on the part of the viewers to reconcile the pictures with the words used to describe them. This one required a herculean effort. One large color photograph showed a view from the northwest, with the tower superimposed on the existing site. The caption read: "The proposed tower in harmonious composition with the church and surrounding buildings." The tower was a huge, faceted prism of mirrored glass, fifty-nine stories high. It rose almost 200 feet higher than the neighboring skyscrapers and 400 to 500 feet above the dome of St. Bartholomew's. It dominated the church the way the superstructure of an aircraft carrier dominates the flight deck.

It was even less harmonious when seen from the southwest. The architect claimed to have saved the old Community House by pasting a remnant of its brick-and-stone facade onto the base of his design. It was an architectural hangnail on the toe of the new tower.

The addition was set back from Park Avenue the same distance as the existing Community House. It was narrowest at the entrance, where the old facade clung to the new. As it got farther from Park Avenue, it stepped out sideways, toward the church. To obtain the greatest volume, the architect cantilevered part of the tower over the sanctuary. The corner of the main thrust came within thirty feet of the dome and looked as if it would puncture it.

"Bowers's Tower of Power," as it was inevitably labeled, was the logical outcome of a search for "the biggest bang for the buck," a phrase used unabashedly by one of Tom's own fans. It was difficult to imagine a less appropriate building for a landmark site. Zuccotti's guess about the public's reaction was on target. Almost everyone without a vested interest considered it a monstrous joke, a textbook example of the developer's dream and the preservationist's nightmare. Those who spoke in favor stressed income value, not architectural virtue. The design community unanimously condemned it. Brendan Gill, a fixture of New York architecture criticism, pictured the church "huddled in forlorn shadow at the base of a grotesquely over-scaled needle. If this is not a mutilation of Bertram Grosvenor Goodhue's masterly original design, what can it be called?" Christobel Gough, a tenaciously effective Greenwich Village preservationist, drew more than a few chuckles with her image of St. Bartholomew's after the Fall: "We know that heaven is not literally up. But modern man still considers that his prayers fly up. The idea that they would do so through desks, chairs, wastebaskets and ashtrays would be something of an anticlimax."

The most stinging attack, however, came from an insider. It was not a critique of the building but an indictment of the motives and methods that had led to it. David Trovillion was now an ex-verger of St. Bartholomew's. Back in 1981 he had briefly locked horns with the rector when his modified cartoon had poked fun at the development idea. The rector's displeasure at the gibe and Trovillion's financial need to hold on to the verger's position had led him to keep a low profile from then on. The soft-spoken midwesterner was so successful that the hostility of his true feelings brought audible gasps from unsuspecting friends in the audience.

> The way [the rector and vestry] have gone about this project from the beginning has been a ruthless all-or-nothing contrivance by a group of aesthetically depraved bullies. . . . To them, God is on the side of the materially destitute; on the other side is the vast majority of New Yorkers. Their exploitative and condescending defense of the poor, although prompted by Christian sentiments, crowds out the rest of Christianity.

In late June 1984 Reverend Tom Bowers received a letter from Gene Norman, chairman of the Landmarks Preservation Commission. The proposed tower failed to relate in "texture, material, style or proportion to the landmark," and the commission therefore found it an inappropriate alteration. The commissioners did not think the design could be modified to make it acceptable.

From the beginning, the rector had been pessimistic about a success at Landmarks and had volunteered that view in public. "Those bimbos and dummies on the landmarks commission" were "jerking [the church] around for the fun of it," as he put it. Consequently, Tom Bowers was unmoved by the mass of criticism laid at the church's doorstep after its presentation to the commission. In any event, as far as he and the vestry were concerned, the affair would probably not end at Landmarks, should the commission's decision be unfavorable to the church. The main concern of the church fathers was that they touch all the legal bases in their appearances before the commission since that was the only way they could be certain that the case would not be summarily dismissed when and if they eventually challenged the constitutionality of the Landmarks Law in federal court.

Father Bowers's distrust of the landmarks commission was based upon the different interpretations that the church and the commission placed on two particular paragraphs in the 1967 designation report of St. Bartholomew's Church.

These reports usually describe various architectural details of the building being landmarked and, when appropriate, its role in important historical events. For the most part, St Bartholomew's report read like hundreds of others, but the two paragraphs in question contrasted noticeably with the tone of the rest of the report and even appeared to undercut the protective purpose of the designation:

The Landmarks Preservation Commission recognizes that the Landmark and the Landmark Site are used by St. Bartholomew's Church for religious and charitable purposes and that, in the future, the Church may consider it necessary to alter or expand the existing structures or erect additional structures on the Landmark Site. *By this designation of the Landmark and Landmark Site, it is not intended to freeze the structures in their present state or to prevent the alteration or expansion of existing structures or the erection of other structures needed to meet the church's requirements in the future. The Commission believes it has the obligation and it has the desire to cooperate with owners of Landmarks in such situations and looks forward to working with representatives of St. Bartholomew's Church should such contingencies occur* [emphasis added].

The Commission is also aware that several times in the

past, due to changes in the character of the neighborhoods in which its Church has been situated, St. Bartholomew's Church has found it necessary to dispose of its Church structures and erect others elsewhere. The Commission recognizes that such a condition may recur making it advisable for St. Bart's to dispose of the Landmark and Landmark site and that the proceeds of the sale of the Landmark and Landmark Site will be required in order to effect a relocation.

The commission had not promised to roll over and play dead if the rector and vestry wanted to slice the dome off St. Bart's, but it is easy to see how the church could believe that the commission had obligated itself to go out of its way to accommodate necessary changes in the buildings. Past and present church leaders had thought of these paragraphs as an escape clause, protecting, if not assuring, their right to change the buildings to suit the church's needs. That interpretation gains credibility with the knowledge that the church's attorneys, Milbank, Tweed, Hadley, & McCloy, had worked with the landmarks commission to refine the language of the report and make it acceptable to the church.

Why did the commissioners agree to language that could be seen as defeating the intent of the new law? Probably because they had little choice. The perception of the purpose and impact of the Landmarks Law has changed enormously over the twenty years of its life. Even some real estate developers are now willing to admit that it has served the city well. But no one knew what its effect would be when the commission first came into being, and the infant agency found itself in an awkward position. Many owners of potential landmarks had to be convinced that a designation was not also a kiss of death in terms of property values. In its earliest days, therefore, the landmarks commission moved with caution to avoid stirring up an organized opposition that might emasculate the law before people got used to having it around. Frank Gilbert stated the strategy behind the paragraphs in testimony submitted at the first St. Bart's hearing. The paragraphs were "part of our effort to gain the understanding of property owners," he wrote to the chairman of the commission.

It is difficult to imagine how these paragraphs would have increased understanding but easy to imagine they might make an owner more willing to accept a designation. Substituting "pacify" for "gain the understanding of" in Gilbert's letter would probably give a more accurate representation of the effect of the language. The deferential tone would surely have assured uneasy owners that what seemed to be an immutable process could be painlessly reversed, affording what proved to be an ill-founded sense of security in St. Bartholomew's case.

Gilbert defended the commission's early strategy by pointing to almost identical paragraphs in other early designations—Trinity Church, St. Paul's Chapel, and the Flatiron Building, among others—which only bolsters the notion that they were designed to placate. Guardians of other potential landmarks would have been no less leery than Dr. Finlay and his vestry.

A few weeks after receiving the letter of rejection, Tom Bowers formally advised his parishioners of the commission's decision. "Accordingly," said the announcement, "the vestry plans to pursue this Constitutional issue in the Courts in September unless it finds a satisfactory alternative solution meanwhile."

Ron Alexander had been a vestryman for a year and a half when the church received its first rejection. Several times during that period he had casually suggested the church should probably go straight to court if the first tower was turned down. Only later did it occur to him that those cavalier speculations might have led Tom to think of him as a reliable person to have on the building committee, for Tom, too, thought the courts were the correct next step. Whatever the reason, Alexander received a telephone call shortly after Labor Day 1984. Father Bowers wanted new people on the building project, and he hoped Ron would come aboard. Two other vestrymen, E. Theodore "Ted" Lewis and Fletcher Hodges, joined then, too. The three men accepted their appointments on a curious condition: The explicit agreement was that Tom would stay out of the building project. The rector's talents for dividing the parish with his caustic tongue was acknowledged even among supporters, and Alexander and the others did not want to operate under that handicap. Tom promised he would make no public statements that might do political damage to the church.

By the time Ron penetrated the inner circle of the development project, there had been weeks of heated discussion over Tom's statement about going to court. Less dramatic options were available, and moderates thought they would produce better results. By that line of reasoning, the next step was not a lawsuit but a hardship application.

While the committee considered the options, it also looked at two recent decisions handed down by the state court, which reinforced the Landmarks Law. The first involved Marymount School, an independent Catholic school on Manhattan's Upper East Side. The court agreed with the commission, saying it had interpreted the law correctly in granting the hardship plea and permitting Marymount to build a gymnasium on top of its landmarked structure.

The second decision concerned the United Methodist Church of St. Paul and St. Andrew, on Eighty-sixth Street and West End Avenue. St. Paul and St. Andrew had been the unwilling recipient of a landmark designation in 1981 and chose to fight it. Far poorer in worldly terms than St. Bart's—with no endowment, and around $20,000 in the bank—the congregation decided not to seek relief via the administrative route but to challenge the constitutionality of the law directly. The people at St. Bart's knew the details, because someone from St. Paul and St. Andrew had been invited to a vestry meeting to speak about the case.

In the spring of 1984 St. Paul and St. Andrew lost in the lower courts. The case was not "ripe," said the ruling. The church should have applied for relief under the law before asking the courts to invalidate it. (It later lost its appeal, and the Supreme Court subsequently refused to hear the case.)

St. Paul and St. Andrew marked a dangerous soft shoulder on the curving landmarks road. By itself, that should have led the vestry to keep the first design and file a hardship application, but several things made them steer a different course.

As diplomats learn to decipher the nuances of international communiqués, those who deal with city agencies try to guess what, if anything, can be read between the lines of offical pronouncements. The commission had roundly rejected the first proposal yet made a point of saying the Community House, terrace, and gardens were not "inviolate or unalterable." Was it a come-on, a suggestion that a more graciously designed building might meet with approval? Perhaps the church would be able to build an income-producing tower after all, without baring its financial heart or pursuing a costly and uncertain constitutional course.

The church was also concerned with the effect the apparent come-on might have at some later date. If it ignored the hint that a better-designed building might pass, some judge down the road might say it had failed to pursue all the administrative options. It was also thought that submitting a smaller building, which did not need special approvals, would give it stronger legal leverages in the future. It was easy to imagine a judge being reluctant to get the robes of justice caught up in the machinery of church/state litigation when the cause of it all was a building that could not be built under existing zoning regulations. Returning to the commission with a smaller building would also put the church in what Ron Alexander called the "high moral position of trying to be cooperative." Finally, by placing itself within the protective walls of the Landmarks Law rather than assailing it from without, as St. Paul and St. Andrew had done, the vestry thought it would end up in a better position for its eventual legal attack. "The [smaller building] will test the genuineness of the Landmarks Commission's statements regarding possible solutions contained in its rejection of the big building," wrote Anthony Marshall. So the church submitted a second design.

Had the first tower been built, St. Bart's would have had about 50 percent more area for its Community House. During the last months of 1984 representatives of the church, the architect, and the developer undertook the painful task of robbing St. Bartholomew's to pay the landmarks commission. The architect cut ten stories off the original design and retracted the cantilever that had imperiled the dome. In compressing its bulk, the rentable square footage was reduced by half, so while the first scheme would have netted the church almost $10 million a year, the figure for the new design was closer to $4.5 million. If it was a financial disappointment, it was a design triumph compared with the first. But that was to compare a catastrophe with a mere disaster.

In late January 1985 architect Peter Capone presented the second tower to the commission. The garish mirrored glass was traded for lower stories of warm-toned brick trimmed with white limestone (a motif borrowed from Goodhue's church), which metamorphosed into glass as the skyscraper rose beyond the dome of the church. The western and southern facades were flattish, Mayan-like pyramids, with a series of setbacks that broke up the still-considerable bulk of the tower and made it seem smaller than it was.

The drawings showed mainly the bottom half of the new design, which used the church's decorative motif. Capone presented a stunning, full-color, photomontage showing the tower, church, and adjoining buildings. St. Bart's was awash in brilliant sunshine, from brick-and-stone arches to crowning dome. Next to it, but pulled back, sat the tower; it was slender, sympathetic in materials, and apparently more discreet in its relationship to the church. It seemed large in the picture, but not grossly oversized. However, what you saw was not what you got. The montage seemed to show the whole tower, yet only the lower half was visible. The rest ran off the top, out of the field of vision.

The entrance, which people would see most often, seemed prosaic, at best, from what one could make out. The designer must have thought so, too, for he took care to camouflage it. Architects deploy vegetation the way admirals used to lay smoke screens.

Capone spoke about a positive visual relationship between the tower and the church, but the eye refused to believe the ears. If the two-dimensional presentation fooled anyone, the brutal truth was clear as soon as you laid eyes on the model. The gigantic sliver of a building was wedged between St. Bart's and Fiftieth Street. "Shoehorned" was the expression that leaped to mind.

If the rector and vestry thought this one might succeed where the first had failed, it was not apparent from the lawyer's presentation. John Zuccotti opened his testimony as though the sole purpose of the hearing were to lay the groundwork for the constitutional case to come. He ticked the items off his list, insurance that no judge could say they had not cooperated fully with the commission. The new tower had been redesigned in response to the criticisms of the first scheme; its materials were now similar to those of the church (at least at the base); it stood only on the Community House side of the site and stepped away from the church as it rose rather than overhung it, and so on.

When Reverend Bowers spoke, it was a brief but emotional statement. He suggested the church would take the commission to court if it did not approve the design.

Patience is a virtue demanded of commissioners. Supporters and opponents had a right to have their say. The second St. Bart's hearing began shortly after its assigned ten o'clock starting time and continued into the late afternoon with a brief break for lunch. Speaker after speaker rose from the pews, squeezed by fellow watchers, and walked to the lectern to speak his or her piece. The commissioners shifted from haunch to haunch, in soft leather chairs, as the day dragged on. The audience, on hardwood pews, shifted with greater frequency.

Once again the commissioners considered much of the church's testimony irrelevant. The vestry had submitted hundreds of pages detailing the problems it had raising money, but fundraising difficulties were not apropos. The job at hand was to decide if the new building was aesthetically in tune with the church, and questions from the dais were directed accordingly.

As in the first hearing, most of those who testified opposed the tower. Each time a voice spoke out against it, Commissioner Anthony Tung, an architect, asked if the speaker thought it was possible to design a skyscraper for that site that would be acceptable. Preservationists answered without hesitation: It was impossible. Architects willingly acknowledged the beauty of the landmark, but none dared impugn the competency of the profession by saying it was impossible to design a commercially viable tower that would also complement the church.

The impression among onlookers of both persuasions was that the commission would not approve this building either. Some who had followed the proceedings over the months wondered aloud if the commissioners and churchmen didn't think of it as a grand and tiring charade.

The landmarks commission holds two kinds of public meetings: hearings, where testimony from all sides is taken, and executive sessions, where the commissioners discuss the testimony among themselves. The first invites public participation. The second convenes after the public record is closed but permits visitors to play fly-on-the-wall. Because no testimony is heard, audiences are considerably smaller, and the commissioners meet in the nondescript conference room on Vesey Street. Guests and staff enter through the same double doors. Visitors sit at the entry end of the room, on loosely ordered ranks of folding chairs, which seem to hold back piles of drawings and models stacked casually against the back wall. The audience forms a protective reef between the sea of application material and the commissioners' island, a large mosaic of conference tables at the other end of the room.

If Tom Bowers was correct and the commission was just "jerking" the church around, it was not apparent from those sessions. The discussion sounded meticulously, almost unrealistically, unbiased. Was it possible that after more than a year of testimony none of the officials had been swayed one way or another? Perhaps the impression had something to do with the classical dilemma of the anthropologist, the observer altering the response of the observed.

A single executive session may cover several projects. There was no change in the commissioners' demeanor when talk shifted from minor facade modifications of this or that landmark to St. Bartholomew's application. The audience perked up, however, for it was made up almost exclusively of partisans of one side or the other.

All the testimony, as well as most of the explanatory material— stacks of paper at least a foot high—was piled neatly in front of each commissioner. Unless a final decision is to be made, the discussion at these sessions is limited to bits and pieces of additional information the commissioners have requested. (The rector said he looked upon those requests as the commission's way of making the church waste even more money, part of the broader bureaucratic conspiracy to do it in.) One commissioner asked for more precise information about the tower's "footprint"—where it sat on the site, the shape of the ground-floor plan, and how close it came to the church. Another doubted the accuracy of the shadows on the photomontage and asked for more information. Old hands at these hearings wondered if the query was a setup or just naïve. The architects obviously picked a time of year when the tower's shadow on the church would be least noticeable. If that was from 12:15 to 12:18 on the day of the summer solstice, and shadows cloaked the sanctuary the rest of the year, so what? Architects are in the business of painting the rosiest picture. The executive sessions were unsatisfying for anyone who hoped to divine the commission's collective mood.

Commissioners have ninety days to make up their minds once they close the public hearings. St. Bartholomew's was discussed at several executive sessions during those three months. The last was in July 1985, at the end of the ninety-day period, when the verdict was due.

Gene Norman, chairman, opened the meeting. Like the bishop, he is an ex-marine. He is also an architect who has worked in private practice and for various government agencies. He went on record saying what Sinc Armstrong and Rob Morris, who were closely following these events, had already suspected. The commission had received a series of letters from the rector and vestry of St. Bartholomew's asking that the decision be postponed. Why had the applicant requested a delay? No one knew, but Norman suggested the church was "a many-headed creature," a reference to its several lawyers. Before reaching any decision on the request, the commissioners passed on to other aspects of the application.

For several minutes there was nothing but small talk, as the commissioners sniffed around the matter of the tower like dogs around a fire hydrant. Then one asked a question that must have stunned church supporters: "Should the commission permit the demolition of the Community House?"

The chairman quickly jumped in, saying past discussions implied they would consider tearing it down. The first tower had not been rejected because it eliminated the Community House but because the new design was inappropriate.

Architect Tung disagreed, and at that point the conversation took what appeared to be an unchoreographed turn. The commissioners had never implied or said outright that they would tolerate the destruction of the Community House, Tung continued. The first scheme had at least kept the facade. If the second one looked better next to the church, it had eliminated even that paste-on remembrance and had entirely destroyed the garden. In a Byzantine twist, the commissioner argued: "The application just seems very backward to me. It should be possible to build something here [but] you can't build something [appropriate] on a landmark site of this quality by tearing down the landmark."

Another architect, Frances Halsband, reminded everyone that the buildings had been designated as a group. A new design would have to be at least as sympathetic to the church as the present Community House.

Church backers were as appalled as the opposition was elated. Nothing in the hours of cross-questioning at the public hearings or the discussions in the public executive sessions had offered the faintest hint that the commissioners felt the Community House could not be destroyed.

The chairman interrupted, again noting that the first letter of rejection had said the Community House, terrace, and garden were not inviolable. No one in the executive session had disputed that, he observed, in apparent contradiction of Commissioner Tung's comments. Was St. Bart's being "jerked around"? wondered some in the audience.

Depending upon your point of view, the commission's opinion either "jelled" or "surfaced" at that point. In any event, the death knell for the second St. Bart's tower was sounded. The "landmark" here is "more than the church," said Norman. "I don't hear any voices speaking for [the proposed tower]. Therefore it's 'inappropriate,' and therefore the chair will entertain a motion."

Dorothy Miner interrupted. Last-minute matters of the legal record had to be tidied up. Like a mother hen collecting her brood, she began gathering bits and pieces of ideas thrown out that morning to weld into a formal rejection. The commissioners needed a motion saying the garden cannot be demolished, she said, but the no-demolition phrase should not come first. The legal maze took on yet another layer of complexity as Commissioner Tung read what appeared to be a prepared statement. (The commissioners had met privately before the public session and had presumably agreed on the gist of what the audience had just witnessed.) The landmark was a trilogy (church, Community House, terrace and garden), forming a whole, read Tung. It was the larger experience that the present proposal ignored by removing the Community House and reconfiguring the garden. In addition, the materials, colors, proportions, and style at ground level did not "recall the spirit of the old building." The application to demolish and build should be denied.

Tung acknowledged that the St. Bartholomew's site presented a difficult design problem but felt both submissions were so far off the mark that neither seriously tested the commission's earlier statements that the Community House, terrace, and garden were not inviolate.

Commissioner Adolf K. Placzek, an architectural historian and librarian emeritus of Columbia University's Avery Architecture

Library, then spoke up. He doubted that anything acceptable could ever be built on the site. Architect Gene Norman disagreed.

The vote to reject was unanimous.

The stage was set for the hardship drama. Rarely do the intimate financial details of a church's life, particularly a wealthy one, promise to surface in such juicy detail. The public would not be disappointed.

The commissioners might well have decided earlier that designing a building of any size for the location in question was a task for Superarchitect. But they were in an inescapable bind. They had to approach each submission with an open mind, for their job was to decide on the merits of each submission, not to assume the task was impossible.

The commission rejected St. Bartholomew's towers because of their inappropriate materials, colors, scale, and style. Although each of the church's neighbors suffers from these same faults, in greater or lesser degree, none is as disturbing as either of the proposed towers would have been. Have the buildings just been around so long we are used to their disharmony? Not really; there was a more basic problem with the new towers. They sinned by violating the architectural privacy of the church.

Some years ago fashionable designers mused about the sociological implications of architecture. The concept of "personal space" usually came up in those discussions, the notion that each of us carries around a bubble of space, a sphere of privacy. The size of the bubble varies from culture to culture and determines the comfortable distance between you and your spouse, a family member, business associate, or stranger. We know the bubble exists because we are uncomfortable when someone invades it by coming too close to us in a given situation. An analogous bubble exists around buildings, varying in size depending upon the site and the type of the building.

The grid pattern of New York City makes the block the basic spatial unit. St. Bartholomew's takes up a clearly delineated half block of space; its orthogonal bubble of personal space is marked on three sides by Park Avenue and the cross streets, on the fourth by its tall neighbors to the east. The church dominates its space, and, in doing so, satisfies a cultural expectation rooted in some 1,500 years of Christian symbolism. The only structure that is permitted to rise above a sanctuary in its own precincts is a steeple or bell tower, either of which is clearly an adjunct. But steeples and campaniles are too skinny to lend themselves to commercial use. So while they would be acceptable architectural forms to insert into St. Bart's personal space, they are unthinkable for a development scheme.

Although grotesquely out of scale and style with the church, the neighboring skyscrapers do not disturb it because they do not puncture its bubble. And because they are so outrageously out of scale, they do not compete. Instead, they focus attention on the church, their similar size binding them into a neutral backdrop against which the church stands out dramatically.

The size of the bubble is critical. It must be properly proportioned if the church is to seem comfortable in it. The Community House half of the site provides the necessary architectural breathing room. There are many New York churches without these bubbles—St. Thomas, on Fifth Avenue, for example. They are still valuable architecturally, but in the larger context of the city they are greatly diminished by the loss. As long as St. Bartholomew's commercial neighbors do not intrude, they do not offend. The building that shoulders into the church's space will transform the gracious dowager, secure amid the commercial upstarts, into an architectural bag lady who seems to squat on a corner of midtown turf.

Throughout his year and a half of dealings with it, Tom thought the landmarks commission was persecuting his church. He sensed something sinister in its rejections and in the lightning-swift negative judgments that descended on each of his towers from almost every corner of the public sector. Bishop Moore agreed with part of that assessment. "In the long range," said the prelate, "one regrets the overdevelopment of midtown Manhattan, but I feel we're being discriminated against in not being allowed to put one skinny office building there."

Both priests wondered why the city should prevent St. Bartholomew's from doing what has always come naturally to landowning New Yorkers. The bishop pointed to several examples. The dusky cliff of Olympic Towers dwarfs St. Patrick's Cathedral. The Villard Houses, across Madison Avenue from St. Patrick's, were ravaged by the Helmsley Palace Hotel. The Racquet Club, McKim, Mead & White's urban palazzo, backs up against the garish green glass of the Fisher Brothers's tower, a cheerless exercise in architectural revisionism. In a city where cheek-by-jowl is the rule rather than the exception, why couldn't St. Bart's follow suit? The bishop implied that the city's history of architectural desecration should have immunized New Yorkers against that kind of insensitivity.

The thrust of the argument was that the church was the only important part of the landmark grouping. There is an elementary aesthetic misunderstanding in that point of view, albeit a comprehensible one given the church's situation. By itself, the Community House is not a work of major architectural interest. But it was not meant to stand alone. By itself, Meryl Streep's nose might be thought too thin or finely chiseled. But Ms. Streep's nose was also not designed to be seen alone. Indeed, it is hard to judge the value of a nose on its own, because the aesthetic virtues or failings of parts of the anatomy, while they may be commented upon in isolation, can never be fully appreciated until they are viewed in their context. The same must be said of bits of architecture that belong to larger compositions. The balance which the Community House gives to the asymmetrically sited church is essential to the aesthetic experience of the unit designated a "landmark."

As publicly pessimistic as Tom Bowers was about the church's fate at Landmarks, he expected little better treatment in the lower courts. Some of those judges were "subject to bribery," he confided. "I see it every day in this business. . . . There isn't organized crime in New York City, New York City is organized crime." It was not the judges' fault, the rector said by way of explanation. They were poorly paid and so, like the policemen, were easy marks for people with money. "The devil is in all of us, but in this thing the devil is really at work." Only after the case reached the federal courts did Tom Bowers expect a fair hearing.

Kent Barwick thought the clerical persecution complex was exaggerated. A tall, quiet man who attends Grace Episcopal Church, Barwick has been a powerful presence in preservation and art circles since the late 1960's, as chairman of the Landmarks Preservation Commission, member of the New York State Council for the Arts, and, during the St. Bart's controversy, head of the Municipal Art Society.

"I do not subscribe to Tom's theory that he is the victim of a cabal," said Barwick, "where everybody else gets away with murder but they're not going to let him do it because he's an Episcopalian or something. There are not a lot of people sitting around thinking how they can make life difficult for this guy Bowers." Barwick suggested Tom's problems might stem from internal, rather than external, forces. Whatever aggravation he suffered at the hands of the media came, in Barwick's opinion, because he refused to keep his foot out of his mouth.

Barwick was not the only one to make that assessment, and it was not entirely off the mark. Early in the affair Tom Bowers compared New York City's enforcement of its Landmarks Law to the barbarisms committed in Nazi Germany, an analogy that showed an ignorance of history as well as an insensitivity to his neighbors (New York has the largest Jewish population of any city in the world). He also ventured an opinion about Jackie Onassis and Brooke Astor, two of the city's better-known citizens who publicly opposed his tower. Brooke Astor is probably the most impressive, single philanthropic presence in New York City, and few, except a newcomer from Atlanta, would question the good deeds of the former first lady. "You think those two care about poor people?" he was quoted as saying. "They despise poor people. Do you think Mrs. Astor thinks about Harlem? Do you think Mrs. Onassis knows what it is to starve?"

That sort of remark gets people's backs up, suggested Barwick, particularly when it comes from someone who lives in a twelve-room luxury apartment on upper Park Avenue and makes around $125,000 a year—almost half of which is tax-free.

Barwick found it odd that Bowers thought everyone who wanted to save the buildings was a politically conservative old fogy, while everyone who wanted to level them was a liberal. He seemed to be saying that if you "signed on for Christ," you didn't care about living in an inhumane environment. That took no account of the positive impact of beautiful surroundings. The issue was much more complicated, Barwick explained. People who want to save buildings are also concerned with the spiritual life of New Yorkers; it is destructive to draw the lines so simplistically—to claim a choice must be made between feeding people and having a humane city. Go down a list of exceptional buildings in New York City—the Metropolitan Museum, the Public Library, St. Patrick's, and so on—and take every dollar you could get from developing those sites and see how many homeless it will feed. It would not help the poor greatly, he said, and would impoverish the city beyond measure.

The head of the Municipal Art Society than added another variation to the "blue-gray" theory, which attempts to explain the rector's impact on some New Yorkers in cross-cultural terms. "I don't think Tom is really at ease in New York," Barwick said earnestly. "I don't think he's comprehended the style, and it is unfamiliar territory."

Barwick was not alone in thinking Tom had put on a hair shirt of his own making, then claimed it was tailored by others. Tom did not stub his toe in Washington or Atlanta, noted the argumentative Don Chappell, a fellow Virginian. "Why then did he come here and fall flat on his face, making an ass out of himself almost instantly?" Tom offended by his belligerence, said Chappell, first inside the parish, then in public. "He comes in and doesn't ask anybody any questions. 'I want it my way or no way. If you don't do it my way, then you're against me.' He has no class. It's intolerable to have someone like that as rector of St. Bartholomew's."

Tom seemed to gather kindred spirits around him. Leslie Sloate has served as public relations adviser to the church since early in the struggle. Sloate was a news liaison person for Nelson Rockefeller years ago but quit when Nixon returned to the Republican picture in the late 1960's because of a mutual dislike (a curious turn, since the ex-President and the ex-press secretary look very much alike). For a PR front man, Sloate had a decidedly off-putting manner. After four unreturned phone calls, one journalist looking for an interview with the rector was informed imperiously: "You will take us [Bowers and Sloate] to a relatively inexpensive Chinese or Japanese restaurant in midtown." Sloate is also a man of aesthetic contradictions. He writes on esoteric and refined topics ranging from Rembrandt to hieroglyphics but can push away a half-eaten plate of sukiyaki and plop his napkin into it.

*   *   *

Under certain circumstances, making a hardship application to the landmarks commission is perfectly straightforward. The statute says a hardship finding will be returned if:

1. There is a firm agreement to sell or lease the property "with reasonable promptness."
2. The landmark is incapable of earning a "reasonable return" (6 percent).
3. The landmark is no longer "adequate, suitable or appropriate for use."

Once those tests are satisfied, the burden of preservation shifts to the public. The commission must relieve the hardship or permit the alteration of the landmark. Relief for commercial owners of landmarks normally comes through a reduction, exemption, or remission of real estate taxes. If the offer is rejected, the commission has six months in which to find a buyer for the property who will maintain it as a landmark. If none is found, the city may take it over or may give up and let the owner go ahead with the requested demolition, alteration, or reconstruction.

Two of the three tests mentioned above apply to any landmark owner: a firm offer to lease or buy and unsuitability to the owner's purpose. The other—that the property produce a reasonable profit—applies only to commercial owners, not to nonprofit groups. Therefore, when the commissioners met to consider St. Bartholomew's hardship testimony, Miner advised them that the last test ("adequate, suitable or appropriate" for use) would be the critical one in terms of the statute.

Many of the city's religious leaders have made it clear in recent years that they think the landmarks statute cannot be applied to churches because its hardship provision demands a profit be shown. The failure of the written law to address the difference between profit-making and charitable owners was recognized long before St. Bartholomew's tendered its hardship application. Harmon Goldstone said the commission "realized [in the 1960's] that the relief written into the law had all been conceived of for commercial operations. It did not apply to nonprofit organizations, and there was a gap, a very real gap, in the equity of these situations." The sale of air rights was designed to help correct that unfairness, but the judicial system was also working to rectify the inequity. The tradition of common law allows the legal system to compensate for inadequate statutes through the accretion of case law. As judges interpret an ambiguous law, a body of precedents that complement the statute and make it applicable to circumstances unforeseen by the original authors slowly accumulate.

Case law on hardship, which had been building up since shortly after the commission came into being, provides what is known as the "comparable judicial test" to determine if a designation places a financial hardship on a not-for-profit owner. Because the statute was admittedly inadequate, this test became the primary means for determining not-for-profit hardship.

The judicial ruler that measures the penury of not-for-profits came out of a case in which a Staten Island home for retired seamen sued the commission to have its designation removed. In the late 1960's Sailors' Snug Harbor said it did not want to sell or lease its property (a requirement in order to qualify for hardship under the statute) but to develop it itself. Since the Landmarks Law provided no "self-development" option for not-for-profits, Sailors' Snug Harbor claimed the law did not apply to it.

It lost the case, but the appeal provided the key test for charitable hardship. After saying the law's weakness was not enough to make it unconstitutional, the appellate division decided a comparable test for charity is where the maintenance of a landmark" either physically or financially prevents or seriously interferes with "its charitable purposes. The point at which that interference begins depends on several things. Does the cost of preservation interfere with the charitable purpose? Can the building be converted at a reasonable cost to serve that purpose? Does the cost of maintaining it without use entail "serious expenditure." Each question must be considered "in the light of the purposes and resources of the petitioner." The appellate division sent the case back to the lower court to see if the designation did interfere with the charitable purpose, but the city bought the property from the trustees before it came to trial.

Other proceedings eventually buttressed the Sailors' Snug Harbor test. In the 1970's the Lutheran Church of America found J. P. Morgan's town mansion too small for its vastly increased administrative responsibilities. Like Sailors' Snug Harbor, *Lutheran Church in America* v. *City of New York* was a "nonalienation" case; the church did not want to sell or lease its property but to develop it itself. The landmarked mansion was to be replaced by an office building. The commission thought that was an inappropriate alteration. The court of appeals again found the law itself constitutional but said this application of it was an overregulation that inhibited the charitable purpose. The designation was rescinded.

The Society for Ethical Culture, located on Central Park West, decided it wanted to replace its landmarked Meeting House with an income-generating apartment tower. Again using the

Sailors' Snug Harbor test, the lower court overturned the landmark designation, saying it interfered with the purpose of the nonprofit organization. The Penn Central case intervened, however, and saved the commission.

Penn Central wanted to build a skyscraper atop Grand Central Terminal, at Park Avenue and Forty-second Street. It argued that the Landmarks Law stripped it of its Fifth Amendment protection against uncompensated confiscation of property by the state. The case eventually reached the Supreme Court, which found in favor of the city and its landmarks commission. The decision established the principle that the owner of a landmark was not entitled to the so-called highest and best use of his property, as long as he enjoyed a reasonable use. On that basis the commission took the Ethical Culture Society to the court of appeals, and the lower court verdict was overturned. The society failed to meet either the Sailors' Snug Harbor or Lutheran Church test. It had not shown that its charitable purposes were disrupted by the designation, merely that it was not able to make money without developing its property. "[T]here simply is no constitutional requirement that a landowner always be allowed his property's most beneficial use," said the court.

The society entered one other argument on its behalf, which would also be taken up by St. Bartholomew's. It held that the law encroached on its First Amendment right of free exercise of religion. The court disagreed.

As a result of these decisions, St. Bart's came before the commission knowing it had to prove the following points if it expected to satisfy the hardship provision:

- That the landmarks designation interfered with its charitable purpose
- That the cost of renovating the building to suit that purpose would be too great for the church to bear
- That the church could not afford to maintain the buildings in its present financial condition

Each particular had to be proven in the context of the larger framework of the church's "purposes and resources."

John Zuccotti directed the hardship presentation, as he had directed the earlier submissions. He is tall and heavyset, with dark hair. A veteran of such proceedings, he approached the lectern with a measured gait, neither anxious nor optimistic, but rather like a seasoned long-distance runner at the beginning of a marathon. He attempted to show, in his opening paragraphs, that St. Bartholomew's met the requirements of both the statutory and judicial tests. The church would provide "evidence as to the theological basis of the church's purposes, the nature of its activities, and the inadequacy of the physical facilities." He advised the commissioners that the church's precarious financial position forced it to choose between maintaining its buildings or funding its ministeries.

Three public hearings were held on the hardship application between October 29, 1985, and January 21, 1986. The church's arguments did not change over the three months, but at one hearing Zuccotti introduced a new element into the church's official testimony, venturing a few remarks on what he thought to be the constitutional implications of the case: Despite the court's comment in the Ethical Culture case, the lawyer contended that denying St. Bart's hardship application would violate its First Amendment right to the free exercise of religion.

Dorothy Miner, counsel to the commission, is intensely committed to her work and fiercely protective of the institution and its statutory birthright. Sinc Armstrong, who had occasion to work with her on this case, commented on her fine legal mind. Miner shatters the TV cliché of the tailored lady lawyer, cultivating a casual, almost frumpy style—no makeup, loose dresses, hair in benign disarray. The combination of unexpected dress and an intensely focused concern sometimes presents a frazzled impression. But when John Zuccotti suggested the future course of the St. Bart's case, Miner appeared anything but frazzled. She bolted like a Thoroughbred from the starting gate. "I'm sure Mr. Zuccotti understands that the Commission isn't the properly constituted body to review the constitutionality of its law," she shot back. "He is seeking to establish a [court] record, I believe, for his purposes."

Before the church could begin to make its constitutional claim, however, it had to prove that the law prevented it from carrying out its charitable purpose and to establish a claim to that purpose.

Vestryman Fletcher Hodges was the point man for the second task. Tall and slim, with a lined and weathered face worthy of a *Mayflower* descendant, he had been a parishioner for twenty-five years, the last five of them on the vestry. President of his own investment banking firm, he has solid credentials as a concerned citizen. Active in the 1960's civil rights movement and the New York Urban Coalition, he worked with Whitney Young at the National Urban League and is *pro bono* president of the East Side Service Center, one of the largest drug rehabilitation centers in the city. He has been a consultant to the Board of Education, the Metropolitan Museum, the American Jewish Committee, and the Economic Development Office of the City of New York, as well as cochair of the vestry building committee.

Religion was more than simple worship to the people of St. Bart's, he told the commissioners. It meant helping others. In the 1970's the Community House had many outreach programs. Tom Bowers hoped to start many more with the proceeds from the building project. Two years after Bowers came, a Task Force for Ministry in the Community Outside the Parish had been set up to plan new programs. By 1982 its volunteers had formed an umbrella organization for all outreach missions at St. Bart's, the Council on Community Ministry. Much of this information had already been submitted at previous hearings. Hodges reiterated it, and added more. There were now senior citizens activities and a counseling center handling groups and individuals. Volunteers helped several churches in the South Bronx by lending their expertise in improving Christian education programs, sharpening fund-raising capabilities, and maintaining buildings. Detailed testimony was given about two of the outreach ministries at St. Bart's, the Clothes Closet and the feeding program.

The Clothes Closet opened in 1982. Within two years it was handing out free clothing to nearly 1,500 people a year. Some came for survival wear—the minimum needed to face winter in the streets. Others were "repeaters," who turned up each week in search of clean clothes, often just so they could go to a job interview in a presentable shirt and pants.

Lack of space was its greatest hardship. The Closet was actually a closet. Only a small stock of clothing could be kept on hand, and the cramped quarters forced visitors to line up on the street rather than in the comfort of the corridor. Fifteen volunteers ran the program, donating a total of 350 hours a year.

Gene Norman asked what the budget of the Clothes Closet was. He was told it cost St. Bartholomew's Church $1,700 a year, including petty cash for buying socks and underwear.

Betty Hudson, chair of the Council on Community Ministry, explained the feeding program. In four and a half years it had gone from feeding 30 people a day to feeding 160 to 180 a day twice a week. Between 10 and 15 volunteers prepared the food and set up tables and chairs. Her main complaint was also lack of space. The guests ate in the Memorial Chapel, which could hold only 55 people per sitting. That meant three seatings an hour, which rushed the guests and "greatly affect[ed] the quality of our ministry" because it did not give the staff time "to get to know them, and see if they need other services." The chapel was also awkwardly located. The food was prepared in a kitchen just off the Community House auditorium, and volunteers carried it down a flight of stairs and under the church to reach the chapel.

Fletcher Hodges then reclaimed the lectern to explain the shelter program. While the city had asked the church to take in more people, the bathroom facilities were inadequate, and there was room to sleep only ten men and women, six nights a week, in the narthex (the interior entrance porch). With some frustration, Hodges said the beds and bedding had to be set up each evening and taken down again the next morning.

Expert testimony also came from outside professionals, hired by the church to do special reports. Keith Keppler is president of the New York office of Walker Associates, Inc., a firm specializing in planning interior spaces. He had just begun his statement about the church's need in terms of additional space when a conspicuous swell in the background noise outside the hearing room caused heads to turn. Seconds later a door opened and in strode a tall, lean clergyman. The half dozen or so priests in the hearing room flew their pew perches and gathered around the newcomer like a flock of white-banded blackbirds. The planner's testimony was interrupted in deference to the Right Reverend Paul Moore, Jr., Bishop of New York.

Although the annual Diocesan Convention was under way that day, the bishop had slipped away to give his testimony in person. He leaned comfortably on the podium and launched into his speech with characteristic verve. His voice was spirited and forceful, the intonation normal, except when he quoted Scripture. Then, without changing any other aspect of his demeanor, he shifted vocal gears and intoned in the singsong melody that infects anyone who spends time in a pulpit. "We are here fighting for the life of one of the city's most beautiful and most useful resources. We are fighting for our very survival," the bishop said. Jesus showed the way in His parable of judgment day (Matthew 25:33–46).

The bishop's speech was not as impressive as it might have been, for although it was rendered in the imposing, stentorian tones of the professional, most of the images he used had already been heard several times that morning. He did raise one new point, however. While its commercial neighbors had reaped millions over the years, tearing down luxury apartment buildings and replacing them with corporate headquarters, St. Bartholomew's had preserved the beauty of its complex for all New York. Was the city now going to discriminate against the church because of the generosity it had so unwisely shown? "We claim the right to do the same."

In closing, Moore pressed home a legal point which had already been made in one way or another by each of the previous speakers for the church: Preventing St. Bartholomew's from building this tower was nothing less than an "infringement of the Constitutional right of the Episcopal church to serve the poor." However, before returning to the cathedral, he muddied what had until then been clear waters by expanding the conflict from the parish to the diocese. The law impinged not only on St. Bartholomew's right of free exercise but on the privilege of other churches in the diocese to profit from that right. "Under our polity, all churches and institutions of our diocese which serve the poor are dependent on churches like St. Bartholomew's." The financial viability of large city parishes was essential if the diocese was to carry on its ministry to the poor: "Will you deny us the right to practice our religion? Will you deny us the means to pick up as best we can the burden of the poor that the public sector has so shamelessly laid down? Will you prevent us from sheltering the homeless, feeding the hungry?"

Having established the theology foundation of outreach and the historical fact of St. Bart's charitable service, the church set about showing the correctness of its hardship claim relative to the Sailors' Snug Harbor test. The financial information the rector and vestry had eagerly presented at earlier hearings, which the commission had considered irrelevant to the aesthetic aspect of "appropriateness," was now germane. Commissioners were not only willing but obligated to listen, for each point affected St. Bartholomew's ability to carry out its charitable purpose. To that end, the rector and vestry produced testimony to show:

- The cost of repairing their buildings and maintaining them in "landmark" shape was insurmountable.
- A depleted congregation had reduced the church's ability to raise income through traditional means.
- Capital fund drives were unrealistic in St. Bart's case partly because of its depleted congregation and partly because its corporate neighbors would not support sectarian causes.
- While its endowment was imposing, it could not be used for operating expenses. Access was choked off by donors' restrictions on how the money could be spent. Only a tiny percentage of the total was available to maintain the church's buildings and fund its ministries.

If they could prove these points, the commission would have to conclude that the burden of landmarking made it impossible for St. Bartholomew's to carry out its Christian mission without developing its property. The rector and vestry produced a series of witnesses who testified to that effect.

When the church first appeared before the commission, Peers Brewer, the treasurer, said it would cost almost $8 million to rehabilitate the buildings. The declaration was supplemented with a bare-survival list of repairs ranging from waterproofing the roofs of the sanctuary to replacing the marble entrance columns and the heating and ventilating systems. It included $325,000 for a new sound system and $295,000 for lighting, the existing lights not being able to "produce the proper effects for a wide range of liturgical and other events." There was also a $120,000 computer, to manage the 1,600 names on the membership list.

The inventory of repairs had been revised by the time the hardship hearing came—the lighting and sound systems were gone, along with the computer—but many new things were added. Before the hearing was an hour old, the commissioners learned that the original deferred maintenance figure of $7.5 million had swelled to nearly $12 million in two years' time. The church had asked O'Brien-Kreitzberg & Associaties (OKA), a nationally known engineering firm, to find out what had to be done to make the Community House safe and habitable. It submitted a report titled "Required Repairs," which went into extensive detail and substantial figures. Fixing the fire escapes on the Community House would cost $200,000; another $200,000 was needed to mend the front steps. The bronze doors to the main sanctuary were falling off their hinges—$165,000. The marble columns flanking the doors were deteriorating, as were the smaller columns of the upper gallery—$559,000. The Community House balcony needed almost $1 million; new mechanical systems took an additional $1 million, plus more than $800,000 for plumbing and electrical work. In the language of *Sailors' Snug Harbor*, the buildings could obviously not be converted "to a useful purpose without excessive cost," and the "cost of maintaining them without use would entail serious expenditure."

To prove the inadequacy of the Community House, the vestry commissioned a space study. The president of Walker Associates (who had been interrupted earlier by the bishop's arrival) told how his firm had analyzed existing conditions, interviewed staff members about special needs, and then calculated the amount of space needed to carry out the church's charitable purpose. Eye-catching flow charts were said to show a straightforward conclusion: The physical layout of the Community House prevented St. Bart's from doing what it wanted to do. It was 8,000 square feet too small.

The building committee had also commissioned a financial report from the church's accountants, KMG Main Hurdman. Nearly an inch thick, the bulk of it consisted of annual reports. In a comment that made the commissioners perk up their ears, Edward Martin, a partner, testified that *the church has been in essentially a break-even position,* [with] *minor surpluses or deficits"* over the past ten years (emphasis added). After that rather startling statement the accountant wound up his presentation with a carefully worded conclusion, which relied wholly on the figures presented in the O'Brien-Kreitzberg report: ". . . in light of the information from the engineers, that significant repair and rehabilitation must be performed on St. Bartholomew's property . . . [t]here is convincing evidence that some form of funding must be found . . . because St. Bart's, as it is now constituted, does not have the resources to meet those needs."

Having amassed a mountain of expenditures and lengthy testimony about the inadequacy of the present building and the need for new sources of income, the rector and vestry moved on to prove that they could not raise enough money by traditional means to pay the bills.

From its first public comments, the church's rationale for choosing development had been based on the irreversible decline of a traditional source of income—parishioners. The reason for that appeared to be simple. In its early years on Park Avenue, St. Bartholomew's had nestled among the kinds of blocky, brick-faced apartment buildings that still line the upper avenue. Those fashionable addresses held plenty of wealthy families to fill the polished pews. As posh apartment houses gave way to posh corporate headquarters, St. Bart's congregation slowly dwindled, gradually moving uptown or out of town. Young singles or retirees replaced families. The first group was just beginning its climb toward peak earning power; the second was over the crest. Neither had much left over at the end of the month to give to the church.

The loss of parishioners would have been bearable had the corporate newcomers taken up the slack. But it was more difficult to raise money from them than from the depleted congregation. In 1983 the church sent out a plea for corporate donations from forty-five major corporations in the area with an obvious stake in the quality of life of the neighborhood. Not a penny came in.

Although deprived of its wealthiest old families and hemmed in by corporations, Tom and the church fathers had made one grand effort to raise money through traditional channels—a $12 million capital fund drive, in 1980—but it had been a flop, and they had had to cancel it. Nor could the church's princely endowment lighten its financial load. On the contrary, it offered one of the prime arguments for development. H. Peers Brewer, the banker who was treasurer of St. Bartholomew's, had sworn that 95.5 percent of the $12 million was untouchable and that the unrestricted portion was "virtually exhausted." Only the investment income—some $1.3 million a year—was left to meet the day-to-day needs of the church, and even some of that was restricted. With annual budgets running between $2.5 and $3 million, normal sources of income were not enough to keep the sanctuary operating and still support the church's ministries. In the terms of *Sailors' Snug Harbor*, that seemed enough to get the church off the landmark hook.

Tom Bowers took the lectern late in the day and attacked the commissioners head-on, chastising them in a slight southern accent. His church had presented its hardship case years ago, "but you refused to entertain it at that time." Theologically, the church was not and never had been a building. The true church was "the body of Christ, that divine organism which is to continue the life and work of Jesus in every generation and to witness for the love of God for the people of this earth . . . [and] my task is to help that community stay alive, and to do its work, and to further its mission, which is to feed the hungry, shelter the homeless, clothe the naked, celebrate the sacraments, preach the gospel. And if it is to continue that mission in that location, that important location in this city, it must have the use of all its resources." When a law demands he care for his church first and his ministry second, "that law is wrong." The rector announced his willingness to go to jail to demonstrate that wrongness, then pursued a potent metaphor, likening the Landmarks Law to a neutron bomb, killing the community of believers but leaving the buildings unscathed. "This will be our last appearance before you," he said. "We have fulfilled all the so-called administrative remedies. We have expended much too much time, energy, and money required by this unjust . . . law, and if we get no relief we must go immediately to the federal courts to have our constitutional rights adjudicated. We have no choice."

The commissioners asked no questions.

VI

As the Battle of St. Bart's unfolded over the years, Tom's enthusiasm for his point of view sometimes led him to make public statements that contained an element of truth but were also somewhat misleading. As one priest who worked with him put it, "I think Tom is a great dissembler, I think he can dissemble and rationalize— the end justifies the means." In one brief talk before a Baltimore meeting of the National Trust for Historic Preservation, he:

- Declared that the landmarks statute discriminated against not-for-profits because the only way to prove hardship was to fail to make a reasonable profit. He ignored the body of case law that covers not-for-profit hardship, although his lawyers were discussing that topic with the vestry with regard to the hardship application.

- Pointed righteously to his bishop's wholehearted support for the scheme, while neglecting to tell the out-of-towners that the diocese had also been offered as much as half the income from the venture.
- Complained of costly legal fees stemming from parishioners' suits against the church but did not say that he and his vestry had opened the legal floodgates by suing those parishioners first.
- Said the church's only benefit from the new building would be more space, failing to mention that it also expected $9 million a year in rental income.
- Said the landmarks commission had refused to hear its hardship case at the first hearing "on a technicality," although lawyers had advised him that the commission was obliged to judge appropriateness before considering hardship in such cases.

Some of the arguments presented at the hardship hearings also suffered from closer scrutiny.

The commissioners registered relatively little outright skepticism in the public hearings. They were waiting for the verdict of their own experts.

Bronson Binger was the first of these. He is the assistant commissioner in charge of capital projects for New York City, and oversees the repair and maintenance of thousands of old buildings. An architect himself, Binger took a team of nine engineers and estimators into the Community House to see how its mechanical systems were faring. He was a particularly interesting witness because he had spent several years supervising the restoration of the Church of the Heavenly Rest on the Upper East Side. That church was just two years younger than St. Bart's Community House, and much of its mechanical equipment and many of its service systems (electrical, plumbing, heating, and ventilating) had been made by the same companies that had supplied those items to St. Bartholomew's.

Binger spoke at an executive session. The questioning was informal, but the commissioners were mindful of the litigation to come. Since the record was officially closed, they underlined the propriety of their action before inviting Binger to give his report. In what appeared to be a carefully planned exchange, Commissioner Tung and Chairman Norman stated that Binger and his associates were "consultants" to the commission, rather than "witnesses" and therefore were giving "information" rather than "testimony."

In addition to visiting the Community House, Binger had studied the OKA report and found that several of its conclusions should not be questioned: Some of the entrance columns had obvious fractures, and he agreed that aesthetics demanded they all be replaced at once. There was less agreement in most other areas.

OKA's report described aged machinery, grinding away in the basement of St. Bart's, healthy in the era of Chaplin's *Modern Times* but barely able to drive the church's life-support systems nowadays. Binger disagreed completely. The systems were more than adequate and, for the most part, were superior to what is available today. There was deterioration, mainly because of poor maintenance, but it would cost less to repair the equipment than to rip it all out and start from scratch. Binger spoke of grimy ventilation fans and beautifully wrapped electrical coils with an affection and reverence practical people often show toward things well made. The guts of those buildings could have mechanical immortality if they were lovingly attended by a maintenance staff. The beauty of the old systems was that they did need almost daily maintenance. Since someone was always looking after them, the problems were uncovered before they did real damage.

Binger thought the dollar figures in "Required Repairs" were totally unrealistic. The Department of General Services did estimates on 300 to 400 old buildings each year, and his experience told him OKA's basic premise was wrong. Because it treated the Community House as though it were a new building rather than a renovation, costs were calculated on a per-square-foot basis, with an assumption that none of the old equipment could be salvaged. All the old cast-iron radiators appeared to have been thrown out, for instance. Ridiculous, said Binger. They would last another fifty years, and whatever they might be replaced with would fall to pieces long before that. OKA had also recommended bringing the buildings up to modern fire code standards, which involved replacing all wooden doorjambs with metal ones ($97,000) and removing all wooden corridor floors ($56,000). Binger said no fire department in the country required that kind of retrofitting.

Then there was "double dipping," a quaint expression for including one item two or more times. Two hundred thousand dollars for electrical work turned up twice, to take one example. No one suggested the repetitions were intentional, but the "dippings" did inflate the final figure considerably. Finally, OKA had multiplied its totals by a factor of about 1.5 because the building was a landmark and therefore required special care. Yet the mechanical repairs were almost exclusively on the interior, and that was not designated.

In a later statement James J. O'Brien said he stood behind the figures as solidly as Binger did behind his. He claimed his firm's report had not recommended replacing every piece of old machinery and said it made little sense to do a Band-Aid job on that kind of renovation.

Binger still called the estimates "irresponsible [and] exaggerated beyond reason." He apologized for using such strong language when speaking of a firm of high repute but stood by his conclusion. "It's a hell of a way to do a report." His own estimates were five to ten times below those and were for a "first-class job" which in many specifics would outlast what O'Brien-Kreitzberg had proposed.

The Polonia Restoration Company examined the church's estimates for external repairs. It figured a maximum of $1,141,903 would have to be spent over a five-year period; another "optional" $500,000 could be spread over the following five years. That contrasted dramatically with the OKA figure of $6,308,782 (including fees and contingencies) for immediate repairs. Polonia, like

Binger, had very different figures from the OKA report on most particulars. The repairs to the Community House terrace offer a typical example. Some tile damage was apparent, particularly around the drains and near the southern retaining wall. "Required Repairs" earmarked $250,000 for it. Polonia's technicians said most of the tiles could be saved and estimated that both the terrace and retaining wall could be put into excellent condition for $46,000.

Other "required" items in the OKA report were even more surprising. For years the church had told the public that its auditorium balcony was unusable because of a fire code violation. (The auditorium is the home of an amateur theater group known as the St. Bart's Players.) It became an architectural stigma, tangible proof of the validity of the church's quest for relief. OKA said it would take $360,000 to make it usable again.

The balcony had apparently been damaged by a small fire in the church basement in early 1979. The blaze (from a gas clothes dryer) had been put out easily enough, but the department issued a violation preventing the church from using the balcony for seating. Everyone assumed it had been damaged—perhaps weakened by the heat of the blaze. When Landmarks staffers checked the records in 1986, they found no building or fire code violations on St. Bartholomew's. A bit more digging showed that nothing had ever been wrong with the balcony itself. The inspector had said the basement needed a sprinkler system, and until one was installed, he had put a limit on the number of people who could use the auditorium above. The easiest way to do that was to put the balcony off limits. St. Bartholomew's had installed the sprinkler in 1983, a year before it first applied to Landmarks, and the violation had been removed. From then on, ticket holders should have been filing back into the balcony, but it remained, instead, a visible sign of hardship.

Like the other experts who testified for the church, Walker Associates, the space analysts, had been hired only six months before the hardship hearing. The eleventh-hour nature of the church's requests for expert opinions disturbed the commissioners.

The thoughtful owner who finds a building ill suited to his needs generally asks a professional's advice before deciding to tear it down, not afterward. Knock out a wall here, put one in there, and the problem might be solved in less time and with considerably less investment than it would take to destroy and rebuild from scratch. Yet the rector and vestry waited more than five years before asking if there might be an easier way.

The commissioners did their own analysis of Walker's space studies. They compared them with the schematic plans of the new building and with the working drawings of the present Community House and came away in disbelief. The report said the new space was flexible, the old space was not. They thought it was the other way around.

The Walker report said the Community House had a massive structural system of load-bearing walls, which made it difficult to adapt its spaces to different uses. But the Community House did not have load-bearing walls. The experts seemed to have misread the original working drawings, and what they thought were "massive" walls were actually fill-in partitions between supporting columns. They could be knocked out easily, and the columns themselves were small and far apart (only a foot square, with a thirty- to forty-foot clear span in between). The columns in Ronson's tower were typical of skyscrapers—massive (around six feet square) and in places only eleven feet apart. If the church was concerned about flexibility, it was jumping from the frying pan into the fire.

Other details also made the commissioners wonder why the tower was an improvement. Almost all the usable rooms in the Community House are aboveground; two-thirds of its space in the new tower was to be belowground. Finally, noted the panel, if the Community House did not meet the church's present ministerial demands, precious little additional space appeared to be needed. After a careful study St. Bart's space planners provided the community ministry programs with a mere 400 square feet more, presumably for new bathrooms.

The space in the tower would have provided the church about

7,600 square feet more than it now has in the Community House. During the hearings the commissioners learned that it could have had almost three times that amount by simply adding a few floors to the present building. In the late 1970's the church had asked its own architects to see how the Community House could be expanded. They had found ways to add 20,000 square feet to the present building.

Firsthand impressions are always the most accurate, so the commissioners arranged to tour the disputed battleground themselves. Nothing they saw pointed to the kinds of problems claimed by the church and its experts. The worst problems were some stains on the women's locker-room ceiling, which they traced to clogged terrace drains above. Cleaning the drains and patching the tiles would stop the leaks.

While they saw no serious damage, they also saw little evidence of a solid maintenance program. In addition to clogged drains on the terrace and roofs, Binger found ventilating fans pumping air into dampers that looked as though they had been shut for a generation.

The lack of day-to-day maintenance could have come about for any number of reasons. Ron Alexander said the vestry thought one of its main "hardship" problems was that the church did not look run-down enough. An effective maintenance program would have only exacerbated that. A defector from the vestry told the following anecdote, to explain the reaction to this dilemma.

Shortly after the first landmarks commission hearing, someone noticed that the organ pipe fastenings on the north side of the choir were loose. It was mentioned at a vestry meeting, and a colleague suggested leaving them that way to call attention to the church's hardship. The idea was nixed when the question of liability was brought up, but the fastenings were not repaired. Instead, an "ugly scaffolding" was put up to spotlight the problem. The badge of hardship stayed in the nave until a parishioner earmarked a gift for the repair.

Had the commissioners been able to browse through the vestry minutes of a few years earlier, they would not have been surprised at the generally good condition of the buildings. In November 1979 vestryman John McNeely presented a "recently" completed report on his "inspection of the Community House properties." He had walked over each floor, carefully noting any signs of deterioration. The report read, in full:

Inspection of Community House, 3:30 P.M. Thursday, November 8th [1979]

—Passenger Elevator needs painting.
—Rooms 52 and 53 and Men's Lavatory all in good condition.
—4th Floor—Staff dining room, kitchen dining room and lounge all in good condition.
—3rd Floor—Offices O.K. Lounges 35 and 38 O.K. Men's. Ladies Rooms O.K. Door to hall needs painting.
—2nd Floor—Library and offices O.K. Door to hall Stairs needs painting.
—1st floor—Door to stairs needs painting.
—Auditorium O.K.
—Where are portraits of Bishop Greer and Vanderbilt? (Vanderbilt responsible for building Community House. Bishop Greer past rector.)
—Ground Floor—Hallway beyond switchboard toward Ladies room has not been painted since Mr. Bourne last had it done—three years ago. Needs to be painted.
—Light fixtures have no shades—just bare bulbs.
—Choir room needs new carpeting.
—Verger's office needs paint job.
—Entrance hall across from switchboard chipped and in need of repair.
—Doors in Basement need paint.
—Exercise Room O.K.
—Several shower heads leaking in men's shower room.
—Door to gym needs paint.

—No one in gym or exercise room—lights on full blast and in other unoccupied rooms.

—Sign should be at light switches asking that lights be turned off when room is not in use.

Eleven months before the church decided to raze the Community House because it was too expensive to fix, the most glaring defects McNeely found were a few leaky shower heads, some chipped paint, and a choir room in need of new carpeting.

The church's testimony about what was "required" conflicted on virtually every point with that of the commission's experts. Honest men and women may disagree, of course, and honest differences might even account for the roughly $10 million spread separating the church's final figure from that of the commission's consultants. But it is also possible the different figures were elicited by different questions. The commissioners wanted to know what had to be done to make the buildings sound and workable. While the title of the OKA report suggested differently—"Required Repairs and Rehabilitation"—St. Bartholomew's had given the engineering firm a license to paint a hardship picture of operatic breadth. As co-chairman of the building committee, Ron Alexander had issued the directive.

The day after the second tower was submitted, early in 1985, Ron began preparing the hardship presentation. One of his first official acts was to commission the OKA report. He told the experts to "maximize" their findings, to suggest the most that could be done. Replace the floor when a tile is cracked; never mind that the city does not require retrofitting to make existing conditions conform to new fire codes—renovate to make them conform. "If you're on the church's side in litigation, you want a big number for maintenance," Alexander said matter-of-factly in an interview. The Sailors' Snug Harbor precedent required proof of an intolerable financial burden. This report was to drive that point home. He wanted "a mountain of material," something so daunting that even St. Bartholomew's, with an $11 million endowment, could not scale it.

*   *   *

In defending its decision to develop, St. Bart's stressed the changed composition of its parish, now made up mainly of young and old singles. Its own study, done in the early 1980's, appeared to contradict that: It showed 47 percent of the membership earning more than $50,000 a year and at or nearing its peak earning power.

The specter of a shrinking congregation also played a key role in the hardship argument. The flight to the suburbs had been under way for decades, and since people go to church in their own neighborhoods, St. Bart's naturally lost out.

The vanishing parishioner argument would have been more convincing if the church's treasurer had not lived in Wilton, Connecticut, its junior warden in Middletown, New Jersey, and its rector forty blocks north, on Park Avenue. Those stalwarts attended a church outside their neighborhoods. Why not others?

There were more than 1,350 names on St. Bartholomew's parish list as of the 1986 vestry election. Only 193 had the same zip code as the church (two other Episcopal churches share it as well), while 550 on that list lived in other zip codes on the Upper East Side and passed as many as fifteen other Episcopal churches on their way to St. Bart's each Sunday. Another 140 or so lived on the West Side of Manhattan, home to thirteen more Episcopal churches, and 120 in lower Manhattan, with nine of its own Episcopal churches.

The list of qualified voters is smaller than the parish mailing list, but equally dispersed. Of 594 voters in that same vestry election, 400 lived outside the church's zip code, and 11 percent were from out of state.

The peppering of the city and nearby states with St. Bart's parishioners is not the result of an Episcopal diaspora precipitated by the commercialization of midtown Manhattan. It reflects a truth of Episcopal life: People choose a church because they like it, not because it is nearby. Trinity Church is buried in the heart of the financial district and presides over an 8:00 A.M. to 5:00 P.M.

neighborhood much like that of St. Bartholomew's. It has had virtually no round-the-clock constituency in its immediate neighborhood for the better part of this century, yet it has never lacked parishioners. They come from the five boroughs, Connecticut, and New Jersey. It is not the convenient location that attracts, but the cachet of the premier Episcopal church in the country—and perhaps the richest single church in the world. (In the eighteenth century Trinity was given most of the land on the west side of Manhattan, from below City Hall north to what is now Houston Street. The greatest part of that was slowly sold off, but Trinity still earns roughly $25 million a year from the remaining 4 percent of the grant.)

Each church has its special character, and an Episcopalian considers all facets—architectural, musical, and, of course, liturgical—when looking for a parish. St. Bartholomew's was always known as a church of the wealthy, if sometimes the nouveau wealthy. Old hands say Grace Church was home to the older, more prestigious families of New York. The fabled music program attracts many to St. Thomas. (It has not lost members in recent years, although it is just two minutes' walk from St. Bart's.)

The style of the liturgy may be the most important element in determining who attends which church. The Book of Common Prayer provides the matrix for Episcopal ritual, but the final form of the service varies dramatically. St. George's, just above East Fourteenth Street, continues a nineteenth-century tradition of relative simple Low Church services. At the other end of the spectrum, St. Mary the Virgin, in the West Forties, boasts rituals so elaborate and incense-filled, the like is rarely found in the modern Catholic church. (Episcopal clerics call it "Smoky Mary" and joke about the Catholic priests who go there to learn how to conduct a proper mass.)

The business of attracting parishioners is more decorous than the scramble for Nielsen ratings but only slightly less competitive. Proximity is not necessarily an asset; distance, certainly no obstacle. Father William D. Persell, of St. Ann and the Holy Trinity in

Brooklyn Heights, found no truth in the gravitational theory of congregants: that people are drawn to the nearest congregation of the appropriate faith. His first three years in the Heights taught him how difficult it was to hold on to parishioners. "There is no shortage of Episcopal churches here," he commented, yet many locals still disappear into the subways on Sunday morning, to reappear a few minutes later at Trinity, Wall Street—or, a little later, at St. Bartholomew's or St. Thomas. "The churches of Manhattan should minister to the people of Manhattan," said the Brooklyn rector, with only a hint of humor.

If the membership of St. Bartholomew's did decline since the 1950's, it is probably not for the reason offered by the rector. There has been an across-the-board loss of membership among mainline denominations in the past three decades, and Episcopalians were hit particularly hard. Yet there were exceptions to the trend, and Tom's previous parishes were among them. While the national church was losing members, his were adding them, first St. Patrick's, then St. Luke's. His power to attract was not dwelled upon at St. Bartholomew's, however, at least not after the landmarks controversy had boiled up.

The development scheme forced the church fathers into an odd corner when it came to reporting on the health of the parish. They had to hold firm on the depleted parish argument but did not want it to look as if the new rector—hired to revitalize—was presiding over a moribund congregation. Therefore, while decrying their diminished income base, year after year they reported that membership and pledging were up. The budget, which Brewer had claimed would be $730,000 in the red by 1984, was balanced in 1985, and the $11 million endowment had swelled to nearly $13 million. By 1986 pledges were up 135 percent over Dr. Finlay's last year, although the number of pledging households was down 21 percent. Total receipts from plate and pledging were up 344 percent during the same period. On the surface at least, things appeared to be rosy, and getting rosier each year, in the declining parish of St. Bartholomew's.

While the contributions seemed to be on the rise, another

important figure appeared to be in decline. The church lost 150 members between January 1982 and January 1985, said Rob Morris, a figure that took into account the new members Tom attracted. (Morris officially monitored the vestry elections for the Committee to Oppose between 1982 and 1986, signing the tally sheets along with the head teller for the church.) That was almost one paying member a week, each week of the year, walking out of St. Bart's and pledging her or his money to another Episcopal church. The slide, while not catastrophic, suggested to Morris that Tom's magic was not working on Park Avenue as it had in other parishes.

The rector and vestry needed an extraordinary financial burden if they were to reconcile an apparently healthy parish with the need to develop. They took a step toward that end by establishing a prodigious figure for deferred maintenance, but they also had to show that because traditional remedies were not the answer, development was. Whenever the media asked the rector about fund raising, a look of frustration would cross his face, and he would say a few words about the big capital drive of 1980. St. Bart's had tried for $12 million but aborted the campaign on the advice of a professional fund raiser.

Few parishioners on either side of the fight remembered that campaign. Rob Morris doubted it ever took place. "That's a crock. That is a statement contrary to fact. If they had capital drive in 1980, it was a very closely guarded secret. Nobody that I know in the entire parish, except Marc Haas and Tom Bowers, knows that such a capital campaign occurred."

The rector and vestry did apparently embark on a $12 million capital drive in late 1979 and did give it up. But it is not clear that they abandoned it solely because a professional said they could not reach their goal.

The vestry notes of John McNeely contained an outline of the 1980 drive that detailed some important particulars the church had left out of its account of that effort. The genesis of the campaign might be traceable to the fall of 1979, when McNeely jotted the following note in the margin of his vestry minutes from September 10: "Expansion costs prohibitive—Start a capital Fund Drive?," an apparent reference to the architect's study for expanding the Community House. McNeely cited three reasons for the capital drive: increasing expenses, building maintenance, and the "receipt of [a] most generous gift as a beginning of such an effort," nearly $1 million from Marc and Helen Haas.

The minutes of January 14, 1980, record that the rector's secretary was preparing lists of prospective donors. Tom was moving ahead just as one would expect on the basis of previous performance. On February 11 he announced to the vestry the formation of a capital fund committee, headed by vestryman Edward Ridley Finch, Jr. By March the vestry was reviewing long lists of prospective donors.

Knowing the schedule of the drive is critical to understanding not only why parishioners knew so little about it but why it was abandoned. Active solicitation was to last four years, with pledges coming in over another three to five. The $12 million was to be in hand by 1989. The "Gifts Required for a $12 Million Campaign" were apportioned as follows:

1 of $1,000,000	=	$1,000,000
2 of 750,000	=	1,500,000
4 of 500,000	=	2,000,000
10 of 250,000	=	2,500,000
25 of 100,000	=	2,500,000
50 of 50,000	=	2,500,000
Total		$12,000,000

In phase one, to begin in the fall of 1980, the church fathers intended to approach "certain parishioners and friends of St. Bart's . . . who have the capacity to give large amounts." They would canvass corporations and foundations between 1981 and 1983; securing pledges from them would not be easy, but the vestry was confident it could be done. Parishioners would be approached only in 1984; that explains why troops on both sides of the line knew nothing about the mammoth undertaking. But the campaign was canceled in the summer of 1980, months before the first phase had even begun. It was not aborted, however. Rather, it vanished in the womb, a kind of immaculate deception. Years later, when the tower made fund raising a serious issue, spokesmen would say it was stopped on the advice of a well-known fund raiser, Robert Duke, vice-rector of St. Paul's School, Bishop Moore's alma mater. The church was vague about the moment of contact with Duke, but he recalled it as "midyear," or the summer of 1980.

Why would the vestry ask for a feasibility opinion in the summer of 1980? Strategic planning had been under way for more than six months by then, and the initial solicitations—which might have given an indication of how things would go—were another three to four months away. The crisis of confidence is doubly surprising in light of Bowers's style and past record. The professional fund raiser who had told him it couldn't be done in Atlanta had been invited to go back home—or stay around and see how it was really done. Tom had raised $1.7 million in about four months there, in a parish with none of St. Bartholomew's national renown. Duke himself put his finger on the key: "One doesn't have to be in the fund raising business long to know that leadership is the most important element."

One more curiosity: The rector and vestry gave up after cracking the most difficult nut. The $1 million donation was already in the treasury, courtesy of Mr. and Mrs. Marc Haas, when the drive was killed.

An observer of those events said the drive was canceled because a better opportunity presented itself, one of immensely greater financial import, which would have been mortally wounded had the effort come anywhere near its goal. In July, recalled the observer, someone came to the rector's office and made an offer to develop the entire site. That coincides with Duke's recollection of the timing of St. Bart's inquiry and puts the offer in the church's hands eight or ten weeks before it appeared in *The New York Times*.

From the first day he stood in the pulpit, Tom had made it plain he wanted a parish known for its outreach. Here was a heaven-sent gift that would let him do it, and do it in style. He was ecstatic, recalled the observer. "Tom just couldn't believe it, he was so excited. It was almost like he was rubbing his hands together, and saying he couldn't wait to tell Bob Parks [then rector of wealthy Trinity Church]."

It is not sure that Tom told anyone on the vestry about the offer right away. At least one vestryperson recalled hearing about it only days before it became public knowledge. Like news of Sutter's find, however, word that a rare vein might be tapped on Park Avenue flashed around the real estate community. That rumor, according to the observer, probably prompted Marc Haas to call the September news conference and reveal the $100 million offer. (Tom's antipathy toward Rudin, the owner of the building behind the Community House, apparently stemmed from that time, for he blamed his neighbor for starting the rumor that led to the public revelation.)

At the time, however, there was nothing but jubilation on the church's side. And in the midst of all the rejoicing, the $12 million capital drive died of an embarrassment of potential riches.

The restrictions on the endowment provided another key argument for development. Peers Brewer had sworn that only a fraction of the $11 million was unrestricted. Several members of the vestry questioned that figure, according to Ron Alexander, but their polite inquiries were always met with a "Trust me" from the treasurer.

Sinc Armstrong and his group did not know what to make of the finances. Assuming the treasurer's analysis was correct, they feared the vestry was illegally spending the restricted endowment to finance the speculation venture, but they did not have access to the records, and therefore had no way to dispute what appeared to be a simple matter of bookkeeping. Alexander eventually did get to the information, and what he found prompted him to defect from the Bowers's camp and side with the opposition, not because he disagreed with what the rector wanted to do but because he could not countenance the way he went about doing it.

Ron was nervous about the state of the endowment for much of his time on the vestry. His discomfort dated from the first few meetings:

"Tom would open a meeting with a prayer. Fine. He would say a few words. Fine. Then we'd move to the agenda. The first thing would be the treasurer's report. Peers [Brewer] took the floor. 'The projected deficit is a hundred thousand dollars or so, and we have so much left in unrestricted funds'—it varied between a hundred eighty thousand dollars and five hundred thousand dollars. And then he would go on to talk about a few other things: 'We're going to spend so much here and so much there,' and then he'd be done. Tom would say, 'Thank you so much for your report,' and we'd go on to the next item on the agenda. I was flabbergasted. The treasurer had just told us at the low point that we have less than two years to live, and everyone is nodding their head and going on to listen about the Sunday school."

Money came out of the unrestricted endowment to cover annual deficits, which were hundreds of thousands of dollars in the early eighties. As a trustee of the religious corporation, and therefore legally responsible, Alexander was uneasy. How long could a tiny, unrestricted endowment cover such substantial deficits?

He was a successful tax attorney, and the confidence it takes to get that far, relatively early in life, is not normally associated with timidity. Yet Ron was also the the youngest member of the vestry, a hallowed institution at St. Bartholomew's. "Wonderful," Alexander thought the first few times he heard Brewer report on the endowment, "just two meetings on the vestry, and already about to make a fool of myself as a 'young Turk.' My quandary was understanding how the others on the vestry—well-educated business and financial professionals—could sit there month after month, saying nothing, doing nothing, planning nothing. Would they wait until the last dime was spent before rising from their quiescence?"

As time passed, he decided to look in on the executive committee sessions. Perhaps they handled the important matters there, he reasoned. "If you think the elders of the church sat down and said, 'What are we going to do about the endowment . . . about going broke in two years?' you have another think coming."

When colleagues voiced similar concerns, Brewer would come to the next meeting with an upbeat announcement. He had adjusted the inflation figure, which increased the spending power of the investment income and therefore erased the predicted deficit. "Then everyone cheered," quipped the ex-vestryman, "and they all went home. It was a card trick, a sleight of hand."

Three or four others also felt the treasurer's performance, and the acquiescence of the rest of the vestry, verged on the incredible. They would go out for a beer after the meetings and marvel that no one seemed the least bit concerned about the catastrophe that must soon overtake their church. But Alexander did little more than that during his first two years on the vestry. Tom sat by quietly as the question-and-answer sessions ran their course.

"Are you sure that is all the unrestricted funds?" Alexander queried on one occasion. "We could be broke now, and spending money for which trustees are personally responsible."

Brewer was certain.

"Where does your information come from?"

"I did a study."

"But you are neither a certified public accountant nor a lawyer."

Brewer was a banker, however, and had read all the memos attached to the gifts that had been given over the years and was aware of their conditions.

"Has the financial history of the endowment ever been thoroughly examined?"

Brewer said the records went back so far it would be impracticably expensive to have the accountants look over the entire endowment. Besides, they had seen the treasurer's notes and said they were okay.

Alexander approached the question in terms of a lawyer's

safeguards. "Would the accountants give a letter saying they have reviewed your work?"

They were not willing to give such a letter, said Brewer.

That was a "red flag," Alexander remarked later, but he had no authority to pursue it at the time. Brewer was the only person who could commission an endowment study unless a majority of the vestry asked for one, and that seemed unlikely.

Eventually the vestry did balk—but at the deficit, not the illusive endowment figure. The crisis came when Tom proposed a 1984 budget which was $500,000 in the red. Within weeks the church governors had inaugurated their first serious cost-cutting measures. That was in December 1983—more than three years after Brewer's original doomsday cry, and just weeks before the church's initial appearance before the landmarks commission.

- The $135,000 diocesan assessment was first on the chopping block. It was "written off to zero," Ron Alexander observed, "with no apparent thought about the implications for the diocese."
- The maintenance staff was cut back. (A confidential vestry report of the time disclosed that St. Bartholomew's staff was nearly three times the size of those in other New York churches of comparable size and wealth.)
- The church began charging admission to its renowned musical program. (Begun by Leopold Stokowski around 1905, it had been supported largely by voluntary contributions; those, as well as attendance, fell off under the new policy.)
- One part-time priest was given his walking papers, and the salaries of some others, including the rector, were cut. (The extent to which those reductions were felt was a topic of lively, if informal, debate within the church. Scuttlebutt among the volunteers and staff was that they were paper cuts; they assumed Marc Haas had written checks to cover the difference. His generosity had already paid for one clergy salary the vestry did not want to cover. Tom had hired

a priest over the objections of the vestry a few years before, and Haas had written a $15,000 check to cover the first year's salary.)

• The 9:30 A.M. Sunday service was dropped. (It was the only one still using the 1928 prayer book, and the gesture appeared to be as much a grudge cut as a stab at reducing expenses. The retired priest who conducted the service was not on salary, so there were no savings there, and since the building had to be opened for the 11:00 A.M. service anyway, the meager gain in utilities and security would barely make a jingle in the collection plate.)

• The decision to close the main sanctuary six days a week was the most visible cut, but it, too, may have been more gesture than substance. No one who testified for the church at the hardship hearings knew how much it saved. Since the chapel stayed open, the church still needed security, and as most churches are normally not heated during the week in any case, it was difficult to see a substantial saving.

• Leslie Sloate, the rector's public relations adviser, was put on a deferred salary of $1,500 a week a few months after the first landmarks hearing. If the church was successful in developing its property within ten years, Sloate (or his heirs) was to receive $2,000 a week until the total that had accrued was paid off. (He retained the use of an office in the church.)

Alexander was enthusiastic about reducing the deficit, for it lessened the chances of eating into the endowment. But he was still far from comfortable with the continuing Alice-in-Wonderland approach to the endowment. Only when he joined the building committee did he have a chance to change that.

Ron was helping to organize St. Bartholomew's hardship presentation in the first months of 1985. Still skeptical of the treasurer's figures, he wanted precise information on which funds were restricted and which were not. "If I were a judge, and St. Bart's came to me asking for relief, I would ask how you can be broke with eleven million dollars in the bank. If you can't answer that question, you can have piles of documents and data and aren't going to win anything."

He approached Brewer again. Was Peers positive only 5 percent of the endowment was available? According to Ron, the treasurer went home, pushed the numbers around, and returned to tell him they might be able to free a total of 10 percent if they stretched it. The margin of error didn't seem out of line, yet caution still counseled the need for an unbiased opinion to present to the commission. As chairman of the building committee Ron could authorize a study, and he did.

The review was not the gargantuan task Brewer had made it out to be. The accountants' fee was a mere $5,000; the church expected to pay $270,000 in lawyers' fees alone for the hardship application. The preliminary report was on Ron's desk in a few weeks. He was stunned. He asked Main Hurdman, the accountants, to recheck the figures. The final report arrived in early April 1985, the figures unchanged. The treasurer had miscalculated the unrestricted endowment by $6 million. (The additional money was available because New York State law permits earnings on restricted gifts to be spent, unless they are specifically restricted by the donor.)

Alexander immediately called the rector. Tom had made some strong statements at the recent landmarks commission hearing about going broke, and Ron suggested he rein in a bit until he saw the study. He presented it first to members of the executive committee. They refused to believe it. Ron suggested they meet with the accountants and lawyers to see how they had arrived at the figure. The specialists verified their work to an incredulous audience.

When the full vestry saw it, they could not believe the accountants had dug through 150 years of church history in so short a time. A "shoot the messenger" mentality prevailed, and Ron was ridiculed for being dumb enough to believe anything so absurd.

Again the accountants and lawyers were called in, and again

they confirmed that they had examined all the vestry minute books and all the fund consolidations. Their findings were accurate, give or take 10 percent. The vestry had to believe.

The experts left the church fathers to deliberate in private. Discussion was lively, and while it was going on, Alexander began thinking he would try to calm things down; a mistake had been made, but they could recover. Just tell the truth, and go ahead with the project. Before he could get that thought out, one of his colleagues suggested they declare the entire endowment restricted, by motion of the vestry.

Ted Lewis, the only black on the vestry, resigned from the building committee on the spot. He would have to think more before deciding if he would also leave the vestry. He told the quieted group how often he had spoken in favor of the project, to parish and friends, and how he now felt he had been an instrument of deception.

The idea of restricting the entire endowment appalled Alexander. It was legal, of course, but meaningless, and did not begin to address the moral dimensions of the situation. He announced his own resignation from both the building committee and the vestry.

Everyone present knew a double resignation would not look good from the outside, particularly since it accounted for two-thirds of the building committee. Alexander, sensing the possibility of a compromise, suggested they cool off and call a special meeting in a few days to talk things over. Tom, who had been quiet up to that point, agreed to the meeting.

The adrenal surge of the moment gave Alexander the courage to push things a bit farther. A few people there had some questions about other things, he said (later he called them "profound underlying management problems"). Could those also be addressed?

They could.

When the meeting broke up, Alexander was treated to another shock regarding the endowment. Anthony Marshall, the church's business manager (who had the same name as the junior warden), said the endowment news had come as no surprise to him. Alexander could not imagine what Marshall was driving at and thought perhaps he was trying to diminish the impact of the new information. Not so. The business manager produced a memo that placed the unrestricted endowment at $1.9 million. It had been written by Peers Brewer in the summer of 1982, just six months after the parish had been told it should vote for development because only a pittance of unrestricted endowment remained. That was distressing enough, but the memo went further. The treasurer had cited all the relevant sections of New York State law that the accountants later used to show there was $6.5 million in unrestricted endowment.

"The implications were staggering. I couldn't believe what I was being given," said Alexander. As early as 1982 Brewer and the vestry had known there was probably much more money available than what they talked about to the parish or public. None of that information went beyond the vestry. Worse than that, Peers Brewer had given sworn testimony before the landmarks commission on two separate occasions, saying only half a million was unrestricted.

Alexander assumed Brewer's 1982 memo had been written to pacify the principled and curious Mark Green (the vestryman whose embarrassing memo of the same time had turned up on Armstrong's desk). Alexander knew Green and guessed that he might have compared the high budget deficit to the tiny unrestricted endowment and begun to squirm a bit, wondering how the church managed to stay out of hock. Brewer's report would have eased his mind in two ways: It increased the church's available funds by a factor of four and pointed out that the vestry could find more if it wanted to go looking.

Did no one on the vestry notice that the memo contradicted what it had been telling its parishioners? Or was the discrepancy ignored because of the stakes involved? That is, were the vestry members bumblers or connivers?

"Haas is bright," said Alexander. "Tom is bright. Peers is

bright. You have to conclude, I think, that—between connivers and bumblers—given people with those talents, they must be connivers."

Within a few days of the accountants' presentation Ron and five vestry colleagues had drafted a letter outlining the areas of church management that they felt needed more attention. It was not a manifesto, just an agenda. They sent Tom a copy.

The day before the special meeting Tom made a grand and public faux pas. It was unrelated to the endowment but disturbed Alexander deeply. *The New York Times* ran an article on the occasion of the Landmarks Preservation Commission's twentieth anniversary, which quoted from a story Tom Bowers told about Andrew Stein, then borough president of Manhattan. Tom said Stein had called him up sometime after the building project first became public and said they would have no trouble getting city approval if they worked with Donald Trump. The rector confirmed his authorship of the remark to the *Times* reporter before the story went to press.

It was too much for Alexander. He and the others had agreed to serve on the building committee only because Tom promised he would make no more public statements about the real estate deal. This was the worst kind of publicity at the worst possible moment. The building committee was putting together what Alexander thought would be an impressive hardship presentation, which he hoped might convince the commission to compromise. If the church found itself in negotiations with the city, it would need all the goodwill it could muster. Slandering the borough president did not enhance St. Bart's chances for success. Alexander called it stupidity verging on self-destruction.

The atmosphere at the special vestry meeting was electric. Ron promptly made plain his annoyance at Tom's meddling in the building project and then did the unthinkable. The junior vestry-man suggested the rector consider resigning.

Tom was outraged. Ron and his cadre were on the vestry only

because he had put them there. They had no support in the parish. His church was vibrant and growing. Everything was fine. Charles Scribner (who had become senior warden when Marc Haas retired) claimed Alexander's actions indicated psychological problems. None of the five who had signed the agenda letter to Bowers risked the rector's wrath by taking Alexander's side, although most quit the vestry within the year.

Alexander submitted his resignation from the vestry the next day. A week later Ted Lewis also resigned.

As in the old cowboy movies, the black hats were run out of Tom's parishes, one way or another. He demands loyalty to the cause. Fletcher Hodges regularly called for loyalty votes in the vestry, recalled Diane Calvert, and at one point presented a resolution that would have barred anyone who disagreed with Tom and the development scheme from working in St. Bartholomew's outreach programs. To the vestry's credit, the proposal was voted down. Hodges stayed on the vestry building committee after Alexander and Lewis resigned.

"Tom's a good nurturer until you cross him," said Calvert. She resigned from the vestry nine months after the endowment affair and then stopped going to the church she had belonged to for a decade. None of the priests, including Tom, ever called to ask why she no longer came to church. "St. Bart's is a wonderful, exciting place. There's a niche for everyone, until you find out too much and become disenchanted. Tom is a caring person to those who agree with him," she said with difficulty, "but he surrounded himself with mediocre people on the vestry—yes-men—and when some of us said, 'Wait a minute,' the rest of the yes-men outvoted us. I hope the church wins, but I also hope there's a parish left if it does. . . . I love him dearly as a man, but I don't think he's a good rector."

By late 1986 at least five more people—in addition to Mark Green, Ron Alexander, and Ted Lewis—had quietly left the vestry. Tom handpicked the replacements, recent arrivals chosen not because they were leaders in church activities but because they were loyal to him.

Alexander knew the revelation about unrestricted endowment had implications for the bishop and the diocese. St. Bartholomew's had chosen not to pay its assessment the year before (1984), claiming it was strapped for funds. While the bishop later said it was not unusual for a church to default on a payment, a priest who follows these dealings said it never happens to parishes of St. Bartholomew's financial stature.

The bishop had come to St. Bartholomew's to plead for the money only a few months before Alexander learned about the endowment. He had not come officially, he told the vestry, but as a friend. The diocese was in trouble to the tune of $140,000, the exact amount of the unpaid assessment. St. Bart's had always been a keystone of diocesan support, he said, and now the diocese needed its help. He even said he was willing to help it raise money from other parishes in the diocese.

Tony Marshall, the junior warden, had politely acknowledged the bishop's request and followed it with an impassioned statement of his own, in defense of his church. With no money to pay its assessment, would he please tell them which priest they should fire in order to support the diocese? "He gave the most eloquent rebuttal of a bishop I've ever seen," said one vestryperson. It was a mesmerizing speech, and "everyone in the room believed that every single word Tony was saying was true."

Moore backed off immediately, thanked the vestry for hearing him out, and left the room. The door had barely closed behind his lanky frame when a spontaneous cheer broke out in appreciation of Marshall's moving defense. Unfortunately Moore apparently had difficulty finding the men's room, and when he returned to ask its whereabouts, he opened the door just in time to hear the impromptu celebration.

A few months after the bishop's visit, and only weeks before

Alexander received the endowment report, the Diocesan Adjustment Board reduced St. Bartholomew's assessment from $140,000 to $80,000. The Reverend Joseph Zorawick, its chairman, sent Brewer a letter that hinted at hostile reactions in other parishes: "This by no means indicates there will not be any 'flack' about its [the Adjustment Board's] decision. However, with your vestry's intent to, firstly, meet with other members of the Diocese to discuss St. Bartholomew's position . . . we believe most will see the rightness of our actions." The resentment toward St. Bartholomew's which was festering in other parishes in the diocese did not subside when the conditions of the reduction became known. St. Bartholomew's was to pay $80,000 of its $140,000 1984 assessment immediately, the other $60,000 "when possible." The 1985 assessment was to be paid on time and in full. If the church's condition was as bad as it said, how did the Adjustment Board expect the church to pay anything toward the 1985 assessment, let alone all of it? Cynics assumed the whole idea behind the failure to pay the diocesan assessment was directly connected to St. Bartholomew's application to the landmarks commission. The decision not to pay had coincided neatly with the church's first appearance before the commission, and the publicity surrounding the application carried news of a great Episcopal church that was in such dire straits it could not afford to contribute to the support of its diocese.

Alexander had watched the exchange between Bishop Moore and Anthony Marshall, never doubting the accuracy of the warden's stand. When facts proved otherwise a few months later, he was profoundly embarrassed. Assuming the worst, said Alexander, some of the vestry had always known the money was there and had lied to the bishop from the start. If it was an honest mistake, however, they should tell Moore and immediately settle the diocesan debt.

But the vestry appeared to be in no hurry to do that. Quite the contrary. When it heard the endowment news, its first reaction had been to hoard the riches, not to give succor to sister parishes.

Alexander made it plain that he thought the vestry should tell Moore, but he resigned before he could do anything about it.

Ron kept in touch through friends who stayed on, however, and one of them, Diane Calvert, was concerned enough to try to contact the bishop on her own. Alexander did not pursue the matter, therefore, thinking Diane would get the message through. He did see Tom a few days after his resignation, however, and inadvertently let something slip out about Calvert's wanting to contact the bishop. When a month went by and nothing was said to either the parish or the bishop, Alexander called Calvert. She revealed that Fletcher Hodges had spoken to her on behalf of others on the vestry and had told her she had absolutely no business going to see the bishop about parish affairs. Calvert responded that she would see her bishop whenever she pleased and did ask Moore for a private meeting. That was the beginning of summer, however, and Calvert was leaving shortly for Europe. No meeting could be arranged before she left, and by the time she returned, there was no need.

When Alexander learned that no one was telling the cathedral anything about the new endowment information, he decided to do it himself. It was not a wholly altruistic move; like Mark Green before him, Alexander had a professional reputation to guard. In his view, and that of his lawyer, New York law required him to make certain disclosures. He did so in a letter dated May 21, 1985. The bishop was advised that, between 1981 and 1985 the vestry of St. Bartholomew's had made many statements about the endowment to the parish, diocese, city, and editorial board of *The New York Times*—some of them under oath—which were now known to be "substantially inaccurate." He hoped the bishop would encourage the vestry to make a correcting statement and use his influence to heal the wounds in the parish.

Moore called Alexander and said he would look into it. On June 20, the former vestryman met the bishop and three officials of the diocese. One of them had already been to see Charles Scribner, who had said St. Bartholomew's was ready to make a full disclosure. "I am overjoyed that so felicitous an outcome to a very delicate question now appears to be developing," Alexander wrote after the meeting. "This is very heartening indeed." The system seemed to be working.

The churchmen extracted a promise from Alexander that he would drop the subject once a disclosure was made. The disclosure came in a letter to the parish sent out in early July. It was an innocuous document, with nothing to draw attention to the revelation it contained. The new endowment figure was there but buried in pages of figures where it was difficult to notice.

Moore then wrote to the ex-vestryman. Had the letter satisfied him? It had, replied Alexander, for in the most narrow and technical sense, the figure had been put before the parish, "[b]ut, were I now on the vestry, I would read the letter of July 3rd and not be proud. . . . A trained, careful and inquisitive reader, undaunted by the prospect of wading 12 pages deep into an accountant's report, will therefore be directed to a schedule which corrects previous pronouncements by officers of the vestry. It is doubtful whether, for the untrained reader, this constitutes a fair presentation given the prominent and unambiguous character of the vestry's previous statements on this question. . . . Is stealth the mark of a Christian? Is Christ's mission thus advanced?"

The ethical questions continued to chaff. In the months that followed the July letter of disclosure, Alexander urged Moore to use his godly counsel to smooth things out within the parish: ". . . it would be a tragedy of the first magnitude for these matters to be vented publicly. Only you have the personal prestige, the dignity of office, and the authority of the Church Canons to prevent it. An unsullied tunic in the midst of a carnage, worn by one who could end the slaughter, is no badge of honor." The bishop said he was sincerely concerned about the general state of St. Bartholomew's, but had been in close touch all along over the past few years, approved of the way the vestry was handling the matter, and therefore would not intervene.

Reflecting on that turbulent summer a year later, Alexander

recognized that the main concern of both the bishop and the vestry had been to keep him quiet. He was a thorn that threatened to puncture the development balloon and jeopardize the financial future of the parish and the diocese.

While Moore did not want Alexander trumpeting the news about, he did not hesitate to have the diocese profit from it. St. Bartholomew's anteed up the remainder of its 1984 assessment soon after the letter to the parish. Moore claimed the disclosure played no part in the diocese's good fortune. A priest close to the review committee said the correlation was direct. A short time after the new endowment figures had arrived on Moore's desk, he met with respresentatives from St. Bart's, and the church withdrew its request for an adjustment.

It was an affair of conscience for Alexander, and the anguish it brought on did not soon dissipate. Weeks after disclosure had officially closed the episode, Alexander was still passing sleepless nights. During one of them he penned the following letter to his rector:

Tuesday, 30 July, 1985, 4:30 A.M.

Dear Tom,

It's the middle of the night. I've just crept from bed where I've spent at least the last hour talking with you. We've been standing in the entrance hall of your apartment. I've been explaining that I didn't know whether to give you a big hug or to find the biggest damned 2 × 4 and break it over your head.

The fires within you make you a brilliant beacon in a land of spiritual desolation. But those same fires consume you with distrust of everyone around you, including, most especially, yourself. Consequently everyone loves you and everyone is exasperated by you. You both inspire and infuriate your greatest admirers.

As a vestryman, I wanted to give you support and guidance, but as a trustee I had to clobber you with that 2 × 4 if things got too far out of hand and nothing else got your attention.

Now I feel like I'm writing my collected letters entitled "[T]he Bishop and I." Maybe the Bishop's got a harder 2 × 4, mine's all splintered.

Tom, I'm getting pretty tired of seeing your ugly face at 3 A.M.! Will you kindly get your act together so I can get some sleep. Or else ask Margaret to tell me what kind of wood she uses in *her* 2 × 4.

Love, Ron.

Eventually Ron did precisely what the vestry and bishop had been trying to prevent. He went public. He testified at the December 3, 1985, hardship hearing, startling the room into silence with a lengthy and detailed statement citing a chronology he thought established a pattern of intentional misrepresentation:

- October 1981: The vestry report, "Securing the Future of St. Bartholomew's," reported to the parish that they had $533 thousand in spendable money.
- July 1982: Memo from treasurer Peers Brewer to the vestry said there was $1.9 million in unrestricted funds, and cited the New York State law that ultimately provided a full $6.5 million to the church. (Not made available to the parish.)
- January 1984: Anthony Marshall, junior warden of St. Bartholomew's, testified before the Landmarks Preservation Commission that the church was going broke.
- January 1984: Peers Brewer, in a sworn affidavit before the Landmarks Preservation Commission said the church had only some $500,000 available.
- April 1984: Brewer repeated the same testimony in a second sworn affidavit.
- Between 1982 and 1985: Peers Brewer made several statements to the diocese and the Diocesan Assessment Adjust-

ment Board to the effect that St. Bartholomew's had approximately $500,000 in available funds. Similar statements were made during the same time to *The New York Times* editorial board.

- April 1985: Main Hurdman drafted a report, the first comprehensive accountants' and lawyers' study of St. Bartholomew's endowment, which showed over $6 million in funds available to be spent.
- Fall 1985: In filing their hardship application before the Landmarks Preservation Commission, the vestry claimed they had only $317 thousand remaining in spendable funds.

Thorough to the end, Alexander sent courtesy copies of his testimony to Bishop Moore, and John M. Allin, then presiding bishop of the Episcopal Church. The replies spoke eloquently about each man, recalled Alexander. Allin's handwritten note was a model of concern for the spiritual over the material:

Dear Ronald Alexander,

Thank you for your thoughtfulness in sharing the account of your experience re: St. Bart's project with me. I pray, of course, that the building project does not become the end, if it cannot be a means to Christian mission. I told Tom Bowers there is much good to be done there with or without the new building. Failure must not be the threat. Best to you.

Faithfully, John M. Allin

Moore's typewritten response displayed annoyance at the blow dealt the development project and resentment at its author's continued hassling.

Dear Ron [Alexander],

I cannot help but be upset by what you've been up to. I see no constructive result from this continuing hassling.

I felt that when we met in my office a while back and were able to bring about the opening up of the books, that this would satisfy you. In fact, you told me it had satisfied you. I was therefore enormously surprised and displeased that you continued with the law suit, and so forth. Will this hassling ever cease?

Sincerely, Paul Moore, Jr.

Long after all the facts were public, Moore seemed puzzled when asked about Alexander, as though he had never understood what had distressed the tax attorney: "Ron Alexander is a rather eccentric fellow. I don't believe a lot of the allegations he made."

A priest who knew all involved thought Ron was a conscientious fellow who had objected because the vestry—of which he was a part—had apparently lied. "That was a self-conscious choice," said the priest. It bothered the lawyer more than it did the bishop.

After Alexander's testimony made the affair public, the church and its counsel maintained that the size of the unrestricted endowment was irrelevant; a church shouldn't spend its endowment or the interest from it. Alexander had a different view. The law said endowment income could be spent prudently. If the church was going to be bankrupt in a few years, prudence certainly dictated spending some of its endowment earnings. If it was not teetering on the brink of bankruptcy, however, the story St. Bartholomew's had been circulating for years was a complete fabrication.

The final building block of St. Bartholomew's hardship plea was its outreach ministry. Bookkeeping is as much art as science, and the financial statements showed what the church wanted them to show. Some information was remarkably detailed: One sheet showed that precisely $28,858 had been spent on maintaining the organ, $12,888 on air conditioners; $1,406 had been given in gratuities to its staff, and $2,791 went for flowers for the church and Community House. Yet it was difficult to ferret out any information

on specific expenses connected to the community ministry programs. Despite their importance to the church's case, facts about
outreach ministries were meager and incomplete.

During the five years of controversy Tom often spoke about
the shelter program at St. Bartholomew's, leaving the impression
that the church paid for it and that with more income it could care
for more indigents. Sinc Armstrong always questioned the rector's
broad statements. "Bowers says 'We're doing this great charity for
the homeless,' " he scolded, "[but] that program is not funded by
St. Bartholomew's church. Out of his $2 million of income . . . he
supplies the crypt and janitorial service. That's it. The actual
funding of that program comes from an outside source. I just have
to tell you that this guy is not a person whose judgment as to what
Christian charity is I respect."

St. Bartholomew's provides space for the homeless, but it
costs the church little or nothing. The shelter program is 100
percent subsidized by the city, part of a city-wide system for
housing the homeless which began in the early 1980's at the
prodding of Mayor Edward I. Koch. The church sleeps ten guests,
five nights a week. These are screened by a private agency and
bussed to St. Bart's at the city's expense. (The difficult or dangerous
ones go to city shelters.) The city provides beds, linen, and
blankets and delivers clean sheets and towels each week when the
dirty laundry is picked up. St. Bart's is even reimbursed for cost of
heating and utilities, according to Partnership for the Homeless,
the nonprofit organization that is the liaison between participating
churches and the city.

The church's testimony at the hardship hearings failed to point
out that its other community ministries are also self-funding—by
vestry decree, according to Ron Alexander. The volunteers who
ran the programs also raised the cash to pay for them. No money
was diverted from weekly plate collections, annual pledges, or
investment income to support the church's good works. The
expenditures were in addition to, rather than instead of, income
the church would have received had those ministries not existed.

To use the most obvious analogy, St. Bartholomew's outreach expenditures were not a slice cut out of the budget pie but a topping added on.

Church documents appear to bear this out. In recent years the treasurer repeatedly told parishioners that annual pledging was rising at a healthy clip at the same time funding for the community ministry was on the rise. In a confidential letter describing its funding sources, the St. Bartholomew's Council on Community Ministry told the rector and the vestry that volunteers had taken in more than $50,000. Nearly half came from parishioners' gifts, another 20 percent from government and corporate grants, the remainder from fund-raising events run by the volunteers. The letter conceded that the council expected no funding from the church: "We realize that in order to finance the community outreach activities of St. Bartholomew's, fund raising must become a major function of the Council on Community Ministry."

Part of the money given for outreach customarily covers overhead. The 1984 Community Ministry budget was about $75,000. Overhead took approximately $35,000, including $28,000 in salaries. (St. Bart's is one of the few churches with a full-time priest overseeing its outreach.)

It is not surprising that St. Bartholomew's outreach ministries were self-funding. Most church programs are. It is surprising that the rector and vestry pointed to those programs so often, and so melodramatically, to account for why the church needed a far richer source of general income.

Armstrong claimed the church was intentionally underachieving in order to spotlight the difficulty of carrying out its Christian mission without development: "I don't object to having scruffy people sleeping in the narthex—in terms of scruffy people destroying whatever it is that makes our church 'nice.' But I think it's tokenism. It's done to make a show of doing charity. I don't think it's a significant amount of charity, and I don't think it's the right kind of charity."

Some clerics from the diocese openly doubted that money

from the tower would ever get to the poor. They might get some attention at the beginning, said one priest; but it was the church's money, and the rector and vestry would end up using it for what they wanted to—a reference to the electronic church. Another priest suggested the bishop should have his own accountants audit the books if he wanted to be sure to get his share.

Other naysayers suggested that the equation implicit in St. Bart's arguments—*more income equals more outreach*—was far from proven. The size of a congregation, magnitude of endowment, and amount of annual income do not necessarily influence the scope of outreach ministry. Diocesan records indicate that St. Bartholomew's had more than 2,100 baptized members in 1985, and an operating budget of nearly $3 million. In that same year its volunteers raised between $75,000 and $100,000 for outreach, about 3 percent of the total operating budget of the church. (The feeding program served 19,000 breakfasts that year, 180 a day, twice a week.) The composite parish of Calvary-Holy Communion-St. George's is located on the Lower East Side of Manhattan. St. George's Church is about the same size as St. Bartholomew's, twice as old, and plagued by proportionately greater maintenance problems. The parish has 1,280 baptized members, and an annual operating budget of around $700,000, and raises $150,000 a year for outreach ministries—21 percent of the church's annual operating budget. The Church of the Heavenly Rest has 1,370 baptized members, a budget of approximately $460,000, and raises an additional $140,000 to fund outreach ministries—30 percent of the budget.

Then there is Holy Apostles. This tiny church, with 170 baptized members and an active congregation of close to 90 people, occupies a charming but rickety landmarked building at Eighth Avenue and twenty-ninth Street. With approximately one-twentieth the membership of St. Bart's, virtually no endowment, and an operating budget of $186,000, its volunteers raise $450,000 each year to fund the Holy Apostles Soup Kitchen. In a tiny facility (about the same size as the Mortuary Chapel at St. Bartholomew's),

Holy Apostles provides 185,000 meals a year—more than 700 a day, five days a week, fifty-two weeks a year.

The program at St. Bartholomew's is commendable, and comparisons are not meant to disparage or belittle the hard work of the volunteers who make them possible. Yet skeptics thought it reasonable to ask why they should assume St. Bart's would do appreciably more with an income of $7 or $8 million than it was presently doing with an income of $3 million.

St. Bartholomew's complemented its arguments for development by claiming it could not raise money from secular corporations. Other churches do. "It is difficult to get money from corporations, but to say you can't do it is not accurate. It's how you do it, and on what basis." That observation came from the Reverend Hugh Hildesley, rector of the Church of the Heavenly Rest, a well-to-do parish on upper Fifth Avenue. The tall, soft-spoken rector with a hint of an English accent knows about such things, for he spent twenty-two years in the world of business—as an art appraiser, auctioneer, and then senior vice-president of Sotheby Parke-Bernet—before answering a call to minister. He still runs an occasional art auction.

Reverend Bert Draesel, of the Church of the Holy Trinity, on East Eighty-seventh Street, has an approach to funding outreach projects that is being seen in more and more churches. Holy Trinity recently established a secular, nonprofit corporation to operate its outreach ministry, for secular corporations have little difficulty soliciting funds from secular sources. Draesel expects support to come mainly from church-related sources at first. Once the organization has proved itself capable, however, the resourceful rector is confident it will also get secular funding. "That's the way things are."

The Brooklyn Heights Church of St. Ann and the Holy Trinity offers a more unusual example of putting the secular sector to work for a church. The Landmarks Conservancy, a private organization devoted to preservation, helped evolve a plan to finance the restoration of St. Ann and the Holy Trinity, which turned it into a small alternative to the Brooklyn Academy of Music. St. Ann is now home to many groups that need performance space but do not have the drawing power to fill the academy. The arts do not generate the income, said Reverend William D. Persell, but the "arts angle" secularizes the church enough so corporations and foundations feel comfortable giving to it.

Some preachers find it easier to wrest funds from private sources when their churches are landmarked. Organizations are often more willing to support a building they think will be around in the future for their enjoyment. In the course of his own ministry, Persell has "never seen a church or priest held back in terms of doing important things because they had a landmarked building. I've seen lots of other things that hold people back—[lack of] imagination or courage—[but it] doesn't take a lot of money to do good things."

Despite its protestations to the contrary before the landmarks commission, St. Bartholomew's did receive donations from corporations. "We have always gotten money from Exxon and other corporations for community ministry," said Tris Pough, a parishioner who helped found St. Bart's Council on Community Ministry. When he last saw the outreach budget (in 1983), 25 to 30 percent of it came from corporate donations.

One important question was seldom asked inside the walls of St. Bartholomew's: Was Tom Bowers's notion of outreach the right one for his church? Some of his fellow priests thought not.

"Money isn't going to save that church," contends David Garcia, rector of St. Mark's. "If Tom had a hundred million dollars, he wouldn't be able to save that church, because money cannot finance vision. That is the issue at St. Bart's." Garcia and others think Tom set out to minister to the wrong people in insisting on following the path he took in earlier parishes. "Outreach at St. Bart's is a red herring. I think he talks about the soup kitchen and beds ten homeless people down at night . . . to taunt the [opposition], rather than to organize and build something." St. Bart's should not be feeding people, in Garcia's view. That is important, but a small-scale issue, something "frontline" parishes like Holy Apostles should handle. St. Bartholomew's has the resources in wealth and expertise to confront the more substantial theological issues facing the Episcopal Church—how cities grow, where their tax bases come from and go to, the importance of landmarks, the importance of spiritual life to a city.

Garcia is an intense, well-read man of early middle age, who spoke lucidly on this complex theme. Beginning with an admittedly Marxist interpretation of Episcopalian shortcomings, he energetically accuses his church of having failed miserably to counteract the corrosive mythology of individualism, which he thinks is responsible for the spiritual decay of the middle class. White-collar alcoholism is only the most obvious symptom, one of many problems of the affluent which the church should be attacking.

The rector of the East Village parish has an unlikely ally in his theory about St. Bart's proper mission. Hugh Hildesley also thinks St. Bart's has "misread its mission for that territory and that time" and is foundering because of it. He doubts that any rector could fill the church on Sunday, no matter what he or she did. But it could be filled during the week, if it offered services the neighborhood at large needed—not aid for the indigent but help for the business community.

Other agencies minister to the hundreds, even thousands of street people in midtown Manhattan, yet hundreds of thousands, perhaps millions within a ten-block radius of St. Bartholomew's have equally serious spiritual needs which are not being looked after. If their pathologies are not as visible, people in the business community still take a terrible beating. "What is 'quality of life'?" asked David Garcia. "They may live in eight-hundred-thousand-dollar duplexes, but does that mean they're happy? Not at all. What does religion mean to them? It's primitive and underdeveloped. If one had spiritual directors who addressed those issues, it would be far different. That is the mission for St. Bart's."

Critics of this bent think St. Bartholomew's would best serve its neighborhood as an uptown Trinity. (Enrollment in its business ethics seminars rose sharply—and attendance at noonday Holy Eucharist doubled—after corporate raider Ivan Boesky was indicted for insider trading.) St. Bart's should offer similar fare for needy office workers and executives: counseling before and after work and during lunchtime, stress clinics, help for white-collar alcoholics, discount lunch-hour memberships in the Community Club, an inexpensive day-care center for working mothers.

From early in the struggle Tom defended his "ministry over architecture" position by arguing that the church is not a physical thing but the body of Christ. If every church building in the world were destroyed, he said on one occasion, the church would still be the church. The word "church," in the architectural sense, rarely occurs in the first four gospels of the New Testament, and even those references could be interpreted figuratively: "And I say also unto thee, that thou art Peter, and upon this rock I will build my church; and the gates of Hell shall not prevail against it" (Matthew 16:18). As Bowers rightly claimed, the more frequent term is the Greek *ecclesia,* meaning "those who are called out"—that is, the congregation, not the building.

To bolster this argument, Tom held up the early Christians as exemplars. Theirs was the most vital time in church history, said he, yet they built no architectural monuments. Father Bowers neglected to mention other possible reasons for the dearth of Christian monuments before the fourth-century conversion of the emperor Constantine changed the pagan Roman Empire into the Holy Roman Empire. Before Christianity became the religion of choice, the Romans persecuted Christians with disheartening regularity. The visibility that goes with monumentality was just not desirable in the days when the Colosseum scoreboard read "Lions 1, Visitors 0."

Some biblical scholars have suggested that the lack of New Testament references to the physical church might have been the result of Jesus' assumption that the Second Coming would take place within a few years of the crucifixion; therefore, there was no need to raise temples to endure for millennia. Nevertheless, the rector's critics do note that Jesus attacked the money changers, not the temple.

Is the true mandate of the church to save the architecture or the people? It would appear to be both, if we take history as a guide. Among the countless, niggling diputes of dogma that have torn at the fabric of the church for 2,000 years, clashes between beauty and mission are rare. These needs of religion have coexisted in the past, and many Episcopalians feel St. Bartholomew's can accommodate both of them today.

The love of beauty in worship took as firm a hold on the empire's new religion as it had on the old. Even during the persecutions Christians lavished wealth on the utensils of the young faith to ensure their beauty. The temporal triumph of Christianity only led to a greater investment of wealth in religious artifacts. The most substantial symbol of the new faith, the church building itself, was the most commanding temporal witness of the Christian God's presence. Throughout the ages, these buildings have been the spiritual as well as material gifts to city, town, and village.

The Anglican Church has always been fond of majestic architecture, and its American cousin is no different. The Protestant Episcopal Church of America has no official theology about its architecture, but the faith of many is embedded in its brick and mortar. "This is our praise," says the Reverend George W. Wickersham II, "and we are unable to stifle it. We build because we have to. Insensitive the person who can enter that house and not be moved." The Reverend Wickersham II, now retired, was born and raised near New York City. He traveled to England in his seventeenth year and had an extraordinary experience on his first visit to Salisbury Cathedral. "I will never forget my astonishment. Could it be, I thought, that God was that important to those people? Was He that real to them that they should construct an edifice of this stature in His honor?"

The challenge of the church is not to bring God closer to people, he said, but to bring people closer to God. "This is why we build great churches and cathedrals: if only to make the statement that all the great buildings of our burgeoning cities are of little ultimate avail unless our society is deeply affected by the remembrance of Almighty God." A church testifies not only to the importance of God "but to the kind of God He is. They are human responses to the Divine Spirit." St. John the Divine exudes "creativity, graciousness and above all, joy," wrote Father Wickersham. He has worked for the building project at St. John and if he thought that church would someday be chopped up for commercial development, he would try to stop one more penny from going toward its completion. The dismemberment of St. Bartholomew's is just as wrong. "That great block between 50th and 51st on Park is a witness. . . . In the midst of hundreds of citadels of commerce, it stands as a perpetual reminder of the existence of God and of His importance in our lives. To eliminate it, or in any way emasculate it, would only provide a dramatic negative witness to our basic belief."

Yet many who favor development cannot understand why anyone would oppose such an eminently sensible proposition. The deal is unquestionably well conceived, and the opportunity may be lost if it isn't acted upon soon. At some point the zoning law could be changed to prohibit building these huge towers in midtown; that would make the site worth considerably less. In short, development now is an incontestably good business decision.

That, of course, is what adversaries of the building project have long contended. A simple but sound business decision came to be supported successively—and after the fact—by theological, financial, functional, and ultimately constitutional underpinnings.

*   *   *

The commission met in private executive session late on the afternoon of February 24, 1986. It was nearly 3:00 A.M. the next day before they voted. St. Bartholomew's hardship application was denied. The rector and vestry could now pursue their ultimate strategy, to challenge the constitutionality of New York City's Landmarks Law in the federal courts.

Before the constitutional case could get beyond a preliminary exchange of documents, a decision in an earlier suit brought by the Committee to Oppose stopped it in its tracks. The committee had challenged the vestry's right to pursue its revised development plans without a new parish approval. The case hinged on J. Sinclair Armstrong's first formal gesture on behalf of the opposition: the submission of an amendment to the church's bylaws in October 1980, requiring parish approval of any development plans. The vestry had eventually adopted a similar amendment and won the first parish vote on development, in 1981. But the deal had changed, and the bylaw prevented the church from going ahead with any action connected to development—including constitutional litigation—until it had another vote of approval.

The second parish vote on the building project was held in the Community House auditorium, also the home of the St. Bart's Players. At nine-thirty sharp on the morning of September 23, Tom Bowers stood center stage, on the set of *Oklahoma!* (the current offering of the Players), and opened the meeting with a prayer to heal his parish. False-front buildings with skewed perspective flanked the rector, while behind him stretched corn-blanketed plains crowned by an endless blue sky. The only ominous note was a painted thunderhead rising in the distance, above the rector's head.

There were some thirty people in the audience, clotted in small groups among ranks of folding chairs. Most parishioners had voted by mail, so the majority of the 643 votes counted that day were already in the rector's hands. None was challenged, and officials completed the count by 1:30 P.M. The resolution was approved, 403 to 240.

The reactions were predictable. Representatives of the church were calmly confident in victory. Tom Bowers was only mildly annoyed that "those people out there" continued to "harass us," gesturing toward a knot of parishioners still camped in what had become the opposition side of the auditorium.

For Douglas Parker, the lawyer handling the constitutional case, the road to court was cleared once and for all. He stood before the cornfields and spoke confidently of eventual victory. Moments earlier the rector had spoken of his determination to pursue the case to the Supreme Court. Parker suggested that would not be necessary if the city would only recognize the futility of its position and concede the church's right to develop its own property.

Although Sinc Armstrong and several other members of the committee had been privately pessimistic before the vote, they never wore a negative public face. A few moments after the results were announced, Armstrong told a reporter he was overjoyed at having the support of almost 40 percent of parish. He seemed no less energetic and optimistic than he had been six years earlier, when he first stood before the rector to submit the amendment that had required this law. Privately he was not so sanguine. None of the committee's attempts to stop the church had succeeded, and the course was now set for a costly prolongation of the battle on a much larger scale.

Rob Morris was also there. He knew the odds against carrying the day had been too great. The rector had "evicted the original population of the church" by his overt hostility toward anyone who opposed the scheme. If more members had been willing to grit their teeth and hang on, the project might have been finished off with this vote. But too many had opted for calmer pastoral waters. The search for peace had taken precedence over "the fact that they were stealing the church right out from under us."

Two weeks before that vote the congregation of St. Bartholomew's had had a surprise visit from Bishop Moore. He came to the Sunday service to proclaim that "the Landmark Commission law must be amended," that religious institutions must be permitted to use their buildings as they see fit. (This time the bishop said nothing about any money being promised to the diocese.) By godly decree, the parishioners of St. Bartholomew's had been directed to change the Landmarks Law: "The vocation has been given you, I believe by the Lord Himself, to carry this burden and to be in the forefront of this struggle which involves the deepest issues of the United States of America's Constitution, the issue of the freedom of religion."

The soldiers had received the episcopal blessing to open the next great front in the Battle of St. Bart's, the drive to lift the preservationist's yoke from all religious institutions across the land.

Epilogue

St. *Bartholomew's Church* versus *the City of New York* challenges landmark laws across the country. Written to protect sites of extraordinary aesthetic value and historical interest, these laws are designed to preserve moments of history frozen in brick, stone, and steel. But when the laws affect religious institutions, they raise questions of constitutional scope. Does the Landmarks Law of New York City, which applies to St. Bartholomew's, deny its parishioners the right to pursue their religious beliefs? Does it take away property without fair compensation? Is it an intolerable government intrusion into religious affairs?

The First Amendment to the Constitution declares: "Congress shall make no law respecting an establishment of religion. . . ." Originally aimed at stopping the practice of taxing everyone to support a favored sect, it has been interpreted as forbidding any law that is not neutral in its treatment of religion. To avoid any hint of conflict, a law must survive a three-part test (*Lemon* v. *Kurtzman,* 1971):

- Is the primary purpose of the law secular?
- Does its main effect neither advance nor inhibit religion?
- Does it avoid an excessive entanglement between church and state?

St. Bartholomew's believes that the Landmarks Law violates the establishment clause and therefore should be rewritten to exempt religious structures. An entanglement inevitably occurs in hardship proceedings, when commissioners investigate the management of a church's maintenance programs, check into its finances, and judge which of its religious activities is essential to its creed and mission.

The city asserts that entanglement is only one-third of the test. The church's reliance on it is a tacit admission that the law would pass the other two tests. Exempting owners of religous landmarks would favor them over secular owners, and that, in turn, would advance the cause of religion, giving religious institutions precisely the kind of special treatment the establishment clause was designed to prevent.

As for impermissible entanglement (the third test), the city claims there is none. Although the commission looked into the church's affairs, it was a "one-time, special event," not part of a continuing relationship. There was no constitutional encroachment because the commissioners accepted the vestry's definition of its mission and purpose and merely analyzed the architectural attributes of the proposed towers to see how each met the church's needs. In rejecting them, the commissioners did not attempt to interpret theology, define mission, or establish religious priorities; they said only that these were inappropriate additions to the landmark, secular judgments that were well within their expertise.

St. Bartholomew's thinks the Landmarks Law violates the First Amendment's free exercise clause as well: "Congress shall make no law . . . prohibiting the free exercise [of religion]. . . ."

The judicial test for free exercise also consists of three parts (*Sherbert* v. *Verner,* 1963):

- Does the regulation place a significant burden on religion?
- If so, is that burden necessary in order to satisfy a compelling state interest?
- Assuming a compelling interest, is there a less burdensome way of satisfying it?

Counsel for the church says the burden is plain. "All of the programs and activities conducted by the church constitute religious activities, and are the means through which the Church carries out its religious purpose." The Community House is too small to support all the ministries St. Bartholomew's feels obliged to carry on. It cannot be modernized, and even if it could, the church has no money to pay for the renovation. When the Commission turned down the towers, it denied income that is essential if the parish is to carry out its Christian mission, a clear infringement of the free exercise clause.

The city insists that not everything a church does is automatically a "religious activity." The right to develop property is a secular right and not protected under the Constitution. The judicial test for free exercise came from cases in which laws placed a direct burden on specific religious practices, such as forcing people to work on the Sabbath when their faith expressly forbid it. The Landmarks Law does not violate the free exercise provision because it does not force parishioners to do anything directly contrary to their religious beliefs. Denying the right to build a forty-nine-story skyscraper does not prevent St. Bartholomew's from raising money in other ways, nor does it prevent it from making "appropriate" changes to its buildings to make them better suited to the church's charitable purpose.

In a friend-of-the-court brief filed on behalf of the Committee to Oppose, Professor John Sexton, professor of law at New York University, argues that free exercise is not inhibited as long as the law in question does not prohibit or directly discourage a religious practice, even though it may have an indirect and unintended negative effect. An expert on First Amendment church-state controversies, Sexton holds that a law infringes on the free exercise clause only if it "is not neutral between religions, or bears so heavily on religious practice that it amounts to a direct prohibition."

As for the second part of the free exercise test, St. Bartholomew's does not think the city's concern in protecting its landmarks is as compelling as other state interests, such as protecting public health and safety by fire, zoning, and building codes. Landmark owners are not excused from these concerns, regardless of the hardships imposed, yet an owner can be exempted from the Landmarks Law if hardship can be proven. The very existence of the hardship exception is cited as proof of the law's weakness on this point.

Lawyers for the city say the Supreme Court firmly established the civic importance of the landmarking in *Penn Central* (1978). While it did not use the word "compelling," the Court recognized landmarking as a substantial interest of the state. The majority opinion maintained that the law was passed because of a conviction that the city's standing as a worldwide tourist attraction, as well as a world capital of business, culture, and government "would be threatened if legislation were not enacted to protect historic landmarks and neighborhoods from precipitate decisions to destroy or fundamentally alter their character."

If there is a legitimate state interest, counters St. Bart's, it can be satisfied by less intrusive means than confiscatory landmarking. The city could condemn the site outright and pay the church the full commercial value of its property just as it would in an eminent-domain proceeding. Or it could reimburse St. Bart's for the difference between the land's value as a landmark and as a commercial property. A third option would be to make it easier to sell air rights. (Transfer is now restricted to contiguous sites.)

The Supreme Court has already rejected the idea of using tax money to buy landmarks, states the city: "The consensus is that widespread public ownership of historic properties in urban settings is neither feasible nor wise. Public ownership reduces the tax base, burdens the public budget with costs of acquisitions and maintenance, and results in the preservation of public buildings as museums and similar facilities, rather than as economically productive features of the urban scene." The city holds that there is no less intrusive way to protect its interests, and in any case, St. Bartholomew's has failed to show that the law imposes a substantial penalty on its religious beliefs. The church does not say development is the *only* way it can carry on its mission work, just that development would provide more money to spend on those activities. Finally, the city argues, the church still has the possibility of selling its air rights, and anyway, there is another path. The church could propose a smaller building that would meet its own needs and satisfy the commission.

St. Bartholomew's believes the Landmarks Law violates its Fifth Amendment rights by denying due process and expropriating property without payment: "No person shall be . . . deprived of life, liberty, or property, without due process of law; nor shall private property be taken for public use without just compensation." Due process was denied because the commission did not admit hardship evidence at the first two hearings and did not permit the cross-examination of witnesses or the rebuttal of evidence submitted after the public hearings were closed. The commission's standards for judging appropriateness and hardship are also challenged in the due process argument; the church finds them vague and ambiguous and believes owners are entitled to know the precise gauge by which they are being judged. Finally, it insists the city has "taken" its property without fair compensation. It is worth $175 million undesignated, only $35 million as a landmark.

The city says the claim that due process requires a full, evidentiary hearing is wrong on two counts. First, the claim incorrectly assumes St. Bart's was deprived of its property and therefore, some kind of process is due. Second, even if the church had been deprived, it had ample opportunity to present its case, and the commission's procedures and criteria for judging hardship and aesthetic appropriateness are more than adequate to protect the church's legal interests. The matter of "taking" was disposed of in the Penn Central decision, which said: "[The notion that] appellants may establish a 'taking' simply by showing that they have been denied the ability to exploit a property interest that they heretofore had believed was available for development is quite simply untenable."

Neither side wanted a trial, and the city agreed to have the case tried solely "on the record," that is, on the evidence that had already been presented to the landmarks commission. In addition the city waived the right to depose the opposition under oath. Sinc Armstrong was both puzzled and disturbed at that decision. None of the evidence—pro or con—had been sworn testimony, and by passing up the opportunity to depose the churchmen under oath, they were missing a chance to find out the real truth about such things as the original $100 million offer.

In the first pretrial hearing, on March 27, 1987, each side asked for summary judgment in its favor. Federal Judge John E. Sprizzo, the sharp-tongued magistrate who was handling the case, promptly showed he had prepared well for *St. Bartholomew's* v. *City of New York*, and dispelled any notion either side might have had of becoming a quick winner. Lawyers for both factions had come to court armed with length statements, only to find—before they had read more than a few sentences—that the man on the bench was acquainted with the points they were about to make and was impatient to get on with his own line of questioning. They endured aggressive grillings as the stocky, balding judge leaned back in his leather chair, peered over the top of his glasses, and fired probing interrogatories.

Judge Sprizzo responded to the requests for summary judgment in a second hearing, on July 10, 1987. In his view, he told the assembled lawyers and observers, the Landmarks Law as applied to churches was not unconstitutional on its face. He rejected the claim that the law infringes on the free exercise of religion: ". . . I cannot accept the argument that . . . because a church is required by its religious mission to take care of the poor, that would entitle it necessarily to do whatever it pleases and to escape legitimate land-use regulations . . . on the theory that they need to maximize their income to fulfill their religious mission." He also discarded the arguments that the Landmarks Law violated the establishment, taking, and due process clauses of the Constitution. Regarding due process, he thought the law was a bit vague, but did provide the church with adequate opportunity to present its case.

Since the law was not unconstitutional in itself, the judge would make his decision in *St. Bartholomew's* v. *City of New York* based on the facts of the case, rather than on the law.

Six months later, at a third pretrial hearing, Judge Sprizzo advised the lawyers that the state was within its rights to expect either a non-profit or commercial owner to expend a reasonable amount to maintain a landmark. He did feel, however, that case law was not clear on one point: Was he required to examine all aspects of a charity's financial status in order to decide what was a "reasonable amount" to spend on the Community House to make it suit the church's charitable purpose? He asked the lawyers to brief him on their views. If it turned out that he was obligated to consider the total financial condition of a charity, the judge stated flatly that he would declare the Landmarks Law unconstitutional and let the case move on to the Court of Appeals. In his opinion, to insist that the state scrutinize the entire worth of a charity in making such a finding would violate the equal protection clause of the Constitution because it could lead to richer charities being treated differently from poorer ones. It would also demand of a charitable landmark owner something that was not demanded of a commercial one. If Donald Trump owned a landmarked building, Judge Sprizzo postulated, and it did not generate a reasonable profit, the landmarks commission could not examine his total finances and then say, "You make a lot of money on other properties, so you can afford to take a loss on this one." For a state agency or a court to determine whether a church should or should not use its other assets to carry a building smacks of entanglement between church and state, asserted the magistrate. It would be discrimination to examine the complete financial condition of a church, when that is not required when dealing with a commercial owner.

Unless the lawyers convinced him otherwise, therefore, the forceful magistrate said he intended to have a trial based upon the testimony that had been placed before the landmarks commission, which would decide if the law was unconstitutional as applied to St. Bartholomew's. In that trial he would look for answers to the following questions: Is the present Community House suited to the church's charitable purposes? And if it is not, what is a reasonable amount to ask the church to spend to make it so? The determination of what is "reasonable" will be made by arriving at a percentage of the value of the property, or replacement value compared to the cost of repair and renovation with the value of the property. If, for the sake of argument, the property were worth $25 million, $2 million might be considered a reasonable repair figure, while $15 million would not. But the owner's worth should play no part in this calculation.

The Committee to Oppose had asked the court for permission to join the case on the side of the city as an intervening defendant. This status can be accorded to one who is not a party to a suit if the judge thinks it will bring out pertinent facts which would otherwise not surface. The degree to which the third party may participate is up to the discretion of the court. John Sexton, who represented the Committee to Oppose at these hearings, asked that it be given the right of discovery—that the committee's counsel be permitted to depose the plaintiffs under oath. He suggested that this might provide additional information, since the city would be inhibited by the potential for a church/state conflict when dealing with clerics, whereas his client would not. Justice Sprizzo stated emphatically that, if the committee were to be admitted to the case, its lawyers would not be permitted any powers of discovery. To let them take depositions would risk expanding the scope of the inquiry beyond the narrow constitutional issue outlined by the court, into the labyrinth of parish politics, which has no place in the court. The committee would, however, be permitted to cross-examine.

Should the court decide it is possible to make the Community House into a usable facility with a reasonable expenditure—but the church says it cannot afford even the "reasonable" sum—the case would move onto a different footing. By taking that stance, St. Bartholomew's would itself be interjecting the question of hardship, and the court would then be free to look into the question of the church's total resources. If it were to find that the church had the money, but chose not to spend it, the court could not ignore the possibility that St. Bartholomew's was using the hardship argument as a pretext to escape the Landmarks Law.

Judge Sprizzo expected to hold the trial in the spring of 1988.

The loser will certainly appeal. Tom Bowers has often said the church will press its case to the Supreme Court if necessary, and the city will be no less energetic in defending its law. Whatever the outcome, estimates are that the Battle of St. Bart's will not disturb the peace of the High Court before the early 1990's, and even then a hearing is not guaranteed. If the justices think the law is clear on this issue, they will deny the application, and the verdict of the lower court will stand.

St. Bartholomew's has substantial backing. Shortly after filing the suit, the rector announced the formation of a National Advisory Board of St. Bartholomew's Church, designed to buttress the cause through contributions of "time, talent, and treasure." The national Episcopal Church has also lent its considerable weight. In a letter to the rector—which the vestry immediately sent to all parishioners—the Right Reverend Edmond L. Browning, presiding bishop of the Episcopal Church, praised Reverend Bowers for the "valiant effort being made by you and the rest of the leadership of St. Bartholomew's Church in defense of the principle that the Church must be free to fulfill its mission without interference in this religious calling by government. . . . The leadership of St. Bartholomew's Church is performing a sacrificial ministry on behalf of the whole Church when it stands for such traditional American values [restraint of government action]. . . . May God's blessings be yours." A bill has already been introduced in the New York legislature that aims at exempting all religious properties from landmarking because such laws violate the free exercise clause. Among its backers is an active, ecumenical group of clerics called the Interfaith Commission.

It would not be surprising if the battlefield eventually broadened to include an alliance between churches and commercial developers. Hopeful litigants across the land will need millions of dollars. Developers have that kind of money and would almost certainly be willing to give it, knowing churches will not be the only ones to profit from aesthetic deregulation.

Should St. Bartholomew's slip the shackles of landmarking and other religious institutions take up the crusade elsewhere, it would be welcome news to many struggling churches. While some will undoubtedly be unwilling or unable to develop their property, others will find the lure of large sums of relatively easy money a formidable temptation in difficult times. If the present struggle is a fair indicator, ecclesiastical hierarchies will not hesitate to encourage even well-endowed parishes to seek the speculative reward, for the assumption appears to be that all the brethren will share in the profit. No one questions the value of the charitable work now done by churches, and much of the bounty from the landmarks windfall would surely be channeled into worthwhile ministries—from soup kitchens to television preachers. How much of it would actually reach the needy cannot be known, for that will depend on the character of each congregation. In the New York Diocese, at least, there is no official forumula specifying the percentage of gross income that should go toward supporting the poor.

Whether it is an affluent St. Bartholomew's or a more needy St. Paul and St. Andrew, the image of the humble Carpenter's Church shifting over into the Kingdom Business makes cynics jeer, as surely as it makes some Christians cringe. Rich and poor congregations used to generate support for their good deeds through hard work tempered by an unshakable faith in their mission, not the marketplace. When they needed help, they inspired generosity by the purity and intensity of their belief. Perhaps there are fewer churchgoers now; perhaps they are less willing to give; perhaps there are fewer who can inspire. Whatever the reasons, critics keep returning to a basic question: Should cities be compelled to sacrifice their landmarks because some churches find they can no longer attract supporters?

If St. Bartholomew of Park Avenue manages to slay the landmarks dragon, the victory will cut the heart out of landmarks laws across the country. The church's own lawyers carefully point out that the faithful have always built monuments and that is why religious buildings make up a relatively large proportion of our small stock of landmarks. The preservationists argue that generations of builders, planners, and architects guided by an urban "slash and burn" mentality have left us with precious little architectural treasure to bequeath to our children, and churches and synagogues are necessarily the jewels in the urban crown. Those who battle against St. Bart's say that losing a substantial number of them would be a cultural calamity that would change the face of America's cities, towns, and villages.

N O T E S

CHAPTER ONE

Page
11 Weeks before this . . . *New York Times,* September 19, 1980, p. 1.
11 Armstrong declined to join . . . Armstrong, interview, October 31, 1984.
11 Philip Alston, an Atlantan . . . Philip Alston, telephone interview, May 6, 1985.
11 Secretary of Defense . . . Letter from Caspar Weinberger to Brent C. Brolin, September 22, 1986.
12 To his detractors . . . Lester Kinsolving, interview, June 26, 1986.
12 Tom Bowers displayed . . . Bowers quoted by Art Harris, "The Pulpit vs. the Preservationists," *Washington Post,* April 25, 1982.
12 "If he went and did . . ." Patty Weatherly, telephone interview, July 15, 1985.
13 "There are two great . . ." Thomas Dix Bowers, affidavit submitted to the landmarks commission, January 30, 1984.
14 Church fathers commissioned . . . O'Brien-Kreitzberg Associates, Professional Construction Managers, "St. Bartholomew's Church Required Repairs and Rehabilitation," June 19, 1985.
14 St. Bart's ability to . . . Letter from Bowers to parish, December 3, 1981.
15 "affect or not . . ." Local Laws of the City of New York, Section 2004, Para. 207-5.0.
18 But most of the . . . Sam Ervin, "The Constitution and Religion," *Free Inquiry,* (Summer 1983), p. 13.

Notes

Page
18 Connecticut, Maryland . . . Ibid.
18 Compared with the . . . *Encyclopaedia Britannica,* 11th ed., s.v. "Protestant Episcopal Church," p. 473.
20 Leonard Young, *A Short History of St. Bartholomew's Church in the City of New York,* 1835–1960 (New York: St. Bartholomew's, 1960), p. 4.
22 Reverend Andrew Mullins, informal history of the Community House, 1973.
22 When parishioners questioned . . . Reverend Dr. David Hummel Greer, quoted in Thomas Dix Bower's affidavit to Landmarks Preservation Commission, January 30, 1984, p. 11.
23 A spokesman "denied . . ." Richard Oliver, *Bertram Grosvenor Goodhue* (New York: Architectural History Foundation, 1983), p. 146, n. 13.
25 "The Mayor's Committee . . ." "Excerpts from Speech Notes of February, 1972, on How the Landmarks Law Happened," unpublished talk by Harmon H. Goldstone.
26 Old friends like . . . Robert Morris, interview, February 22, 1985.
26 "May I point . . ." Dr. Terence Finlay to Alan Burnham, executive director of the Landmarks Preservation Commission, April 26, 1966.
26 It held three . . . Designation report, LP #0275.
27 "As youngsters we . . ." Bob Albergotti, telephone interview, March 6, 1985.
27 Albergotti and other . . . Ibid.
27 He never said . . . Ibid.
28 Sixteen months . . . Guy Friddell, *The Virginian-Pilot, The Ledger-Star,* December 28, 1980.
29 It was in these . . . Ibid.
31 "He made a lot . . ." Richard S. Beatty, telephone interview, May 9, 1985.
32 "Dressed the best we . . ." Brad Currey, telephone interview, January 6, 1986.
33 As one long time . . . Bob Albergotti, telephone interview, March 6, 1985.
33 An ex-parishioner from . . . Hayes Clement, telephone interview, May 7, 1985.
35 It was demanding . . . Patty Weatherly, telephone interview, July 15, 1985.
36 "Here was a mild . . ." Hayes Clement, telephone interview, May 7, 1985.
37 "He got people . . ." William Milliken, telephone interview, May 7, 1985.
44 "He wouldn't pick . . ." Bob Albergotti, telephone interview, March 6, 1985.

CHAPTER TWO

47 According to Bob . . . Bob Albergotti, telephone interview, March 6, 1985.
48 "I knew that this rascal . . ." Brad Currey, telephone interview, January 6, 1986.
48 He said giving . . . *New York Times,* August 15, 1979.
48 The process of getting . . . Charles Sumners, telephone interview, June 22, 1987.
49 "As I write . . ." Tom Bowers to parishioners, in St. Luke's Episcopal Church *Messenger,* April 23, 1978.
49 "He so was loved and . . ." Patty Weatherly, telephone interview, July 15, 1985.
50 "We know that . . ." Larry Lord to Bowers, in *Messenger,* April 23, 1978.
52 As the story went . . . John Chappell, interview, March 13, 1985.
52 "It was a very . . ." Ibid.
53 "Brewer was a treasurer . . ." Diane Calvert, telephone interview, June 5, 1987.
54 "Why bother . . ." John Chappell, interview, March 13, 1985.
57 Rob Morris, treasurer . . . Rob Morris, interview, November 11, 1985.
58 "We talk about it . . ." Armstrong, interview, November 4, 1985.
58 "It is singularly . . ." Rob Morris, interview, November 11, 1985.
59 "The Electric Church . . ." Vestry minutes, St. Bartholomew's Church, March 10, 1980.
59 The Reverend Charles . . . Charles Sumners, telephone interview, June 22, 1987.
59 In Sumners's experience . . . Ibid.
60 "I love St. Bartholomew's . . ." Emmanuel de Olivera, interview, June 24, 1985.

Page
61 "We never had any . . ." John Chappell, interview, March 13, 1985.
62 Besides being a meeting . . . Dr. Robert Norwood, on the purpose of the Community
Club, quoted by Reverend Andrew Mullins in an unpublished history of the club written
in 1973.
63 Anything beyond the . . . Herndon Werth, interview, May 13, 1985.
65 "As he was going . . ." Marion McNeely, in conversation.
65 "Of course, Tom . . ." Ibid.
66 The new faces were . . . Herndon Werth's recollection of conversation with vestryman
Tom Biallo, interview, May 13, 1985.
69 "The Episcopal Church is . . ." David Garrard Lowe, interview, July 16, 1985.
73 "This isn't something . . ." Armstrong, interview, January 8, 1986.
74 "Oh, we had a great . . ." Ibid.
75 "I'm not trying to portray . . ." Ibid.
75 "In a dispute between . . ." Ibid.
77 "I began to learn from . . ." Armstrong, interview, November 4, 1985.
77 "I don't believe there's . . ." Ibid.
78 "I've been out there . . ." Armstrong to Victoria Newhouse, March 24, 1981.
78 Joyce Matz, a public . . . Joyce Matz, interview, May 1, 1985.
78 Armstrong felt "done in" . . . Armstrong to Victoria Newhouse, March 24, 1981.

CHAPTER THREE

82 He said it was Allan . . . John Chappell, interview, March 13, 1985.
83 "Monuments are very . . ." *New York Times*, September 19, 1980, p. 1.
83 The threat of selling . . ." Ibid.
83–84 Princess Grace and . . . *New York Post*, "Page Six," October 5, 1982.
84 He would be good news . . . Armstrong, interview, January 8, 1986.
84 "I really wanted my . . ." Ibid.
86 "Sometime in 1981 . . ." *New York Times*, October 10, 1980, p. 36, quoted in Kelly
Alford, "The Kingdom Business," unpublished thesis, Department of Religion, Princeton University, April 8, 1983.
87 With a note of . . . Peers Brewer, *New York Times*, October 10, 1980, p. B6.
87 "The physical beauty . . ." Ibid., Tom Bowers.
87 That same day . . . Committee to Oppose to the parish, October 10, 1980.
88 Its first letter to . . . Ibid.
88 Was all church . . . Ada Louise Huxtable, "The Sell-Off at St. Bartholomew's," *New
York Times*, October 26, 1980, Section 2, p. 33.
90 After weeks of prayerful . . . Bowers to parish, October 14, 1980. Similar statements
appeared in *New York Times*, October 19, 1980, Section 4, p. 6.
91 "Marc Haas stood up . . ." Rob Morris, interview, February 21, 1985.
93 Yet the statements . . . Bowers, in *St. BartholoNews*, vol. 3, no. 39 (November 16,
1980).
94 "My experience over . . ." Ibid., quoting a letter which had appeared on November 12,
1978.
96 ". . . for the last two . . ." Luke W. Finlay to Brent C. Brolin, September 23, 1985.
96 ". . . fully conscious of . . ." Ibid.
97 With only the barest . . . Armstrong to Brewer, October 22, 1980.
97 The payroll had climbed . . . The 1976 figure is from "Securing the Future of St.
Bartholomew's Church and Its Ministry, a Report of the Vestry," October 13, 1981,
Exhibit "B," "Statement of Income and Expenses for St. Bartholomew's Church, Year
Ending October 31, 1976," p. 3 ($245,127.49); St. Bartholomew's Community House,
Supplemental Schedules, Year Ending October 31, 1976, p. 3 ($92,368.65). The 1980
figures are from the treasurer's letter to parish, November 17, 1980. Other expenses also

Page

rose significantly; printing and postage costs, for example, went from $42,000 in 1976 to $71,000 in 1980.

97 Between Dr. Finlay's . . . Main Hurdman financial statement of St. Bartholomew's Church, dated February 5, 1982; computer printout of clergy salaries, 1986.

97 The rector's total . . . Figures taken from Convention Journals, Diocese of New York, 1975–1986.

98 The rector closed . . . Bowers to Don Chappell, October 28, 1980.

98 "I did not pledge . . ." Don Chappell to Bowers, November 4, 1980.

100 On the contrary . . . Armstrong, memo to committee, December 1, 1980.

100 A few days later . . . Armstrong to Marc Haas, December 5, 1980.

101 Anyone "who had contributed . . ." John C. Nelson, Milbank, Tweed, Hadley & McCloy, to Armstrong, December 9, 1980.

101 "That was a superb dinner dance . . ." from Armstrong to Bowers, January 16, 1979.

102 "I am not quite . . ." Undated letter from Howard S. Armstrong to Tom Bowers, ca. December 1982.

106 Although the blanket . . . Bishop Moore to Reverend Bowers, February 19, 1986.

106 They would file . . . Armstrong memo to committee, January 1981.

107 Recalling the sack . . . The Very Reverend J. C. Michael Allen to Armstrong, March 1981.

107 Three decades in the . . . The Very Reverend David Rhinelander King to Armstrong, June 2, 1982.

107 "I feel it is spiritually . . ." Ibid.

108 The bishop flatly . . . Moore to Armstrong, April 8, 1981.

108 Both the Not-for-Profit . . . Committee to Moore, March 5, 1981.

109 The prelate took . . . Moore to Armstrong, May 11, 1981.

110 As far as Armstrong . . . Committee to Oppose to parishioners, April 1, 1981.

110 Paul Moore, Jr., grew . . . Jervis Anderson, "Bishop Paul Moore, Jr.," *New Yorker* (April 28, 1986).

110 He graduated from . . . Ibid.

111 Jim Dunning had gone . . . Vestry minutes, St. Bartholomew's Church, May 9, 1977.

111 The three were friends . . . Anderson, "Moore."

113 "Anyone in the world . . ." Rob Morris, interview, February 21, 1985.

113 No one wanted to . . . George R. Hayman III to Armstrong, March 22, 1982.

113 Two days later . . . George R. Hayman III to Armstrong, March 24, 1982.

113 "This threat to commit . . ." Armstrong to Hayman, March 29, 1982.

113 "As far as I am . . ." Armstrong to P. K. Leisure, interoffice memo, April 1, 1982.

114 They did not have . . . Armstrong to Moore, April 27, 1981.

115 "I don't see where he . . ." Ann Nestor, interview, June 26, 1985.

115 He then hid behind . . . David Trovillion, interview, July 10, 1985.

115 One involved a forceful . . . Reverend Jesse Anderson, January 9, 1986.

116 Armstrong thought it a . . . J. Sinclair Armstrong, interview, November 4, 1985.

116 They did not have . . . Dave Duggin, from tape of special parish meeting, December 13, 1983.

117 Early in the affair . . . J. Sinclair Armstrong to Bishop Moore, April 27, 1981.

118 Letters went out . . . Armstrong to Victoria Newhouse, March 24, 1981.

119 They wanted to depose . . . Ibid.

119 "In the Diocese we . . ." Ibid.

120 "You have to have seen Donald . . ." Robert Geddes, telephone interview, January 22, 1985.

120 A special "Parish . . ." This and following quotations from "Parish Conference on Real Estate," *St. BartholoNews*, vol. 4, no. 27 (July 26, 1981).

122 That may explain . . . John Chappell to Armstrong, January 16, 1981.

123 The compliment cost . . . Jack and Lewis Rudin, affidavit to Landmarks Preservation Commission, January 1984.

Notes

Notes

Notes

Page

140 "Keep up the good . . ." Reverend David Garcia to Armstrong, December 29, 1981.

141 The letter of intent . . . "letter of intent," October 29, 1981, pp. 2, 3.

142 Contract or not, . . . Armstrong to the committee, January 16, 1981.

143 "What grew out of . . ." Harmon Goldstone, interview, January 22, 1986.

143 George Hayman (author . . . Edward N. Costikyan to Sally Goodgold, chairperson of Community Board Seven, March 15, 1982.

143 Contrary to what . . . Not for attribution.

144 The Roman Catholic archdiocese offered . . . Monsignor Joseph P. Murphy, chancellor of the archdiocese from June 1971 to July 1985, confirmed in a telephone conversation on October 6, 1985, that the property had been offered to St. Bartholomew's before it was sold to Rudin. The vestry verified the archdiocese's offer in later testimony before the landmarks commission: It had asked $4.5 million in 1975 and lowered the price a year later, but "no further action was taken because of the lack of sufficiently available funds. The Cathedral High School was subsequently sold to another buyer [Rudin]." "Complaint," *Rector, Wardens, etc.* v. *The City of New York*, April 8, 1986.

144 One vestryperson mentioned . . . James Dunning, answering affidavit, Index no. 5178/81 (Action 2), September 16, 1982.

144 In mid-January . . . Charles R. Colwell, president of the Standing Committee, to Armstrong, January 20, 1982. See also Armstrong to Colwell, Feburary 1, 1982.

144 The church could sell . . . Jonathan Morse to Peter M. Brown, February 1, 1982.

144 The Standing Committee did . . . Landmarks Preservation Commission, "Determination of Application for a Certificate of Appropriateness to Alter Designated Buildings Inappropriately on Ground of Insufficient Return, February 24, 1986 (LPC 86-0345), p. 97.

145 "If you approve the . . ." Armstrong to Moore, December 23, 1981, marked "personal and private."

145 If he started . . . Moore to Armstrong, March 19, 1981.

145 The canon places . . . Episcopal Canon 21, Section 1a.

146 Two months before . . . "Securing the Future," p. 28.

146 "When one party . . ." Armstrong to Moore, November 4, 1981.

146 Furthermore, it was . . . Moore to Armstrong, November 24, 1981.

146 Sinc answered with . . . Armstrong to Moore, December 17, 1981.

146 Armstrong had seen the . . . J. Sinclair Armstrong, interview, November 4, 1985.

148 By its own calculation . . . Vestry minutes, St. Bartholomew's Church, November 1, 1983.

148 Presbyterians lost about . . . John P. R. Budlong, chairperson, "Report of the Statistics Subcommittee to the Diocesan Convention," *Journal of Convention*, October 25, 1983, p. 25.

148 The thought of . . . Not for attribution.

148 To no one's . . . Bishop Moore to rector and vestry, February 2, 1982. A more detailed letter followed, February 11, 1982.

149 He needed impartial . . . Interview with Brent C. Brolin, May 7, 1986.

149 The bishop's financial advisers . . . Letter from Davies and Davies to Bishop Moore, January 1982.

149 "The Bishop approved . . ." Armstrong to Richard Oliver, February 17, 1982.

150 The bishop set . . . *Heights*, vol. 4, no. 1 (Fall and Winter 1981).

151 James Sargent, a . . . James Sargent to Armstrong, December 3, 1981.

151 It cast a . . . *Financial Times*, November 1981.

152 Some thought they . . . "Investigation of Dwell Constructions, Ltd. Yorks and Lancs Construction Company Ltd., under Section 165(b) of the Companies Act, 1948," by R. G. Waterhouse, QC, and J. C. Steare, FCA (inspectors of the Department of Trade), p. 414.

152 The report clearly . . . Ibid., p. 404.

152 "Mr. P. J. Smith . . ." Ibid., pp. 215–216.

Page
152 The report said . . . Ibid., p. 407.
152 The "[o]verwhelming . . ." Ibid., p. 409.
161 "Our conclusion is . . ." Ibid., pp. 412–415.
161 "The evidence before . . ." Ibid., p. 418.
161 The release quoted . . . "About Howard P. Ronson," news release from St. Bartholomew's Church, November 1981.
162 When the seven-year . . . "Setting the Record Straight," news release from St. Bartholomew's Church, November 1981.
162 According to the report . . . "Investigation," p. 418.
162 The Department of Trade . . . Ibid., pp. 420–421.
163 The next communication . . . Bowers to parish, December 8, 1983.
163 "The original press . . ." This and following references from Mark Green's memo to the vestry of St. Bartholomew's, July 19, 1982.

CHAPTER FIVE

168 There is a way . . . Local Laws of the City of New York, Section 2004, Para. 207-8.0: *Request for a certificate of appropriateness authorizing demolition, alterations or reconstruction on grounds of insufficient return.*
168 Generally the commission . . . Ibid. Para. 207-1.0.v.
169 Anthony Marshall, the junior . . . Anthony Marshall to vestry, September 24, 1984.
169 According to Marshall . . . Ibid., p. 1.
169 If the church . . . Ibid.
170 "If the LC rejected . . ." Ibid., p. 2.
172 "At present the Church's . . ." Thomas D. Bowers, affidavit to landmarks commission, January 30, 1984, p. 14.
172 Tom Bowers assured . . . Ibid., p. 15.
172 According to Peter Capone . . . Telephone interview with Peter Capone, October 15, 1985.
173 Those who spoke . . . Lucy K. Abbott to the landmarks commission, February 29, 1984.
173 Brendan Gill . . . *New York Times*, January 28, 1984, p. 23.
174 "We know that heaven . . ." Christobel Gough, testimony at landmarks hearing, January 31, 1984.
174 "The way [the rector and . . ." David Trovillion, statement read at the landmarks hearing, January 30, 1984.
174 The proposed tower . . . Norman to Bowers, June 21, 1984; written by Frank Sanchis, director of preservation at the landmarks commission, and signed by Norman (see also preliminary handwritten memo, June 18, 1984).
174 "Those bimbos and . . ." Bowers, in conversation after a debate at Union Theological Seminary, April 19, 1985.
176 "The Landmarks Preservation . . ." Designation Report of St. Bartholomew's Church, Landmarks Preservation Commission, March 16, 1967, #1, LP-0275.
176 That interpretation gains credibility . . . Flora Schnall, Milbank, Tweed, Hadley & McCloy, to Frank Gilbert, November 9, 1966.
176 Frank Gilbert stated . . . Frank B. Gilbert to Gene Norman, January 31, 1984.
177 "Accordingly," said . . . Bowers to parish, July 1984.
179 Finally, by placing . . . Anthony Marshall to vestry, September 24, 1984.
181 The new tower . . . John E. Zuccotti to the landmarks commission, dated December 18, 1985, containing the testimony read to the commission.
182 The landmarks commission holds . . . Notes taken at executive session of the landmarks commission, March 26, 1985.
183 The last was . . . Ibid.

Notes

Page
184 In a Byzantine twist . . . Ibid.
185 In addition, the . . . Ibid.
188 "In the long . . ." Bishop Paul Moore, Jr., interview, May 7, 1986.
189 Some of those judges were . . . Bowers, in conversation after a debate at Union Theological Seminary, April 19, 1985.
189 "I do subscribe . . ." Kent Barwick, interview, March 28, 1985.
189 Early in the affair . . . Marie Brenner, "Holy War on Park Avenue: The St. Bart's Landmark Battle," *New York Magazine* (December 14, 1981), p. 39.
189 Brooke Astor is . . . Ibid., p. 36.
190 "Why then did he come . . ." Don Chappell, interview, May 7, 1985.
191 Under certain circumstances . . . Landmarks Law, Chapter 8, Section 207-8.2.c.
191 The landmark is no . . . Ibid., Section 207-8.2.a, b, c.
192 The judicial ruler . . . *Matter of Sailors' Snug Harbor in the City of New York* v. *Platt*, 29 AD 2d 376 (1968). Geoffrey Platt was the first chairman of the landmarks commission.
192 After saying the . . . Ibid.
192 Each question must . . . Ibid. at 378.
193 The Penn Central case . . . *Penn Central Transportation Company* v. *New York City*, 438 U.S. 104 (1978).
194 He attempted to show . . . Elise Wagner, to Zuccotti, "Draft, Personal and Confidential, Attorney Work Product," January 14, 1985.
194 The church would . . . John Zuccotti, testimony, before landmarks commission, October 29, 1985, p. 16.
194 "He is seeking . . ." Dorothy Miner, transcript, October 29, 1985, p. 238.
195 Before the church . . . See checklist in memo, Ron Alexander to vestry, January 30, 1985.
195 Two years after . . . G. Allen Bass, chairman, Task Force for Ministry to the Community Outside the Parish, "Synopsis and Recommendations," May 12, 1980, p. 1.
196 That meant three . . . Betty Hudson, transcript, October 29, 1985.
197 "We are here fighting . . ." Bishop Moore, transcript, October 29, 1985, p. 154.
197 "We claim the . . ." Testimony of Bishop Paul Moore, Jr., before the landmarks commission, October 29, 1985.
197 In closing, Moore . . . Ibid.
198 "Under our policy . . ." Ibid.
198 The financial viability . . . Ibid.
199 It included $325,000 . . . H. Peers Brewer, affidavit to landmarks commission, January 30, 1984.
199 In the language of . . . *Sailor's Snug Harbor*, at 378.
200 In a comment . . . Edward Martin, transcript, October 29, 1985, p. 188.
200 After that rather . . . Ibid.
201 H. Peers Brewer . . . Brewer, affidavit to landmarks commission, January 30, 1984.
201 His church had presented . . . Transcript, October 29, 1985, p. 247.
202 And if it is . . . Ibid., pp. 247, 249, 251.
202 "This will be our . . ." Ibid., p. 255.

CHAPTER SIX

205 As one priest . . . Not for attribution.
205 In one brief . . . Tom Bowers, taped speech at "Public Institutions Versus Public Interest," Thirty-eighth National Preservation Conference, National Trust for Historic Preservation, October 26, 1984.
207 In addition to . . . Unless otherwise noted, Binger's remarks are from his testimony at the executive session, January 19, 1986.

Notes

Page

207 Binger thought the . . . All OKA figures are taken from: O'Brien-Kreitzberg & Associates, Professional Construction Managers, "St. Bartholomew's Church Required Repairs and Rehabilitation," June 19, 1985.

209 Like the other experts who . . . Alexander to vestry, January 30, 1985.

210 The columns in Ronson's . . . Report of James Stuart Polshek and Partners to the landmarks commission, submitted for December 3, 1985, hearing (undated).

211 In the late 1970's . . . Cain, Farrell & Bell, Architects, plans of Community House titled: "Expansion Studies, 1978–1982."

211 The badge of hardship . . . Not for attribution.

212 In November 1979, . . . St. Bartholomew's Church, vestry minutes, November 8, 1979.

213 "If you're on the church's side . . ." Ron Alexander, interview, January 15, 1986.

216 Father William D. Persell . . . Interview, June 4, 1985.

217 The church lost 150 members . . . Rob Morris, telephone interview, March 1, 1985.

217 "That's a crock . . ." Rob Morris, telephone interview, February 21, 1985.

218 The genesis of the campaign . . . "An Outline Proposal for St. Bartholomew's $12,000,000 Campaign," undated, in vestry minutes and notes of John McNeely.

219 By March the vestry . . . St. Bartholomew's Church, vestry parish minutes, March 10, 1980.

219 Duke himself put his . . . Robert E. Duke to Douglas Parker, April 8, 1985.

220 "It was almost like . . ." Not for attribution.

220 That rumor, according . . . Not for attribution.

221 "Tom would open a meeting . . ." Ron Alexander, interview, January 15, 1986.

221 "Wonderful," thought Alexander . . . Ibid.

222 "Are you sure that is all . . ." (and following paragraphs) . . . Ibid.

223 The $135,000 diocesan assessment . . . (and following paragraphs) . . . Ibid.

223 One part-time priest was . . . H. Peers Brewer, affidavit, January 30, 1984.

224 Leslie Sloate, the rector's . . . Bowers to Sloate, April 26, 1984.

225 The accountants' fee was a . . . Alexander to vestry, February 28, 1985.

227 This business manager produced . . . Memo from Peers Brewer to vestry, July 6, 1982. [The treasurer has the] "honor to report . . . minimum of unrestricted funds . . . $1,953,461 as of December 31, 1981. . . . In addition to the above total, investigation of the historic accounts of the Church indicates that: (1) more unrestricted funds in limited amounts are included among the Church Funds; and (2) some funds also may be available under Art. 5, Sec. 513(c) and (d) of the Not-for-Profit Corporation Law of the State of New York under conditions there stated. In brief, Sec. 513 permits the use of realized gains on restricted endowment funds, and unrealized gains from marketable securities in the same funds for the same purpose as the income earned on those funds is designated, unless the instrument of donations provides otherwise."

228 Within a few days . . . E. Theodore Lewis, R. A. Williamson, R. B. Alexander, George W. Sanborn, Judith Anne Beard, and Diane B. Calvert to Tom Bowers, April 23, 1985. The items for discussion were: (1) refining focus of vestry on areas that will help parish grow in membership, mission, and contributions; (2) reorganizing responsibilities in vestry and staff areas (treasury, audit, accounting, and budgeting); (3) establishing solid follow-up procedures; (4) developing a comprehensive fund-raising program, using professional staff to develop and implement programs for: general giving, specific grants (music, housing the homeless), capital improvements, bequests; (5) establishing a vestry personnel committee to review backgrounds and responsibilities of, and give approval to, key parish staff; (6) clarifying goals for clergy staff; (7) "[d]isclosing, to the bishop and the parish, the corrected status of our unrestricted endowment funds."

229 Tom's a good nurturer . . ." Diane Calvert, telephone interview, June 5, 1987.

230 He even said he was . . . St. Bartholomew's Church, vestry minutes, December 4, 1984.

Page

230 It was a mesmerizing . . . Not for attribution.

231 The Reverend Joseph Zorawick . . . Reverend Joseph Zorawick to Peers Brewer, March 26, 1985.

233 "This is very heartening . . ." Alexander to Bishop Moore, June 25, 1985.

233 The disclosure came in . . . Bowers to parish, July 3, 1985.

233 It had, replied Alexander . . . Alexander to Bishop Moore, July 17, 1985.

233 " . . . it would be a . . ." Ibid.

233 The bishop said he was . . . Moore to Alexander, August 15, 1985.

234 A short time after . . . Not for attribution.

236 "Dear Ronald Alexander" . . . Bishop John M. Allin to Alexander, December 19, 1985, complete text.

236 Moore's typewritten response . . . Moore to Alexander, December 19, 1985.

237 "Ron Alexander is a rather . . ." Bishop Paul Moore, Jr., interview, May 7, 1986.

237 "Dear Ron [Alexander] . . ." Moore to Alexander, December 19, 1985.

237 "That was self-conscious . . ." Not for attribution.

238 Bowers says "We're doing this . . ." Armstrong, interview, October 31, 1984.

238 The church's testimony at the . . . Ron Alexander, interview, January 15, 1986. See also: Memo regarding balancing budget, from Alexander to rector and vestry, October 31, 1984: The community ministry and music programs "shall, as in the past, be on a self-funded basis."

238 No money was diverted . . . Internal documents of the Council on Community Ministry.

239 The letter conceded that . . . Betty Brownfield to the rector and vestry, October 1983.

239 The 1984 Community Ministry budget . . . "Community Ministry Budget, 1984, Total of All Programs."

239 Armstrong claimed the church . . . Armstrong, interview, November 4, 1985.

240 Another priest suggested . . . Not for attribution.

241 "It is difficult to get . . ." Reverend Hugh Hildesley, interview, November 20, 1985.

241 "That's the way things . . ." Reverend Bert Draesel, interview, November 18, 1985.

242 The arts do not generate . . . Reverend William D. Persell, interview, June 4, 1985.

242 In the course of his . . . Ibid.

242 "We have always . . ." Tris Pough, telephone interview, November 1, 1985.

243 Hugh Hildesley also thinks . . . Reverend Hugh Hildesley, interview, November 20, 1985.

244 If every church . . . "Public Institutions Versus Public Interest," October 26, 1984.

244 The word "church," . . . See also I Corinthians, 12:14–27, mystical body of Christ being formed as person becomes a part of the church. Ephesians 2:20, Christ as the "chief cornerstone" of the church, the apostles and prophets its foundation. I Peter 2:4, each Christian is like a spiritual stone, making a new temple for God.

244 Some biblical scholars . . . See the school of historical criticism, from the Greek word *kritikos,* meaning "literary expert." "Literary analysis" might be a more accurate term. (See John Dillenberger and Claude Welch, *Protestant Christianity Interpreted Through Its Development* (New York: Scribner's, 1954). Both Luther and William Tyndale (a sixteenth-century Englishman who translated the New Testament and the Pentateuch into the vernacular) opposed allegorical interpretations of the Bible. The strong impetus from the Reformation challenged the Vulgate version and led to a detailed analysis of Greek and Hebrew biblical texts. "As theological leadership passed to the freer atmosphere of the German universities," points out Dillenberger, historical criticism gained wide acceptance. "The goal of biblical study came to be historical objectivity: the task was to be purely factual and descriptive," p. 189. See also the writings of Friedrich Schleiermacher (1768–1834), sometimes called father of modern liberal theology.

245 "This is our praise . . ." George W. Wickersham II, "Why We Build," *Anglican Digest,* Transfiguration A.D. 1984, pp. 10–13.

Page

246 "This is why we . . ." Ibid.

246 They are human . . . Ibid.

246 "That great block between . . ." George W. Wickersham II, unpublished letter to *New York Times*, no date.

248 The rector "had evicted the . . ." Rob Morris, in conversation, September 23, 1986.

248 By godly decree, the parishioners . . . Paul Moore, Jr., "Remarks from the Pulpit by the Bishop of New York," Sunday, Sept. 7, 1986. Tom Bowers quoted this section in a letter to the parish, dated September 23, 1986.

EPILOGUE

252 An entanglement inevitably occurs . . . Mudge Rose Guthrie Alexander & Ferdon, *Complaint, The Rector, Wardens, and Members of the Vestry of St. Bartholomew's Church* v. *The City of New York and the Landmarks Preservation Commission of the City of New York*, April 8, 1986, pp. 27, 29.

252 In rejecting them, the commissioners . . . Beth G. Schwartz, assistant corporation counsel, *Memorandum of Law in Opposition to Plaintiff's Motion for Partial Summary Judgment and in Support of Defendant's Cross-Motion for Summary Judgment*, February 13, 1987, p. 33.

253 "All of the programs . . ." *Complaint*, p. 28.

253 It cannot be modernized . . . Ibid., pp. 23–24, 28.

253 The judicial test for free . . . See *Sherbert* v. *Verner* (1963), *Wisconsin* v. *Yoder* (1972), *Thomas* v. *Review Board* (1981).

253 The Landmarks Law does not . . . *Memorandum in Opposition*, p. 27.

254 John Sexton, et al., *Memorandum of Law on First Amendment Issues Submitted by The Committee to Oppose the Sale of St. Bartholomew's Church, Inc., as Amicus Curiae in Opposition to Plaintiff's Motion for Partial Summary Judgment and in Support of Defendant's Cross-Motion for Summary Judgment*, February 5, 1987, pp. 16, 24–25.

254 As for the second part . . . *Complaint*, p. 27.

254 *Penn Central* v. *City of New York*, 438 U.S. at 109 (1978).

254 A third option would . . . *Complaint*, pp. 34–35, 36.

255 Public ownership reduces the . . . *Penn Central*, at 109 n.6.

255 The city holds that there . . . *Memorandum in Opposition*, p. 25.

255 Due process was denied . . . *Complaint*, p. 33.

255 It is worth $175 million . . . *Complaint*, pp. 21, 30.

256 The matter of "taking" was . . . *Penn Central*, at p. 130.

256 "I cannot accept . . . Transcript of hearing held before Judge John E. Sprizzo, July 10, 1987, p. 31.

257 Six months late . . . Notes taken at the hearing in Judge Sprizzo's chambers, December 29, 1987.

257 It would be discrimination to . . . Transcript of hearing held before Judge John E. Sprizzo, July 10, 1987, p. 23.

259 Shortly after filing the suit . . . "Installation of the National Advisory Board," St. Bartholomew's Church, no date.

259 In a letter to the rector . . . The Most Reverend Edmond L. Browning, Presiding Bishop, to Bowers, September 17, 1986.

259 A bill has already been . . . Flynn-Walsh bill, or "Religious Properties Landmark Designation Exemption," S. 6684/A. 7942, introduced May 25, 1983.

I N D E X